To:

From:

Date:

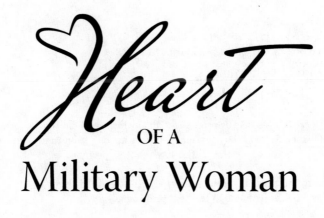

Heart
OF A
Military Woman

Stories and Tributes to Those
Who Serve Our Country

Sheryl L. Roush
and Eldonna Lewis Fernandez

SPARKLE PRESS
SAN DIEGO, CALIFORNIA

Published by Sparkle Press
A division of Sparkle Presentations, Inc.
Post Office Box 2373, La Mesa, California 91943 USA

Send contributions to Sheryl@HeartBookSeries.com

Visit our website at: www.HeartBookSeries.com

First Printing November 2009

Library of Congress Control Number: 2009911568

ISBN 10: 1-880878-24-0
ISBN 13: 978-1-880878-24-8

Library of Congress Cataloging-in-Publication Data
Roush, Sheryl Lynn.
Lewis Fernandez, Eldonna.
Heart of a Military Woman.
Stories and Tributes to Those Who Serve Our Country/Sheryl L. Roush
1. Military 2. Inspirational 3. Women's Issues

Proudly printed in the U.S.A.

Contents

A Day in the Life

Blessings From Above

From the Journals

Gold Stars

HONORING OUR VETERANS

HUMOR IN UNIFORM

LIVING THE DREAM

MILITARY BRATS

MILITARY MOMS

MISSIONS

ON THE HOME FRONT

PASSION, PURPOSE & PATRIOTISM

ROMANCE IN THE RANKS

SETTING THE BAR

SOULS ARE CALLED:
LIVING WITH LOSS AND GRIEF

TIMES SURE HAVE CHANGED

TRAILBLAZERS

TRIBUTES AND ACCOLADES

WISDOM

WITH LOVE, YOUR FAMILY

Introduction

When I sit and think about all the military influences in my own life today, I don't have to look very far. I reflect first on my immediate family tree. My father, Hiram Roush, served in the Army Corps of Engineer, and went on to become one of the best military aircraft design checkers, masterminded the hydraulic wheel lift system on the E-2, and saved the Apollo 11 black box from exploding on impact at the first landing on the moon on July 20, 1969. His younger brother, Henry, was killed in a test flight at Miramar Air Station, taking another guy's shift so he could be with his family. Dad's older brother, James, was a B-52 Bombadier, noted for his accuracy and successful missions. My mother, Beverly, was a Rosie the Riveter, and met my father when working late shifts at the same plant. Several relatives are members of DAR (Daughters of the American Revolution).

Living in a military base town such as San Diego, it was bound to happen that I would meet and marry a man in the Navy, an Air Traffic Controller (Top Gun), stationed on the USS Horne, and later USS Valley Forge. Not sure how "romantic" this was, but he proposed to me during an episode of M*A*S*H. I understand all too well, being a West-Pac Widow, as his ship was assigned to the USS Ranger during the Persian Gulf War. Although he was highly decorated for his merits, he came home a different man, and became an abusive alcoholic. I've since dated a Submarine Senior Chief, and a Marine (not that I'm dating my way through the ranks!).

As a professional trainer, many of my clients are from the military world, not only the individuals and their families, but also their service providers, their hospitals, their housing coordinators, and their transition teams.

I have a certain affinity and a special place in my heart for our military, so I'm proud to produce this book of stories from—and tributes to—each and every one: the service member and their loving, dedicated families.

—*Sheryl Roush*

It's Who We Are!

What is it Like?

What is it like to be a military woman? What is it like? It's like never being alone again in your entire life. It's having the family and discipline that your alcoholic parents could never give you. It's a chance for a high school dropout to turn her life around and make something of herself. It's building a firm foundation upon which to build life and family.

It's always being a part of a team. It's doing service for the United States of America. It's developing a work ethic that will stay with you every day of your life. It's going to the Middle East or Europe or Tunisia or anywhere in the United States and always having a family.

It's a level of understanding that those in the world outside of the military cannot know unless they have been a part of it. It's experiences that you will never forget and relationships that will last a lifetime. It's single moms moving into one house during exercises and splitting the shifts so the kids will have someone there at all times despite the fact that one of the moms is working a 12-hour shift running around a simulated war zone in chemical warfare gear playing "war games." It's walking into a USO anywhere in the world, striking up a conversation with anyone about your time in the Middle East and having an understanding of your situation that your family and civilian friends will never get. It's walking through the airport in uniform and having someone come up to you and saying, "Thank you for your service."

It's not understanding how much you sacrificed because you just saw the military as a way of life and a choice you made to support and defend the Constitution of the United States. It's a military member married to another military member with a family who has to prepare legal documents for someone to take care of their kids should they both be deployed at the same time.

It's being on the Honor Guard, proudly firing the 21-gun salute and presenting a casket-draped flag to the family of a service member who died. It's years of night school between duty assignments, after duty hours and on the weekends to get your college degree. It's hours and hours of studying for a promotion test only to miss it by two points which was the equivalent of one decoration that the supervisor was too busy to write.

It's walking into a newcomers briefing at your base and seeing familiar faces that you can't quite place until you both realize you were stationed at another base together ten years ago. It's flying free on a KC 135-refueler or a C-5 with your kids and watching the loadmaster take them to the cockpit to hang out with the pilot and crew. It's having the world as your backyard and always a place to call home.

It's unexpectedly being named the honor graduate of your class for your ability. It's being well respected and admired by your superiors, peers and subordinates. It's living by integrity first, service before self, and excellence in all you do.

It's crying when you have to return to duty after the birth of your baby. It's being torn between duty to your country and your duty as a mother. It's feeling safe to let your kids play outside or walking to school because you live on base and are surrounded by a fence with military police patrolling.

It's sparing with the neighbor about who leaves their uniform on the longest after getting off from work. It's being able to work on base close to your kids' school and have the freedom to go to their school events. It's being a Girl Scout leader for your daughter's Brownie troop and taking them to London to the Pax Lodge World Association of Girl Guides and Girl Scouts World Center, one of only seven in the world and you are experiencing it thanks to the military.

It's exploring English castles and cathedrals with your kids. It's riding the Chunnel from England to France. It's Harley-riding all over the United Kingdom, across Europe and into Norway. It's taking your photo by Loch Ness, the Swiss Alps, the Venice canals and where the Rhein and Mosel rivers meet. It's walking by Big Ben, Trafalgar Square, the Eiffel Tower, Notre Dame and eating Belgium chocolate.

It's the shudder of your quarters in the Middle East when the C-17's are doing engine runs or the check-points you must go through to leave or get on the base. It's sleeping in a bunk and walking across the base to go to the bathroom or shower. It's working 16–18 hours a day, and people banging on your door on your one day off for you to handle a problem. It's a 141-degree heat index and sweating so much that you have to shower two-to-three times a day. It's sweating and working so hard that you lose enough weight to drop a pants size and you already wore a size small.

It's a few precious moments that you get on the phone with your kids. It's crying because you miss them and are afraid they will forget you. It's watching them walk away as you head to board the plane for months away from them to do your sworn duty and honor your commitment to your country.

It's shooting expert on the M-9 when you barely qualified last time. It's playing paintball as a squadron or having a pie in the face contest and getting the most votes for a pie because you are so well liked. It's the confidence you have gained to stand up and give a speech or briefing and knowing the military has made you the person you are today. It's experiencing your retirement ceremony and knowing you will never again be in that place to have that special camaraderie that only the active duty know. It's the bittersweet feeling that comes when you hand in your active duty ID card and are handed a retiree ID. It's the tears that fall for your lost comrades, and how you wish you were still there to be a part of it all.

What is it like to be a military woman? For this woman, it was an experience that I will cherish forever because the military saved my life, and gave me the foundation that made me the person I am today. The heart of a military woman beats for her children, her family and friends, her community, the people she leads, the people she serves and the country she loves.

~ELDONNA LEWIS FERNANDEZ, MASTER SERGEANT, USAF (RET.)

http://pinkbikerchic.com

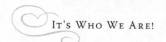

No Creature on Earth

The thoughts that come to mind when I think of the heart of a military woman are not stories remembered, good times shared, or hardships endured, but images, bits and pieces of broken memories of me, and other military women I met throughout my nine years as a photo-journalist and public affairs specialist in the California Army National Guard. Falling atop those memories are the ever present emotions that come forth when I think of my daughter, who was a U.S. Marine and my niece, a Captain in the Army and *Bronze Star* recipient while serving in Iraq.

The heart of a military woman is like the heart of a lion—strong, fierce, tenacious. She will slay an enemy in a heartbeat to protect her country—or her young. She will defend what she believes is right until her last dying breath. She is a tough and formidable opponent if you intend her harm. Yet, her heart will soften and swell with pride as she looks at Old Glory, or the men and women and children she serves and protects. Her allies, her team, her fellow soldiers, sailors, airmen, and Marines are her brothers and sisters; and, she will forever feel the bond they share—no matter how long she served on active duty, and for as long as she lives.

She is also soft and tender. Her heart aches for home and her loved ones. She will do what she says. Her word is an iron promise. She is amazing in her ability to adapt, overcome adversity, do whatever it takes, and still dance the night away if given a pair of heels, a dress, and music. She laughs deeper, loves harder, and her heart knows no bounds. That is the heart of a military woman. There is no creature on earth as tough, as tender, as warm, and giving, as generous of spirit, or as protective as a military woman.

~DEBRA ANN RISTAU

USARNG—California, 1985–1994

www.horsewhispersandlies.com

I Just Didn't Know

The good-byes are the hardest. We've done them with hundreds lingering on the tarmac exchanging letters, hugs, tears and last minute instructions while dreading that final moment. We've done them at home where one last children's toy is repaired before loading the car. We've done them standing in the kitchen rinsing the last plate from breakfast when the dreaded knock on the door occurs.

We've done them at local airports with cars whizzing by, horns honking at us because they want the space and the traffic patrol urging us to move-on. We've done them hurriedly on the phone when the right words just wouldn't come. We've done them standing before a congregation with hands and prayers bestowed upon us, with tears quietly streaming down our cheeks. And each time, I stare at him trying to remember each and every detail of his face. I memorize his smile, the creases that frame his eyes when he smiles, his laugh and the last departing words. I always watch as he walks away and fades into the crowd.

I stand there alone with tears in my eyes, a lump in my gut and a hole in my soul. I offer a silent prayer for his safety. And then I plead in another for faith to replace my fear. I cry all the way home, not knowing when, or if I will see or be with him again.

And then the good-bye is done. It is back to daily living. There is homework to do, school functions to attend, bills to pay, a garage to clean, toys that need new batteries, lunches to pack, household chores, hosting a daughter's birthday party, weeds to pull, oil changes for the cars, grocery shopping, first aid for many cuts and bruises, and simply trying to keep up with the growing list of to do items usually tackled by two. I become, by definition, a single parent, and, often, an overwhelmed one.

And, of course, there is always the car that breaks down, the air conditioner or hot water unit that suddenly ceases, the dryer that won't spin, the washer that leaks, the DVD player that becomes disabled, a relative's emer-

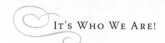

gency, the family of snakes that have taken up residence under the outside AC unit, an essential document that can't be found anywhere and a smoke detector hung from twelve-foot ceilings that seem to always go into power failure at 2 A.M.

All of this, of course, while your husband is unavailable and thousands of miles away. You become adept at fixing things, asking for help or just learning to live with it until he returns. The chore list grows, and so do the weeds. You run late to outings and you run out of energy.

You try to be both for your children and quickly learn you can't. You can't fix things like him. You don't play like he does. You can't build magnificent things with a couple of pieces of wood, some nails and an old hammer. You don't go to the park and play hide-and-seek and do trail walks.

You're not as good at piggyback rides and puzzles. You can't ride the ocean waves with his skill and humor. The milkshakes are too thin. You don't swim underwater and you can't seem to get the bath games quite right. And you learn that this is okay. There is always a place—a space saved and waiting for him here.

And, when their tears flow and their souls are wounded from simply missing their Dad, you know you can't fix that either. All you can do is hug and hold them while saying, "Me too." It hurts, really hurts—for all of us.

You see husbands and dads everywhere. You see them playing at parks, splashing at pools, walking hand in hand at school outings, sitting with their families at church, eating together at restaurants, mowing the yard and riding bikes to school. And we long for him . . .

The garage door doesn't beep at 6:30 A.M. and there is no one for the girls to hug *hello* at the end of a long day, and there is no one to share my thoughts or bed with at night. You go to bed alone with your heart empty and your mind racing. You sigh that you made it through another day—and you pray he did too.

Along the way, there are friends that rush to help, friends that just question and friends that are just there—right when you need them. You cherish the words, "How can I help?" Even though you rarely take anyone up on the offer. You say a prayer of thanks for the friend that insists on taking your kids for the day because she knows you need the break. You reserve your emotions about the friend who just doesn't get it and never will. You cry about a kind note from another that came at the most needed moment.

You are politely excluded from couple outings or you go alone. Either way is lonely and not quite the same. You miss him—you need and want him there with you—just like everyone else.

During birthday parties or events with other families, you watch your daughters search for another Dad that may be willing to swing them in the air, toss them into the water or just play, like their Dad does. And when pseudo-Dad sweeps her into his arms, you are grateful for this wonderful volunteer and the amazing, but brief moments of smiles.

There are the questions. The question from a five-year-old asking, "If Dad is a soldier, does he kill people?" Then there are the questions from friends asking about my stance on the President, the war and the military. The question from someone you have just met, asking if you even believe in war, and if you think that the number of American casualties and cost are worth it. You're asked where Bin Laden is and why we can't catch him. You're asked, "Why can't we just leave Iraq and Afghanistan and let them settle it?"

War is so very, very complex . . . but for you it is simple. You love your husband. You support your husband. You support the missions and tasks he is assigned and his commitment to those. You support his love of God, family and country. You support that his concern for his own life is secondary to his commitment to secure peace and freedom for you, your children, family, and friends and for millions of Americans he doesn't even know. His service is not about war but one of freedom.

You often hear, "You signed up for this." But does anyone know what they really signed up for in life? You didn't know the absences would be so long or hurt that much. You didn't know that you would be glued day after day to CNN hoping for something, anything that would offer you some information and insight. You didn't know that you would shed so many tears for casualties never mentioned by name because you truly hurt for those families . . . and because it could have been him.

You didn't know that not hearing from him for three days would keep you up at night just wondering if he is okay. You didn't know that managing a household could be so overwhelming. You didn't know that being without him could be so empty—so lonely. You didn't know that your children could miss the simple things with him so much.

And, you also didn't know that you could love that deeply or unconditionally. You didn't know that you could fix a faucet or a loose wheel on a bike. You didn't know that you could manage the finances, handle family emergencies and attend parties and events alone.

You didn't know that you would meet so many wonderful friends along the way. You didn't know that you would have spiritual mentors that guided you back to your faith. You didn't know that families would adopt yours at the holidays. You didn't know that a stranger overhearing that your husband was deployed would pay for your meal and thank you for his service. You didn't know that the many prayers and notes from others could offer such peace.

You didn't know that your daughter's teacher would take the extra time to listen and offer hugs in the moments of her sadness. You didn't know that a friend would come get your daughters when you were sick and had no one to take over. You didn't know that your daughters reciting the Pledge of Allegiance and parading a flag about your den could mean so much. You didn't know that the Star-Spangled Banner would make you cry, really cry.

You didn't know that when you married this wonderful man that you and your family would be a part of his sacrifice, as well. You didn't know that this military life could be so painful, so joyful, so difficult—and yet so meaningful. I just didn't know.

~LISA BLACK

Proud wife of Lt Colonel Edward Purnell Black, USAF

www.JustAnotherMom.com

However, with all my military experience and training in Army Family Programs nothing has prepared me for the battle I fight as an Army wife. I am a Veteran, a wife, a mother, an Army wife—and I am a woman.

~CHRISTINA PIPER

www.HerWarHerVoice.com

As an experienced military mom, how do you balance your home life?
One of the most difficult aspects of military life is the frequent changes in routine. Your workload changes significantly when your spouse deploys and you become the sole provider in your home. I find that I need to prioritize during deployments and ask for help. Projects that can wait, wait. I tend to rely on friends and family more heavily during these times. It is also difficult when your spouse returns and resumes helping with the chores, etc. You get used to doing things a certain way and build a routine to make it work. Although you appreciate the help and pray for the day your spouse returns, it is disruptive to the routine you have established and takes a bit to readjust.

~MONICA SHEPPARD, PEDIATRIC PHYSICAL THERAPIST

Wife of Navy Lieutenant Geoff Sheppard, Operations Officer/Speechwriter for Naval Surface Forces

As interviewed by Life Coach (and Aunt), Laurie Sheppard

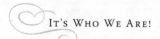

Military Women

We are military women,
Who've never left this land for war,
Our battleground is here at home,
And our home's what we fight for.
Our attire has no insignia,
No ribbons, epaulets, or bars,
No shining medals of distinction,
No gold, or bronze, or silver stars.
Our normal dress is jeans and sweats,
That's a sort of uniform, I s'pose,
Just right for what we do at home,
Thus, they must be military clothes.
Our duty is to keep our homes,
As safe as safe can be,
And to keep the home fires burning,
For dear ones here and overseas.
We're mothers, daughters, sisters, aunts,
We're worriers . . . and warriors,
We stand tall and do not fall
Indeed, we are superior.
We are an army of strong women,
Who do not jump to buglers' horns,
We bear no destructive weapons,
And our jeans are uniforms.
We tend and tend and tend again
To our families and our homes,
With all our might, we fight and fight
To win our wars and hold our own.

~VIRGINIA (GINNY) ELLIS

© *January 2009*

Act as if it were impossible to fail.
~DOROTHEA BRANDE

Your goal should be out of reach but not out of sight.
~ANITA DEFRANTZ

We don't know who we are until we see what we can do.
~MARTHA GRIMES

The real winners in life are the people who look at every situation with an expectation that they can make it work or make it better.
~BARBARA PLETCHER, AUTHOR

The future belongs to those who believe in the beauty of their dreams.
~ELEANOR ROOSEVELT

Look at a day when you are supremely satisfied at the end.
It's not a day when you lounge around doing nothing;
it's when you've had everything to do, and you've done it.
~MARGARET THATCHER

Follow your heart, but be quiet for a while first.
Ask questions, then feel the answer. Learn to trust your heart.
~UNKNOWN

Guess What? I Enlisted!

My Recruiter Was Right

January 1982—I first met my Air Force recruiter on a cold snowy winter day when I was twenty-two. I was looking for a way out of debt and away from the cold. My recruiter was polite, but I could tell he didn't really think I had much to offer. He gave me the introductory speech, asked me a few background questions, and scheduled me to take the Armed Forces Vocational Aptitude Battery test to see if I was smart enough to serve. A few days later, I spent an evening answering the multiple choice aptitude questions. The following week I called to see if my test results were back. I scored well in all four areas; I could choose any career field I wanted.

FEBRUARY 1982   Before signing the delayed enlistment papers, I had a long talk with my Mom. I wanted her advice regarding my decision to serve. From what I'd discussed with my recruiter I felt the structure and camaraderie might fill the void I was feeling in my life. The United States was not at war and, I naively believed we would be at peace for many years to come; however, I had contemplated the possibility of conflict and truly wanted to protect and defend our freedoms if necessary. Once Mom was convinced that I was serious and ready to make a commitment, she gave me her blessing and I visited my recruiter again. I was very interested in computer technology, which fell into the Electrical area; so I choose that as my career field. Unfortunately, there wasn't an open training slot for me until later in the year, so I took the Military Enlistment Oath, and entered into the Air Force Delayed Enlistment program. My recruiter commented that I would be married within a year of my enlistment. I thought that was an odd thing to say. I wasn't looking for a husband I was looking for a career and a chance to serve my country.

JUNE 1982   I flew to Texas for Basic military training. My flight consisted of about fifty women from all across the United States. We marched a lot: to physical readiness training, to the chow hall where we waited in line for meals, to processing locations and to classrooms. In the processing locations, we received uniforms, vaccinations, or testing. In the classrooms, our flight was usually seated on one side of the room and our "Brother" (all male) Flight was on the other side; so our classroom instruction was co-ed, sort-of. We studied military law, history and how to behave in uniform. Along with all the military training, I realized men look similar when they all have the same haircut and uniform on, and men in uniform are *very* attractive.

AUGUST 1982   After Basic, I boarded a bus headed for Tech school. I was looking forward to plowing through a paperback. I didn't get very far in the book since the airman sitting next to me wanted to talk. As I glanced around the bus, I noticed that all the women were being chatted up; it appeared that after 6½ weeks of limited interaction with the opposite sex both genders were ready for some interaction.

SEPTEMBER 1982   Several weeks after arrival, we had enough airmen to fill a class and we started technical training. Six hours of classroom instruction followed by a lunch break. I spent afternoons studying in my room. In the evenings, it was time to relax at the airmen's club. At the club, I learned that when guys out number gals by ten-to-one, that one gal is *pretty popular.* I never had so many guys hanging around me in all my life. I was a few years older than most of the students going through training there so, I dated a National Guard member closer to my age who was at Tech school to learn a new skill.

DECEMBER 1982   Since classes shut down for two weeks, I used some leave to go home, visit family and friends. Upon returning from leave, I had six

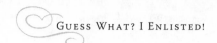

weeks remaining before graduation, and vowed not to get involved with anyone else before I shipped out. Two weeks later, I met my husband.

JANUARY 1983 Airman Raz walked into the classroom and started talking a mile a minute. He would be our instructor for the next block of technical training. My buddy, Dave, was sitting behind me and watching my reaction, later he told me he could see the fireworks going off that very first day; the chemistry between me and Airman Raz was visible to the whole class. Of course, student/instructor fraternization was strictly prohibited, but that doesn't stop people from being attracted to one another. After completing that block of training, Raz asked me out. I accepted, even though it meant breaking the rules; in my mind, it was okay because he would not be teaching my class any more. Four weeks after our first date, Raz took me to the airport; I was shipping out for my first assignment. He teared up as we were saying goodbye, and I decided at that moment that I would not let him get away. To my knowledge, no guy had ever cried because he cared so much about me and was going to miss me, so you can understand why I had to make the relationship work.

FEBRUARY 1983 665th Calumet Air Force Station located on the upper peninsula of Michigan. I managed to arrive between snow storms. I was assigned to a transmitter maintenance team and started my on-the-job-training with Sergeant Vanhuisen. When I wasn't busy learning about, or maintaining, the radar I was writing letters to Raz.

APRIL 1983 Raz and I decided to get married. The plan was to go to a Justice of the Peace for a simple civil ceremony, but Mom got upset when I told her that plan; so, Raz arranged for a Methodist minister he knew to perform a church ceremony to please the in-laws he hadn't even met yet.

MAY 1983 Took leave to get married. We had a very simple afternoon service with a couple friends and immediate family.

Just as my recruiter predicted, I was married before my one year anniversary in the Air Force. One of the best decisions of my life. We'll be celebrating our 26th anniversary this year!
~JULIA BORCHARDT RASMUSSEN
http://juliaras.blogspot.com

Ask for what you want and be prepared to get it.
~MAYA ANGELOU

It takes a lot of courage to show your dreams to someone else.
~ERMA BOMBECK

We've chosen the path to equality, don't let them turn us around.
~GERALDINE FERRARO
The first woman to be nominated as Vice President of the United States

The path to a goal is hardly ever a straight line.
~CATH KACHUR-DESTEFANO

That's the way things come clear. All of a sudden.
And then you realize how obvious they've been all along.
~MADELINE L'ENGLE

The world is terrified by joyful women. Take a stand—be one anyway!
~MARIANNE WILLIAMSON, AUTHOR OF *A WOMAN'S WORTH*

Heart of a Warrior

The night is dark; a deep, bone-chilling darkness without a single star, no moonlight, no lights outside the windows. It's June 21, 1988, somewhere around 2:30 A.M., and you've been traveling since noon the day before. You've been on 'em all: planes, trains, automobiles—and now a bus—a BIG bus. The biggest bus you've ever seen in your short seventeen years of life. This is the farthest you've ever been from home—the farthest you've ever been alone. But you ain't scared; you're a teenager! You know it all and you've got something to prove—to yourself and to the world.

The bus glides to a stop. The airbrakes *hissssss*. Then silence. A silence so loud that you can actually feel it. The only sound you hear is the sound of your heartbeat and the heartbeats of the other souls on the bus with you. You finally acknowledge the *fear*.

All of sudden, the loudest voice you have ever heard bellows, "*Get off my stinkin' bus and put your feet on my yellow footprints—now!*"

That is how I remember my arrival at Marine Recruit Depot, Parris Island, South Carolina. I had arrived at Marine Corps Boot Camp. Let me tell you, in that moment (and plenty of other moments throughout the course of boot camp!) my heart pounded with fear.

Fear changed my life. I was afraid I had made a huge mistake. I was afraid I couldn't handle the challenges I faced. I was afraid to make the drill instructor mad. I was afraid I wouldn't be good enough. I was afraid of my thoughts, so I *quit thinking* and did what I was told to do. I got off the bus.

Ralph Waldo Emerson wrote, "Unless you try to do something beyond what you have already mastered, you will never grow."

When I heard that first unforgettable bellow, I thought to myself, "What am I doing here? Do I have what it takes? I have never really tried to do anything that I didn't know *for sure* I would be good at. Am I good enough to be a leader? Can I be a U.S. Marine? Do I have the heart of a warrior?"

First I had to find out, what being a leader even meant.

The United States Marine Corps defines leadership as the sum of those qualities of intellect, human understanding, and moral character that allow a person to inspire and control a group of people successfully. You see, the Marine Corps has a set of leadership principles (general rules) that have guided the conduct and actions of successful leaders of the past. I had always fought against *rules*. Generation after generation of American men and women have given special meaning to the title *United States Marine*. These same men and women live by a set of enduring core values and principles that form the bedrock of their character. These principles give them strength and regulate their behavior. They form the foundation that allows them to meet any challenge. I had never really challenged myself.

Why was I here? Could I claim the title of U.S. Marine? Was I good enough to be a leader? Did I have the heart of a warrior? On that first day of boot camp, I wasn't so sure. I finally admitted I was afraid. In that moment, I surrendered.

You see, I had been a pretty rebellious kid. Oh, I was smart. And I was athletic. But, I was not the standard Marine recruit. I didn't fit the stereotype. I was going to be "different" from most of my fellow recruits from the get go, or so I had been told by *them*. I had been told I wouldn't be accepted. I would always be an outsider. I was told the Marines were NOT the place for me. I was told I wouldn't make it. *I was told I would fail.*

On the surface, I seemed like a pretty self-confident kid. I had been a varsity athlete in several sports (even had a private coach to see if I really had what it took to try for the Olympics) mostly B's, some A's—without *ever* studying—and was usually invited to all the "in" parties. Inside, however, I was anything BUT confident. I had relied on natural athletic ability, a ridiculously high competitive spirit, and a better-than-average memory/brain to "achieve" all that I had so far accomplished. People seemed to make a big deal out of stuff that just came easy to me. In fact, when anything got too hard, when I actually had to put forth some mental effort, or even push myself, *I usually found a way out of it without being labeled a quitter.*

Back then, I would rather be known as "difficult" or "mouthy" than be known as a quitter or slacker because I could find a way to spin my mouthing off into comedy for the social scene. I didn't respect authority. I didn't respect myself. I didn't have the courage to push myself to my limits. I was really afraid to my very core those first few days of boot camp. I was afraid I would not make it. I was afraid I would lose. I was afraid I would actually have to try. I was afraid because I knew I couldn't get out of it . . . I couldn't quit. Really, I was just afraid to see what I had inside. I had to trust when the drill instructors said that they were there to help, but more importantly, I had to trust myself. I had to believe that I had whatever I needed inside of me. I had to believe I could face the challenge.

Marines know that leadership skills take time, discipline and *belief* to develop, but the payoff is worth the dedication. Marines know that deep within all of us lies the heart of a warrior. Once I surrendered to my fear, I found the courage to act in spite of it. That is the definition of courage— courage is not the absence of fear, it is acting in the face of it. I didn't know I had courage. It was only when I thought I was surrendering . . . *when I quit fighting* . . . that I was able to truly win. I won the opportunity to develop skills (initiative, enthusiasm, dedication, decisiveness, etc.) that will serve me the rest of my life. It was only when I began to trust myself and others, to respect my leaders and learn from them, to believe in myself that I developed the heart of a warrior.

What are you afraid of? Where do you need to surrender?

I believe you have the heart of warrior inside of you. Do you?

~KELLEY MOORE

Former U.S. Marine Cpl. 1988–1993

In This Man's Navy

I had an awesome childhood, at least I think so. Mom did an awesome job by herself. Five children and I was the oldest. She raised us all to be strong and hard working. I give her so much respect, and I cannot express how she has impacted my life. She quit school at 16, and after many years of struggling, she got her high school GED, literally crawled her way up the ladder and retired a government employee, not an easy feat and unheard of, especially in today's society. So, when I came to her at seventeen, in 1981, and asked her if she would sign and give me permission to join the United States Navy, she did not hesitate to say yes.

As a junior in high school, I knew what I wanted to do in my life. It may have been that my father told awesome sea stories during his four years in the Navy, it may have been the poster on the school guidance office window, "Join the Navy, see the world." It may have been the lectures from Mom about not getting pregnant in high school and ruining my life, but I know that I did not want to stay in Ohio. I loved the ocean, I wanted to see the world, and there had to be to more to life than what was in front of me.

I was supposed to fly on an airplane for the first time to Orlando, Florida but it was during an air traffic controller strike and I ended up taking a Greyhound Bus from Ohio to Florida. It didn't matter, even after I joined as a non-rated seaman. I didn't know any better; I was finally out of Ohio and, on my way to something that would change my life forever. Little did I know that Boot Camp was not what I expected. Who wants to be yelled at all day, every day by this person called a Company Commander as soon as stepping off a Greyhound bus? I survived.

My dream was to serve on a Navy vessel. But, unfortunately, in 1981, the Navy was not equipped to have women on ships. Women could only serve on non-combatant ships. So, I listened to criticism from men that "females take up all the shore duty billets." It really got old. I was in Sigonella, Sicily when I was offered my first ship in Norfolk, Virginia. And, I was so excited

even though I was recently married because it meant that I could finally be a sailor. My first ship tour was my first indoctrination into This Man's Navy. I have heard many speeches from high-ranking officials, using the term, but to live those words every day was difficult and challenging.

Three ships, and many duty stations later, I never gave up. I did serve in This Man's Navy and, I'm proud to say so. Throughout the years, the Navy has changed for the better and worse. I believe that the military should be treated and served differently than society. Military life is not for everyone and should not be taken lightly.

I served 26 years in This Man's Navy. I joined as an Enlisted E-1 and retired an Officer O-4 and it was the best 26 years of my life. I am now a government employee working for the Navy and I wouldn't change anything. They were the toughest times, but definitely the best times. I have the closest friends and the best memories that will last the rest of my life.

~TINA MCHARGUE, LCDR, USN (RET.)

Every day we make choices, decisions about what and how our life will be. Each day we go forward or backwards in getting what we want in life. Sometimes we don't make the right choices, but we make the choice we thought best at the moment. We all make mistakes. It's learning from our mistakes and letting them go that determines our future.

~DEBRA PESTRAK

One's philosophy is not best expressed in words; it is expressed in the choices one makes. In the long run, we shape our lives and we shape ourselves. The process never ends until we die. And, the choices we make are ultimately our own responsibility.

~ELEANOR ROOSEVELT, 1884–1962, FORMER AMERICAN FIRST LADY

Getting an Education

I was at home studying. I remember my dad coming in my room and telling me that there was not enough money saved to get me through college. That was when I was in eighth grade. Since that talk, I always wanted to join the military. It was my ticket away from home and a chance for me to go to college. I met all the different service recruiters, but I finally decided to join the Navy at seventeen in the Delayed Entry Program. I went on Active Duty the following year, August 1984. Boot Camp and my apprentice school were both a blast! My first tour of duty was incredible! I went to Washington, D.C., and worked for the oldest Active Duty member in the military at the time, Vice Admiral John D. Bulkeley, a World War II Medal Of Honor recipient. During my tour in D.C., I was accepted in the Enlisted Commissioning Program that allowed me to get my Bachelor's Degree and a commission. I graduated the University of Florida where I was commissioned an Ensign in 1991. Then, during my free time at my next duty station, I took courses through the Florida Institute of Technology earning a Master's Degree in 1995. Several tours later I earned another Master's Degree at the Naval Postgraduate School in 2001. I retired from the Navy in 2005 and later earned an Associate's Degree using my GI Bill. What I learned from going to school is that there is so much information out there. More importantly, the military supports their people going to school and being the best we can be!

My entire Navy career was about constant learning, growing, and evolving as a person and as a sailor whether I was in class or at work. I learned so much about leadership, professionalism, people, and myself. I met and still in touch with many of my fellow sailors, Marines, Airmen, and soldiers. I wouldn't change anything from my service to the Navy and to our country!

~MICHELE RUPPERT, INFORMATION PROFESSIONAL

Lieutenant Commander, U.S. Navy

http://www.micheleruppert.com

Courage is fear that has said its prayers.
~DOROTHY BERNARD

Your talent is God's gift to you.
What you do with it is your gift back to God.
~LEO BUSCAGLIA

Nothing in life is to be feared. It is only to be understood.
~MADAME MARIE CURIE

In the over two centuries since the signing of the Declaration of
Independence, millions of Americans have bravely served our nation in
uniform so that all generations can continue to enjoy those same liberties.
~DOC HASTINGS

My mother drew a distinction between achievement and success. She said
that achievement is the knowledge that you have studied and worked hard
and done the best that is in you. Success is being praised by others. That
is nice but not as important or satisfying. Always aim for achievement—
success will follow.
~HELEN HAYES, AWARD WINNING ACTRESS

You must do the thing you think you cannot do.
~ELEANOR ROOSEVELT

A Challenging Transition

My story might be the mirror of the life of another immigrant woman trying to find the best way to start her life over in a new and completely different world. In this spirit, I decided to join the military with the conviction it was the key to open the door to a world of different opportunities and fresh and rewarding possibilities, and that was exactly what I heard at the recruiter's office. Adventure, opportunity, respect, recognition were some of the words that trapped my interest and made me decide to join right away.

Although it has been three years since I went through Boot Camp, it still brings me memories of the initial challenges I faced for I was not used to being told what to do, where to go, when to eat, to sit or not to sit down, what time to go to bed and even when or when not to make a "head call" (go to the bathroom) and sharing a room with about forty other women.

A couple of months later, a new military experience was waiting for me, apprentice school. Life there was more relaxed even though we had to stick to the military bearing learned in Boot Camp. There, we learned the necessary skills we needed to go face the real deal, *the fleet*. To my amazement, I was sent to an enormous intimidating carrier ship; the one from which I am writing right now. I felt like a diminutive . . . thrilled . . . abandoned . . . insignificant being in the world. I wanted to cry, run away and go back home; unfortunately, I discovered, there was no way back. That was it!

To this day, I still remember the warm smile followed by, "Welcome to the ship and our berthing. We will make it a cozy place for you to live." You can imagine how these simple words change my fears and gave me the assurance I was just going to be all right.

Although getting used to the military life has implied multiple challenges from the very beginning, I have learned that good will and hard work are the main ingredients to succeed in even the hardest environment; even on a ship where daily you have to try to walk through the same small passage way or you have to wait in line sometimes for hours to eat, or more

than twenty minutes to take a shower after having worked for fifteen or more hours a day. All these aspects have taught me a big lesson about patience, tolerance, and endurance. I have learned many valuable lessons from people from all walks in life I never expected to. I feel when my time comes to go back to the civilian life I will have a better perception, a more mature visualization and a higher appreciation of the simple things of life.

The experience has been invaluable since it has helped me to slow down and clarify many aspects of my life I was not really sure about. As a life lesson, it would be worth it especially for somebody who is trying to find their way in life; it is a good beginning. Just keep in mind that challenging experiences have a high component of difficulty and sometimes pain in them. Yet, what makes them rich is precisely their complexity.

~MARIA QUINONEZ

Never do things others can do and will do if there are things others cannot do or will not do.
~AMELIA EARHART

If we did all the things we were capable of doing, we would literally astound ourselves.
~THOMAS EDISON

You do not have to be superhuman to do what you believe in.
~DEBBI FIELDS

The future belongs to those who believe in the beauty of their dreams.
~ELEANOR ROOSEVELT

The Meaning of Teamwork

As a teenage girl growing up in a notorious university party town, I was a little wild. I did not care much for school and certainly did not plan to continue on to college after I barely graduated high school. I was a smart young girl and maybe a little too smart for my own good as I found that I got bored easily and would make up things to do to stir up a little excitement and buzz. I had quite a lot of fun doing that, but as I neared high school graduation, I realized my antics would not get me far in life.

On one unique day, I was in my first period class and I paid attention to the morning bulletin. It was unusual for me to make it to first period or to listen to anything said over the loud speaker. What caught my attention that day was the announcement of the military aptitude testing that was going to be conducted on campus the next day. That meant that if I took the test, I did not have to go to class. I signed-up for the test right away.

After some time passed I received the results from the aptitude test, and to my surprise, I did exceptionally well. Almost immediately, I started getting calls and visits from recruiters. The only thing was that my mom and dad did not know I was talking with recruiters—until after I had made the decision to join the Air Force. My mom took my leaving home very hard, as I'm sure I would if my daughter suddenly joined the military and left home.

Something happened to me the first time I put on my military uniform. I felt strong and confident. I felt like I was part of something big and important and I took it very seriously. I worked hard in my training and even with a few bruised and cracked ribs and a chipped tooth; I made it through the Joint Services Police Academy in the top three-percent of my class. I learned that no matter how hard something is, there is nothing I cannot do. I felt challenged to perform at my highest level and I delivered with 100 percent of my ability.

That young wild child right out of high school grew up quickly. My first duty station was Clark Air Base, Philippines. It was January 27, 1986 when

I got to Clark; and it was the day before the space shuttle *Challenger* disaster. It was also the beginning of a national Philippines' disaster, the *People Power Revolution*.

I stood beside my fellow Airmen as we defended our Base during the tumultuous times leading up to the Marcos/Aquino election, and the resulting strikes against the American presence in the Philippines because of our involvement in aiding the escape of former president and dictator, Ferdinand Marcos and his wife Imelda. I saw firsthand what a foreign terrorist organization is capable of as members of the New People's Army (NPA) injured, kidnapped and killed American's right outside our military bases. One of my best friends, and fellow law enforcement specialist, Steven Faust, was assassinated by the NPA within a mile from my off-base house. You grow up quickly when you begin to realize how fragile life is and how quickly it can all end.

I learned to trust my instincts and to trust in my fellow Airman. When the threat level was at its highest and we had to pull 24-hour shifts, we huddled together sleeping wherever and whenever we could and we watched out for each other. That is when I learned the meaning of teamwork. We were a team in every sense of the word. We supported each other and when one of us was down, someone else would lift us up. We pulled together, kept each other safe, and got things done.

After returning to the states, I became a Desk Sergeant in charge of all law enforcement activity during my shifts at Barksdale Air Force Base, Louisiana. That position quickly taught me how to earn respect and become a leader. Being a female in a male-dominated career field had always presented its fair share of challenges, and being a young female Desk Sergeant increased the stakes just a little bit more. I learned how to communicate with authority and I learned the subtle, but oh-so important, art of being assertive versus being aggressive. I learned how to lead a team successfully, earned many awards including special recognition from the U.S. Military Inspector General, and represented the base as the Female Police Officer of the Year for the state of Louisiana. I had a strong team around me at all times.

I appreciate everything I learned from my eight years in the military. I am who I am today because of what I learned during that time. I gained confidence, learned perseverance, learned to trust and believe in others and myself, I learned the importance of teamwork and I learned how to be an effective leader. I will be forever grateful and proud of my military service. I stand extra tall when I hear our National Anthem and I will always remember and honor those that serve, fight and die for our freedom today.

~ANGELA STRADER, SERGEANT, USAF, LAW ENFORCEMENT SPECIALIST

www.angiestrader.com

Twenty-five million veterans are living among us today. These men and women selflessly set aside their civilian lives to put on the uniform and serve us.

~STEVE BUYER

When we ask American men and women in uniform to fight for this country and to defend this country's interest and then to send them overseas, there is no question we have an obligation to protect them and provide for their safety.

~BYRON DORGAN

Be the change you want to see in the world.

~MAHATMA GANDHI

The Army Connection

I suppose in some ways I was destined to be in the Army and have an Army family. Perhaps it was the fact that my father, who was serving in Vietnam at the time, was informed of my unceremonious arrival into the world via a Red Cross message my mom had sent. Maybe it is somewhat ironic that I have chosen this path because my father was not a career military man. The end of his tour in Vietnam was also the end of his service to the U.S. Army, so I really wasn't what you could call an Army brat. I don't have any memories of my father as a soldier or what it was like to be a child of the Army. So, I don't really know what drew me toward the same U.S. Army when I was a high school senior. Maybe it was the money for school, possibly the hope for some sense of structure after I left home or perchance that little voice we all have inside of us guiding us through uncertainty. I'm still not entirely sure what compelled me to make that commitment, but I know my life has been enriched by that choice.

Since I enlisted in the Army Reserves, you could say I decided to "test drive" the Army before I dove in full-time. This "part-time" adventure opened up a myriad of opportunities for me, allowing me to attend the college of my choice, gain an ROTC scholarship and, ultimately, earn an engineering degree. With that coveted degree in hand, I guess you could say the Army and I both decided to extend this adventure and try it out full-time.

My initial commitment was eight years. Considering all the Army had provided me, it seemed like a pretty fair trade. So, I started a brand new journey after college, first to Fort Lewis, Washington, then Fort Huachuca, Arizona, and then off to Germany, one of my lifelong dreams. I think I grew up a lot there, mostly because I was able to act like a child. It was just me, no responsibilities; I could make mistakes, and they only affected me. I learned a lot about myself, others, and became comfortable in my own skin. And, I met my future husband, who was also in the U.S. Army. We met while we were deployed, no civilian clothes, no alcohol, no fancy dinners or movies, just people living a modest life. We didn't know each other for very long, but there was something there worth preserving, and we both felt the same way. And, so there we were, back at Fort Huachuca, Arizona, married by an Army chaplain.

Ten years later, I had been working as a civilian for almost that long, I had returned to the U.S. Army Reserves; both of us were just having fun and growing old together. We had always wondered if we were right for kids. We liked to travel and live the spontaneous life, and often wondered if a child would overcomplicate things. We decided maybe, and six-months later he deployed for a year to Iraq. I figured we could wait a little longer for the final answer to the question; time was running out, but there would still be a few grains of sand left after he returned. And, maybe, that was our answer.

Two weeks after he left, I found out I was pregnant; I was due in August, three months before his return. And, if I hadn't had a last-minute C-section he could have potentially seen the birth of his son via a webcam. The prevalence of email and other communication methods, have made the necessity of Red Cross messages about the births of children rare nowadays. He was also able to come home to meet his son a few weeks after the birth; a rarity, back then. And, we were able to use a webcam, along with pictures and even a few videos, so he could track his son's progress from far away.

We wonder what path our son will follow. Will he be inexplicably drawn to the military like we were? And, if he is, and starts a family, what will be new and different for them? I just hope I am able to offer them support like my parents did for me while my husband was deployed. And, tell them the same stories about how tough it was back when he was born, all we had was email, webcams, video, and cell phones.

~CARIN SMITH, MAJOR, U.S. ARMY RESERVES

A Day in the Life

To Support and Defend

The El Paso, Texas airport was busy as always. A large group of Army personnel were boarding a plane for a deployment to Afghanistan. Fort Bliss is a stone's throw from the airport and Holloman AFB in Alamagordo, New Mexico, where I was stationed 90 miles away. The airport was busy with troops coming and going.

I walked to the escalator and stepped on. I didn't look back until I got to the top and saw my children and my sister walking toward the exit. They could no longer walk me to the gate to see me off for temporary duty. My heart was heavy as I watched them walk away. National Guard personnel were at various locations throughout the airport, weapons ready. Since 9/11 our country was left in a constant state of alert. It was now my turn to support and defend in the Middle East. As an Air Force Master Sergeant, I was being sent to run an operation. I walked down the long corridor to the plane that would start my journey. With each step I took, I felt the longing for my children and the feeling of separation intensified. It felt like Velcro ripping apart.

I flew from El Paso to Atlanta to board a flight with 200-plus others deploying to various locations in that region. The next leg was Atlanta to Germany for a layover while the plane refueled. The final leg was from Germany to Qatar where I would be spending the next four months of my life in a *tent city*. We all knew of the threat of being blown out of the sky by terrorist forces, so when we were told to pull the shades, and the pilot turned off all the lights for our approach into Qatar, we understood it was so we wouldn't be easily detected.

Touch down was around midnight; it's hot, humid, dusty and miserable. The bags are piled in the middle of the camp—about 1,000 of them. Most people have four bags, two personal and two military-issued gear. Good thing I marked mine with some bright-colored scarves because 400 Chemical Warfare gear bags all look the same. Once processed in, my group of about 30 piled into a bus, and was hauled off to a place called Camp Snoopy, where I would run the Contracting Operation for the 1,000-person base.

The sun was starting to rise as we headed to Camp Snoopy. It was 4 A.M. We arrived at around 5 A.M. to be initiated into the daily process of getting back onto the base. Off the bus, show our ID, sign in, back on the bus to another checkpoint where our ID's were checked again and a large gate opened to let us in. Then, onto yet another checkpoint to get off the bus again, while our vehicle was searched thoroughly for bombs and other objects of terror. This was all a bit unnerving, but part of the territory. It was something we simply dealt with as a normal course of life in a country that was rumored to be a pass-through area for al-Qaida. We're not in the U.S. anymore! Things are different here.

Check-in seemed to take forever. As a Master Sergeant, I was given one of 12 bunks in a small trailer-like facility. The trailer was split into three small rooms, each with four bunks, two top, two bottom, a table in between, two closets and two makeshift shelving units built by a military member who had deployed here sometime before me. There was a window air conditioner on full blast, since the temperature outside was already over 100 degrees at 6 A.M. and approaching 100 percent humidity. I moved my stuff in, and had one bunk-mate who I could reach out and touch.

No time for the weary, I walked over to check-in with my unit, and the guy I was replacing immediately started to brief me on the operation. After all it was already 7 A.M. and the business day was starting. I had only been up for something like a day-and-a-half without sleep. So, I didn't understand a word he said; eventually had to tell him I was zoning out and needed some sleep. It took me a couple of weeks to get my sleep schedule straight.

Once I got settled into the job, I was working 16–18 hour days. We had a recreation tent with several recreation rooms, including an Internet café

to use for e-mailing family members. I was in the Contracting office and we had our own computers and phones so could e-mail and call anytime. There was an outdoor bar in the recreation area with beer and wine, and we were issued a beer card. We had four days per week that we could get three beers or glasses of wine per person.

There were about 700 Air Force, 200 Army and 100 Canadians on this base. We had two chow halls (dining facility) where we ate our meals. I handled the contract to feed the personnel on base. The food was pretty good. One night a week was steak and crab, or lobster. If your birthday was in the month, you could attend the monthly birthday dinner. They roasted a camel once, which was interesting.

One night, the menu was Mexican food. I love to cook homemade Mexican food and missed being able to make my fresh salsa. I asked the cooks if they would let me make homemade salsa. I love to cook Mexican food for my friends, but didn't know what I was in for when I made salsa for 1,000 people! I reported to the main chow hall kitchen several hours before dinner. They gave me an apron and hat, and set me up to roast the tomatoes in a large square cooking surface. I roasted more than two dozen tomatoes that day and it took me about three hours to complete. I added cilantro, fresh garlic, jalapenos, onions and seasoning to make the largest pot of salsa I had ever seen or made! I finished just in time for the dinner meal. Many of my friends and co-workers knew I was making salsa. It didn't last long. By the end of the night it was all gone.

My work in the Middle East was hard and grueling. The heat was almost unbearable. The hours were long and the real world seemed far away. I accepted an opportunity to give back something to a large group of military members who hadn't tasted home cooking in many months. By the speed at which the salsa disappeared, I'd say they were grateful to receive it. My hope is that I will have the opportunity to repeat this experience again in the future.

~ELDONNA LEWIS FERNANDEZ, MASTER SERGEANT, USAF (RET.)

http://pinkbikerchic.com

Undercover Angel:
From Beauty Queen to SWAT Team

Feeling rather proud of myself for my ability to drive a stick shift, I arrogantly volunteered to do a tractor-trailer run downtown with a 32-foot flatbed trailer. I got onto the highway feeling confident. I ignored the usual Saudi road-rage, and felt euphoric driving such a powerful big rig. I dared a Saudi to cut me off in this monster! I now knew what it felt like to power such a huge machine and earn the respect of mortal drivers. When a 32-foot tractor-trailer changes lanes, everyone moves out of the way.

My trip went without a glitch. I picked up the load, strapped down my cargo, and headed back to the base. But as I arrived at the main entrance, my illusion of confidence came to a thundering halt. I had forgotten about the zig-zagging, anti-terrorist barricade that I would need to weave through to get back onto the base. I recalled that, weeks earlier, this had not been an easy task with the 1.5-ton box truck. I came to a dead stop, took a deep breath, and ran a series of options through my mind:

OPTION #1: I could drive around the entire base and ascertain if all the entrances had the barricades.

OPTION #2: I could park the truck and beg the Saudi guard to open what looked like a padlocked entrance a few yards adjacent to the main gate.

OPTION #3: I could swallow my pride, radio the motor pool, and request that a more experienced driver meet me at the gate.

OPTION #4: I could give it a try myself.

An advocate of common sense, I jumped down from the rig and walked up to the guard shack. The guards noticed me approaching on foot and became alarmed; one of them scurried to meet me. He held his weapon cautiously and demanded, "What you need?"

I handed him my identification and said, "I don't think I could get the truck through the barricade—is there another entrance without a barricade, or could you open the side gate?"

"No!"

"No what? No gate without a barricade, or no you can't open the side gate?"

He glared at me and insisted, "This way in only!"

I looked at him in disbelief and said, "Thanks."

I felt fired up and thought, *"I'll show 'em,"* as I climbed back into my tractor, and prepared to fit King Kong through the gerbil maze. I wove through the first barricade with relative ease. But as I started my turn into the next one, I could see in my sideview mirror that I was not going to clear the rear barricade. I was exasperated. There was no way humanly possible to get this rig through such a tight configuration. I noticed chunks scraped from the barricades and black rubber marks staining the concrete—definitely a sign that what I was attempting was no easy task. As I tried to back up and restart a sharper forward cut, I came nearer and nearer to the rear barricade thinking, *"I, too, will be leaving a personal mark."*

Vehicles were now piling up behind me, waiting for their turn to get through the maze. I jumped from my rig and asked the driver of the Jeep behind me to spot me as I tried to maneuver out of this mess. For the next 20 minutes, I backed up and pulled forward, rocking back and forth, inching myself between the barricades. All the while, I was stalling out between reverse and first gear. The cars continued to stack up behind me and the gate guard finally had enough. He approached the side of my truck and barked, "Get this out!" I looked at him with equal rage, and asked, "You wanna try it?" He shouted, "Let's go, let's go!"

I assured him help was on the way, radioed my dispatcher, and humbly asked for assistance. One of the sergeants arrived, laughed at my predicament, and took my seat. I remained outside the tractor and spotted his movement. It took us an additional ten minutes to get through the gate.

When I finally climbed into the passenger seat of my rig he said, "You did pretty good kid."

"What if I told you I just learned how to drive stick shift last month?"

"Then you did great. Be prepared though, they're all laughing at you back at the shop."

It didn't matter, if the sergeant needed ten minutes to get through with years of experience driving a truck, I didn't do so badly. At least I tried. This is something that shaped the way I treated life circumstances from that moment on. I would *always* try.

Ninety days had gone by in a flash. I returned home, free of snakebites and scorpion stings, and the skill of having learned how to drive standard transmission vehicles. I became enlightened about the Muslim culture. I'd experienced the notorious desert sand storms and 130° heat. Also, I'd been unanimously chosen to be interviewed for an article in the *Air Force Times* because of my optimistic view on serving in Saudi Arabia considering the gender issues.

Several years after that experience in 1996, I learned that the condominiums I once called home, the Khobar Towers, had been blown up in a terrorist attack. Nineteen Americans, Saudis and allies were killed, and 500 were injured—this in a time known as "Desert Calm." The terrorists abandoned a fuel tanker full of explosives, just adjacent to the anti-terrorist barricade, and detonated it a short time later.

I learned, for the first time, that there are places where it was not advantageous to be a woman; Mom was right to worry, and it made perfect sense that the Saudi guards were so cautious and ill tempered.

After completing my four-year tour of duty in Boston, I was in a flux. I was asked to re-enlist but had no passion for the transportation industry. There was certainly no future for Tony in Boston, as the Chicago Carpenter's Union was significantly stronger. My goal had been to enter the Air Force to get an education; therefore, moving back to Chicago was the logical solution.

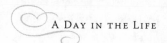

Once home, I entered community college and began working full-time as a private security officer. The more I learned about public safety through my employment and my criminal justice courses, the more interested I became in law enforcement.

While working the security job, I met a police officer who would find a reason to enter my building and engage me in casual small talk. "What's a nice girl like you doing in a job like this?" When I explained that the "nice girl" was a Desert Storm Veteran, he became reticent. Even with that information—and the knowledge that I was married, "Officer Friendly" was clearly in denial. Time after time, this rogue refused to look beyond my shell and mocked my interest in becoming a police officer. He was more interested in trying to cheat on his wife than answering my litany of police-related questions.

As part of my college course criteria, I was required to devote 200 hours as an intern at a police department of my choice. I chose the Chicago Police Department for two reasons: I was aware that Chicago gave educational incentives beyond a four-year degree, and I'd have plenty of opportunities for excitement.

~LISA LOCKWOOD, AUTHOR OF *UNDERCOVER ANGEL: FROM BEAUTY QUEEN TO SWAT TEAM*

Excerpt from Lisa Lockwood's Memoir, Chapter 4: Desert Storm

U.S. Air Force 1989–1993, Desert Storm Veteran

www.LisaLockwood.com

Focus on your potential instead of your limitations.
~ALAN LOY MCGINNIS

Dead Air

When I enlisted in 1976, the Women's Army Corp (WAC) was in the process of being disestablished as a separate branch of the Army. I'm very proud to have been one of the last WAC's, serving during this exciting era in military history. Women were being admitted to West Point. Maternity leaves replaced compulsory discharges, and the umbrella, a traditional military taboo was approved for issue in the name of promoting a positive feminine image. The powers that be even retained a designer to fashion a sporty new mint green, wash and wear uniform. The times they were a changin'.

There were those, of course, who weren't enthusiastic about the trend. I encountered several male soldiers who appeared to be threatened by the growing presence of women in the motor pool, the mess hall, and even in co-ed barracks. Some men attempted to deflate our influence with casual flirtation. Others insisted we carry our weight—equal pay for equal work, by golly. None, however, stood out so predominantly in my memories as a certain surly NCO at Fort Gordon, Georgia.

Even though I'd have to change it here to protect the innocent, I wish I recalled his name. He was a gristly, Old Army type—a field instructor attached to the signal school where I was trained. I was offered only three occupational options; food service, clerkship, or communications. I'd opted be a radio teletype operator—a dinosaur Military Occupational Specialty (MOS), like the WACS that no longer exists. Quaint historical reference makes for great story telling. Ask any veteran, young or old. When two or more gather together, the war stories commence in earnest.

The Old Army NCO taught in the field, training the students to apply classroom academics to the actual equipment we'd use to perform our duties. We knew the basics of setting up and maintaining a radio network, but hadn't learned a great deal about trouble-shooting. His job was to station himself with one network station each day and teach us how to deal with real life obstacles as they cropped up.

His approach was stoic—stand back and let us flounder, making one frantic mistake after another, until the entire network crashed. Afterwards, he'd explain what went wrong and help us to figure out how we could have responded more effectively. In theory, his methods seemed valid enough, but his criticism was often sarcastic and condescending. Locking us in a poker face look, he'd observe every move without offering the slightest hint as to whether we were right or wrong. We never knew what was coming; reward or reprimand. It was excruciating.

One morning, I was manning the network controlling station. By the time he stuck his head through the door of the rig where I was working, I'd already lost communication with one of my network stations. The others were apparently beginning to panic, thumbing through their ciphering and frequency manuals to determine if their settings were correct. Lack of confidence in their own training may have caused them to fiddle with the dials.

The gristly NCO watched while I performed a network check, hailing the other two stations and getting dead air in response. I feverishly typed in the abbreviated commands again and got nothing. Staring at the teletype for a few seconds, I prayed for inspiration. He was expecting me to do something, so I hopped out of the rig and headed toward a nearby jeep.

I slipped on the Morse code key leg strap and began tapping out the commands. The NCO followed. He rested an elbow on the crash pad, leaning in toward me. He didn't say a word. When the keypad failed, I sat for awhile staring at the field phone, knowing that any transmission on it would be unsecured. I glanced at the NCO, but received no encouragement either way.

I decided to go for broke, snatching up the handset and cranking the generator. He was going to chew me up and spit me out no matter what I did, so I had nothing to lose. Via landline, I was able to contact each network station. Careful not to reveal any classified information over the airways, I instructed them to consult their manuals so we were all on the same page.

Afterwards, I jumped back in the rig and ran the network test again. Oh, to hear the glorious beeps, clicks, and whirs of life. We operated the rest of that day without incident. The NCO never uttered a word. Later that day, back in the barracks, I was summoned to the pay phone in the foyer. I greeted the caller, hearing tinny juke box music, tinkling glassware, and raucous voices in the background. Because he spoke so few times, I didn't recognize the NCO's gravelly voice until he introduced himself.

The hair rose on the back of my neck. I must have really messed up if he was calling from the NCO Club to tell me so. Judging by the way he slurred his words, the lecture probably wasn't going to be polite.

When I didn't respond, he continued. "I hate women," he said. "I especially hate women in the Army, so it really hurts to have to tell you this." He paused for what sounded like another slug from his cocktail.

"But you did one heck of a job out there this morning getting that network back up and running." Of course, being Old School, he didn't say "heck," but I took the liberty to paraphrase.

When I caught my breath after the initial shock, I thanked him. He promised that if I ever told anyone about our conversation, one-sided as it was, that he would promptly deny it. With that, he hung up, and I was left listening to dead air again.

I would go on to receive promotions and other honors from the United States Army, but none gratified me as much as a phone call from a gristly Old School NCO with a chip on his shoulder for women.

~SHIRLEY (SISKO) HARKINS

www.dramadrash.org

Nearly all men can stand adversity,
but if you want to test a man's character, give him power.
~ABRAHAM LINCOLN

Master's, Giglines, and PFTs

By the time I joined the military at the very experienced age of twenty-six, I thought I had done all that needed to be done as a woman in my profession. I had withstood the battle on the ordination of women in my church, and been ordained. I had proven my academic excellence and was entrusted with teaching Greek at the seminary I had attended; and, at another seminary in New York City. I was serving a small church and working on my doctoral degree and decided becoming a Navy Chaplain was what I needed to do. I wanted to be where the other young people were.

I had no idea what I would be faced with because of that decision. And I am so ever grateful to my mother and my grandmother who were my female role models for teaching me that I could do, and be anything I wanted, provided I was willing to do the work required to get there. I learned from them I would never have to fight to get what I wanted. I would have to prove that I could do the job and I could go wherever I wanted to go. And I am grateful to my father, who did not know that there were jobs women couldn't do. I had never met a woman minister, never heard of a woman Chaplain before I went to seminary and even there, the numbers were few.

My first weeks in "Chaplain School" in Newport, Rhode Island, were an incredible combination of exhilaration and frustration. The frustration was repetitive but I knew it would end in eight weeks. I was the only woman in the class; a fact I was frequently reminded of. In those first days, as the men were learning how to put their uniforms together, there was no one around to answer my questions about appropriate wearing of the uniforms I had purchased. The classes were all taught by male Chaplains who did not find it necessary to have that information available for women students. I did the best I could by asking questions at the uniform shop but I was still mortified at my first inspection when the Marine Corps Colonel who was conducting the inspection pointed out that my uniform was not regulation. My belt buckle was on the wrong side, it was on the same side as the men's.

(A woman's "gigline" and a man's are different; we button our shirts and zip our pants from opposite side.) The Colonel then proceeded to berate the class leader (an 0-5 Chaplain) for not teaching me the proper way to put on a uniform. I would hear about that too.

I found the class work in school tedious and simplistic. I kept my mouth shut, did my work and didn't rock the boat until the issue was forced. I was asked by one of the instructors why I didn't ask questions and he did not understand when I said I didn't have any. When he pushed it further, I pointed out that my score on the tests indicated that I understood the material perfectly. Class participation was a requirement but there were no discussions . . . just lectures during which the instructor read things to us we had read the night before. When I questioned the class leader privately about the class content, he informed me that we had to teach to the lowest common denominator.

I made another mistake when I commented that I was under the impression that everyone in the room had at least a Master's Degree in something. That was considered insubordination. I wasn't put on report for it, but I was warned. I didn't know it then but that class leader did not want me to succeed in my career choice.

My third strike with the class leader came in the running portion of the fitness program. I am not, and have never been, a runner. I ran with the group three days a week with everyone else and went to the remedial runs the other four days a week to prepare myself for the Marine Corps Physical Fitness Test (PFT) I would have to take toward the end of the school. I would have to do push-ups (not women's), pull-ups or women's bar hangs and accomplish the three-mile run in under 24 minutes. I would have to pass the swim, jump and tread water tests. Even at the beginning of training, I could complete the three miles in less than 24 minutes. I fast walked a lot of it. I volunteered to teach the remedial swimming, jumping and treading water programs for our Chaplains who did not know how to swim. I could do every part of the test except the run at superior levels.

One early morning, I was in my usual location at the back of the pack doing the run, and the class leader came up behind me and began yelling, "Faster, faster!" I picked up as best I could as he continued to hound me. He then started to shove me forward at which point I quickly subverted the desire to push back, and I stopped dead in my tracks. He got in my face and yelled something and started to push again. Finally, I stepped toward him and said "Sir, you are out of line. If you touch me again you will be picking yourself up off the ground." At which time he turned white, turned and ran away. He never spoke directly to me again during the next four weeks except when he had to award me my First Class certificate for the Marine Corps PFT. But he spoke to me in other ways. I conveyed my concerns to a few of my fellow Chaplains and to our training Gunnery Sergeant, and was told to keep a lid on it. So I did. I believed standing up for myself was sufficient to put an end to it.

I was wrong. I was rewarded with a less than glowing Fitness Report at the end of School. Those of you who know anything about Fit-reps, unless you walk on water (in those days) you don't get promoted or retained. Two years later, I had to make a formal statement to the Promotions Board concerning the prejudices of the class leader who had since retired. My work and reputation and the kind words of my commanding General made a difference. And my career was not impacted by the experience.

The exhilarating part will be another story!

~DARCY LOVGREN PAVICH

Chaplain/Stand Down Coordinator, Veterans Village of San Diego

www.vvsd.net

Love what you do for a living and live what you love.

~MARIA MARSALA

The Jug's Up

"Think you can land that Jug of yours short enough to take the first turn-off?" Helen McGilvery said.

"Sure. Can you?" Nancy Batson replied.

"Easy," Mac said. "Let's do it."

"You're on," Batson said.

They left the Officers' Mess, headed for the flight line and, after a word with their respective instructors, each climbed into her single-seat P-47 pursuit airplane.

The two attractive women in flight coveralls had caught the eye of several young male pilots. But it was their conversation, overheard that day at lunch, which *really* got the guys' attention. As Nancy Batson told it years later, "those young fellas didn't want to be outdone by a couple of women— even if we were more experienced pilots than they were."

The Army needed pilots to ferry those sleek, sexy, single-engine, single-cockpit WWII warplanes called pursuits. Using male pilots trained for combat took men away from fighting the Germans and Japanese, so experienced women pilots were being trained to fly pursuits and to ferry them from the factories to the docks. Once the women had delivered them to the embarkation point, the aircraft were lashed to the decks of outbound ships and sent abroad to the battle zones where they were needed.

When the second class of trainee pilots reported to the Army's new Pursuit Training School in Palm Springs, California, December 10, 1943, Helen Elizabeth Schmidt McGilvery and Nancy Batson were part of it. They had been members of the very first women's squadron formed in World War II—28 professional women pilots, civilians, hired by the Army's Air Transport Command to ferry trainer airplanes. They were known initially as WAFS (Women's Auxiliary Ferrying Squadron).

Late that same afternoon, Mac, finishing her practice maneuvers, put her P-47 into the continuous descending left turn that would result in her

final landing of the day. Batson was already down. Mac checked her speed—120 miles per hour—as she eased her airplane over the fence and the patch of sand at the end of the runway. The massive 2300-horsepower engine obscured her forward vision, but peripherally she could see the white runway stripes on both sides of her aircraft.

She pulled the stick back into her stomach and closed the throttle. The P-47 flared and settled. A perfect three-point landing. A tap on the brakes—ever so slight, so that the tail wouldn't come up—and Mac skillfully maneuvered the aircraft onto the first turn-off to the taxiway.

Right behind her came another P-47, this one flown by one of the young male pilots. He chopped the power—too soon. His plane set down in the sand and flipped over on its back. Mac didn't see it. It all happened behind her, out of her field of vision. Pleased with herself and her landing, she taxied toward the flight line. But she did see fire trucks and an ambulance zip by going the other way. She parked, cleaned up her airplane, and alighted.

Batson was waiting for her, all smiles.

That night, as they toasted their prowess with a Seven and Seven in the O Club, they learned about the accident. The pilot, it turned out, was OK—shaken but unharmed. He had crawled free and gotten a safe distance away in case the downed Jug caught fire.

Nancy and Mac were a bit shaken as well.

The following day came the terse order: *"No more short turn-offs!"*

Oops! The two looked at each other, but didn't say a word.

"They never said a thing to us, but they knew," Batson said fifty years later relating the incident and the flight line edict. "Everything you do out there on the field is right out in front of God and everybody!—Everybody knew. And we knew!"

She grinned, shook her head, and chuckled. "Little Mac and me? We were devils! But we didn't try turning off short again—not in Palm Springs anyway."

Helen Elizabeth Schmidt McGilvery—B.A. in English and Literary Criticism from the University of Michigan, 1937—learned to fly in 1940. In 1944, she delivered 138 P-47s, 19 P-51s and four P-38s for the Army. Helen died in a mid-air collision in August 1948 while giving a flight lesson. The 1,102 women who flew for the Army in WWII were known as the WASP (Women Airforce Service Pilots). Some 303 WASP pilots served in the Ferrying Division, Air Transport Command under the leadership of Nancy Love.

The women pilots of the Ferrying Division flew more than nine million miles in 72 different warplane models. They completed 12,650 domestic movements of airplanes and flew 115,000 pilot hours in the 27 months they were in operation, October 1942 to December 1944.

~SARAH BYRN RICKMAN

Biographer, Author of four published books on the WASP

www.SarahByrnRickman.com

It takes a lot of courage to show your dreams to someone else.
~ERMA BOMBECK

I suppose leadership at one time meant muscles, but today it means getting along with people.
~INDIRA GANDHI

Getting ahead in a difficult profession requires avid faith in yourself. You must be able to sustain yourself against staggering blows. There is no code of conduct to help beginners. That is why some people with mediocre talent, but with great inner drive, go much further than people with vastly superior talent.
~SOPHIA LOREN

Blessings From Above

Time for God

My deployment to Prince Sultan Air Base, Saudi Arabia, during the initial stages of the Iraq War was nothing less than blessed. Before the 552d AWACS Operations Group ever deployed to support the war operation, we spent months studying, training in simulators, and working on team dynamics flying as organized crews. Knowing another deployment was around the corner, my husband and I prayed in spiritual preparation for protection, wisdom, and God's will. We sought prayers from family and friends that there would be Christians on my crew, and that we would encourage one another in Christ, and we would be bold in our faith—especially during the harshness of war.

We arrived at the AFB where AWACS crew members had been deployed for the past 12 years for Operation Southern Watch; however, conditions were very different this time. After flying the E-3 Sentry across the Atlantic and making our way through processing and customs at 2 A.M. local time, we needed rest. Rather than barge in on sleeping roommates in our assigned quarters, we found an empty temporary tent set up in the parking lot, and crashed on our cots to get some sleep. When the Giant Voice loudspeaker conducted the daily test sometime around 7 A.M. our night was at an end. The officers settled into rooms that day, while our enlisted crew members chose to stick together in the parking lot tent. Although we were used to rooming with crew members to coordinate sleep and waking schedules for flying, the overcrowded base lodging could not make room for us. My roommates were E-8 JSTARS crew members who flew missions on different days and at different times than me. We did our best to accommodate each other and our varying crew's rest/sleep schedules.

Within that first week adapting to a new time zone and flying missions for Operation Southern Watch, I discovered there were people of like-minded faith on my crew. I plugged into the chapel praise band right away, and I was surprised and glad to see several members of my crew present at the service. My roommate told me her JSTARS crew leadership had led a crew prayer before each flight during *Operation Enduring Freedom* missions in Afghanistan. I suggested the idea to our aircraft commander. He said he'd never done anything like that before, but he was willing to give it a try. Before our second flight, our aircraft commander led an optional crew prayer in front of the aircraft, and almost the entire crew joined us. Soon, it became a routine task, part of our pre-flight checklist—we gathered in a circle and bowed our heads in prayer before each flight.

Distinguished guests assigned to our missions often joined us in prayer. We were encouraged by our chaplain who mentioned that maintenance troops and other crews noticed our crew prayer before each flight, and at least one member of another crew asked his crew to pray before missions. A leader on our mission crew remarked that he was frustrated with one of his subordinates before the mission, but after the crew prayer he was able to take a deep breath and withhold saying things he would later regret. Before we returned home, crew members' spouses heard about our prayer routine and its uplifting effects on other troops.

Although prayer blessed us as it prepared our mental and spiritual focus before each flight, we were amazed that God was using this experience to reach out to others in the military and back home. AWACS crew morale dipped precipitously when the war started in March. Our comrades in arms stationed in Kuwait at Al Jaber Air Base began getting SCUDs dropped on them at a heavy rate and security was increased. We began wearing helmets and carrying chemical gear and canteens with us everywhere, and our movements were severely restricted. As time passed and the threat diminished, we were able to lighten our load and restrictions were relaxed.

In April, a chapel tent was installed in tent city with its own services so that troops did not have to make the half-hour bus ride across base to attend a service. Several members of our crew worshipped together by leading praise at the contemporary service. The praise band was comprised of AWACS crew members (three were from my crew) and two members of the Royal Air Force (RAF) including the RAF chaplain. God's blessings abounded through friendship with a common love for music and the Lord. Finally, we began a crew Bible study that met twice a week; it provided a time to read the Bible together and to exchange intercessory prayer requests. It was such a blessing to be reminded of God's glory and purpose when our situation during the war was uncomfortable or grim, when we were frustrated with decisions made that we could not change, or when we were frustrated with one another. Fellow believers provided one another with an eternity-based reality check.

God answered my prayers to have fellow Christians on my crew above and beyond anything I could ever imagine. Not only were we blessed to find fellowship and encouragement within our crew, but we found fellow believers throughout the AWACS community. My times in the desert during AWACS deployments have been significant spiritual growth spurts for me while on active duty. I have had time away from the daily routine to focus more on God and to reflect upon His word and the many wondrous works He's doing in my life and in the lives of those around me. This deployment to OIF has been my most memorable time of growth in the desert—I cherish the friendships God gave me and the promises He showed me in His word.

~DR. DOLLY A. GARNECKI

Formerly Captain Garnecki, USAF, Electronic Combat Officer and Deputy Chief of B-Flight Training at the 965 AACS

http://www.scoliosisdoc.com

http://travelingwithbaby.wordpress.com

Dad's Nights in the Window

I began my childhood in a Chicago public housing development, Cabrini-Green, on the north side of Chicago. Over the years, Cabrini-Green became infested with drugs and violence, and the neglect of the housing resulted in poor living conditions. During that time, my dad was an alcoholic and he and my mother often fought each other. Through all of that, Mom worked at Montgomery Wards warehouse and Dad worked on the railroad. My parents managed to get us moved to the south side of Chicago. I remember being excited as we drove to our new area to watch our home being built. When we moved in, I was about nine-years-old and the neighborhood was new. As the years went on, it would also become infested with drugs and violence.

My life began to change as I got older. With my parents still fighting and my male cousin molesting me, I became lost. I got into things I should not have, missed school, and ran away from home a couple of times. After barely graduating from high school, I wanted to become a nurse. So, I went to college for one semester and decided college was not for me. Shortly after, I visited a United States Navy Recruiter, took my test, and did my physical. I told my parents I was joining the military. In January of 1979, I departed for Boot Camp in Orlando, Florida. My dad took it hard. That same year he quit drinking alcohol and spent many nights looking at the street lights wondering if I was okay. After arriving at Boot Camp, I stayed in touch with my parents so they would know that I was okay.

While in Boot Camp, I was scared, often wondering what I had gotten myself into. There were two African-American women I hung around. We ate together, showered together, and slept together. One day, as I was walking back from the chow hall with one of the girls, she said she had something to tell me. She went on to say that she was the male in a two female relationship. Because she did not come right out and say she was lesbian and I had never been around people in this type of relationship, I had a difficult time understanding what she was trying to say to me. Finally, she

said, "I am seeing another woman and she don't like me being your friend." I said, "You can assure her that I do not like you in that way." We both laughed. This was my first exposure to this type of relationship, but did not stop me from being her friend because I looked at her as a person.

I realized I was in the midst of something I could be proud of accomplishing, and my direction started to change. In January of 1979, women were not onboard ship yet, but I was a Seaman driving 50- and 60-foot utility boats across the Mississippi River. In 1982, there were 2,185 enlisted onboard 37 ships and I was one of them. As a Boatswain's Mate, I helped with the ship's maintenance to include marlinspikes, deck, boat seamanship, painting (I painted a lot of decks!), up-keep of ships' external structures, rigging, deck equipment and boats. Other times, I spent days or nights on watch up on the quarterdeck summoning the crew with my Boatswain's pipe. During the times of my watch, I would try to drink coffee to stay awake but the coffee only made me nauseated. To this day, I will not drink coffee. I did meet some lifelong friends along the way.

In 1985, I was honorably discharged from the Navy. I wanted to get out because I was married and wanted to keep my marriage alive. I was married to a Marine, so I began to attend school to pick back up on my nursing. We still needed extra income so I joined the U.S. Army Reserve and went back to Boot Camp. This time, I knew the ropes and was the Platoon Leader. Most of the women were younger, so I made it my mission to prove to myself that I could still be number one and I was. I won *Trainee of the Cycle*. I continued to go to school, work part-time as a nursing assistant, and travel with my husband.

In my last two years of college, we were stationed in Hawaii. I was honorably discharged from the Army Reserve. My husband was due to transfer, so we decided it was best that he went overseas while I stayed behind to finish school. I had struggled with infertility and wanted children badly. In my last semester of college, my husband asked me for a divorce. I was devastated to find out he was having an affair with a military dependent overseas. My husband said, "You are just jealous because (she) has children and you can't." During this time, I struggled to finish nursing school. I became depressed and lost all hope after almost fifteen years of marriage.

In January 1995, I graduated with my Bachelor's Degree in Nursing and a broken heart. The hardest thing for me to do was move on without someone I had spent half of my life with. With God's help, I shifted my focus onto others who were hurting. A year later I moved to Texas, started working as a nurse, and met my future husband. Today, I have my Master's Degree in Nursing and two beautiful children. I don't look at my experiences as a mistake, but as opportunities that allowed me to grow. I thank the U.S. Navy for giving me my start and my direction.

~LAMONDA HOPMAN, AUTHOR OF *SARAH'S CHILD*
www.lamondas.com

God Bless and Keep Her Safe

Daughter, sister, wife
Mother, nurse, cook
Homemaker
Undresses
Slips into her other uniform
Straightens her cap
Walks proudly out the door
Praying to return unscathed
God bless and keep her safe

~MARY LENORE QUIGLEY~
Author of Indelible Ink, God Danced, *and* By Fools Like Me
www.Q2Ink.com

Homeless Veteran to Veteran Homeowner

I grew up in Philadelphia, attended Catholic school and was considered a good student. I am an only child with loving parents and family. After getting my high school diploma, I was faced with the choice every teenager is confronted with: go to college or get a job. So I chose school. Then, one evening my mother mentioned that a neighbor's daughter had joined the military and suggested I do something similar.

On July 14, 1975, I entered the United States Air Force and became an Air Traffic Controller. The training was challenging and led to my becoming the first woman rated (Federal Aviation Administration air traffic controller certification) at Kadena Air Base, Japan's control tower. At that time Kadena, was one of the busiest facilities with more air traffic than the famous O'Hare airport. After returning to the United States, I was trained as a Combat Controller to establish and provide air traffic control in combat zones. This was another male-dominated career field in which I excelled. I continued pursuing my degree, as well. In 1983, I was honorably discharged and relocated to San Diego, California, where I embarked upon a civilian career in social services.

After a few years, I was introduced to drugs and began using recreationally. In 1987, I started selling drugs and became engulfed in an unsavory lifestyle. I lost my job, my relationship, was evicted and finally became homeless. On numerous occasions, I would make vain attempts to get my life back on track by returning to school or trying a new career. At the time, it never dawned on me that drugs had taken their toll and my life was spiraling downward.

In 1989, I participated in an event for homeless veterans called the *National Stand Down* where I met Liz, a Veterans Administration nurse, who offered services to assist Veterans in getting their lives back. Although Liz was exceptional in her provision of services, I remained in denial about my substance abuse problem.

Finally, after being arrested numerous times, failing court-ordered drug diversions, receiving two felony convictions, and spending several short stints in county jail, I was living in a 20×8×8 metal storage container and facing a prison sentence. I realized I needed help. It had taken ten years for me to reach a point of surrender and desperation. I was finally there. This time, Liz was able to arrange for my acceptance into the Vietnam Veterans of San Diego (VVSD) program if the courts would approve my request.

On January 5, 1999, I stood before the Honorable Judge Wellington, who held my fate in his hands as he said, "Ms. Borum, before I pass sentence, I want you to know I am giving you an opportunity to become a productive member of society again." Following those words, he sentenced me to VVSD for 365 days with a suspended two-year prison sentence. I realized this was my last chance, get it right or go to prison.

After entering VVSD, I got a sponsor, went to 12-Step meetings and followed directions. I was elected to the Resident Peer Council, appointed to the role of Model Resident and utilized VVSD's Employment and Training services by enrolling in a local adult school. With the assistance of a great instructor, Sara, I learned to type and became proficient in business applications software. To further enhance my administrative skills, I volunteered as the teacher's aide. The skills I received combined with my determination, led to my being hired as a Staff Coordinator at the Veterans Winter Shelter. I had been given a new lease on life and I was starting to take full advantage of it.

After seven months, I was selected to transition to a sober living program where I resided for another year to hone these renewed life skills. It may sound minor, but I set up a budget and opened a checking and savings account for the first time in many years. I completed the court ordered probation, paid off all fines, made restitution, and even had the felonies expunged.

When the shelter closed, I was hired as an Eligibility Specialist for VVSD's Employment and Training Department. I continued attending school and strengthened my computer skills and eventually became the

Webmaster for VVSD. In 2004, I was promoted to the Pre-Apprentice-ship Program Administrator position enabling me to assist Veterans with obtaining training and employment in the Building Trades Industry. In 2006, I was promoted to Assistant Director of Metro Employment Services. In 2008, I was promoted to Director of Development and became the new-est member of the senior executive staff.

More than a decade has passed since a judge saved my life by allowing me to recapture what it means to be an honorably discharged Veteran. A title I wear with pride realizing my oath of enlistment has no expiration date. I continue to do the things I was taught and it is my life's mission to share these gifts with others. VVSD is the foundation for the miracles that have happened in the lives of countless homeless veterans. I take great pride in being an Alumna and staff member of such a remarkable organi-zation. But, without a doubt, my life has been molded by some awesome women: the VA nurse, the continuing education teacher, and my sponsor. I will always be grateful to those individuals who believed in me and gave me hope when I had none.

As a result of these mentors in my life, I have achieved many accom-plishments. I purchased my first home in 2004, became recognized as the *Unsung Hero of the Year* in 2005 by the National Coalition for Homeless Veterans in Washington, D.C., was selected VVSD's 2008–2009 *Veteran of the Year* and nominated for *San Diego County Veteran* of the year. I find it amazing that there are individuals who actually believe someone with my past is worthy of national recognition.

In addition to these achievements, the one thing I am most grateful for is being reunited with my mother after having been estranged from her for many years. Today, my mother has a daughter she admires and respects. After visiting me in San Diego, she returned home able to proudly talk about her daughter's great successes. Now that's a miracle!

Life today is unbelievable and far greater than I ever imagined. I have a host of incredible friends. I take time to travel, both for vacations and for my favorite pastime, tournament bowling. I speak on a small recovery circuit and have aspirations of becoming a motivational speaker, offering hope and inspiration to those who believe there is no way out.

It is my hope to guide others, especially Veterans who want something different out of life. As for my future, I want to obtain a Master's Degree in Organizational Management and have returned to school to achieve that goal.

This has proven to be a great way to live. I am often quoted as saying, "Some days I would pay to be me." It was not that long ago that I would have paid to be anyone else but me.

~SANDY A. BORUM
Director of Development, Veteran Village of San Diego
2008–2009 Veteran of the Year
www.vvsd.net

If you don't like something change it. If you can't change it, change your attitude. Don't complain.
~MAYA ANGELOU

Nothing in life is so hard that you can't make it easier by the way you take it.
~ELLEN GLASGOW

My philosophy is that not only are you responsible for your life, but doing the best at this moment puts you in the best place for the next moment.
~OPRAH WINFREY

Friendly Helping Hand for a Blessed Event

When I first married Raymond, I expected him to deploy. I knew that he just finished Boot Camp with the Marines. I was unaware, however, that I would be six months pregnant when he would leave for Iraq.

We were both very surprised when we found out I was pregnant. It was not something that we planned at that point, but we were extremely happy. We were deciding on where to live close to base, baby names, and lots of other things when he came home with the news that he was deploying to Iraq in five months. He was by my side for all of the doctor appointments, and was very supportive during my mood swings, bizarre cravings, and outbursts. We were both very happy that he was able to leave work early to see the first ultrasound that showed us our baby girl! We thought this was our last opportunity together to delight in our unborn daughter—until he returned 9–15 months later.

After the ultrasound, we decided that I would move back to Ohio to be around family. Don't get me wrong, being around family, especially when you're pregnant and your husband is overseas, is great, but it is not the same as being with your husband.

When he first left, I was a wreck. It took everything that I had to put on a good show for our two-and-a-half-year-old, and as time went by it only got worse. I never told him what it was really like for me with him being in Iraq. His job is a heavy equipment operator. It was not like he was at the front lines, or kicking down the doors, but it is still dangerous. He is still in Iraq. You are not able to talk to the troops over there every day. Not able to see them, not able to really understand what is going on, and when something does go on. It makes you feel helpless, because all you can do is talk to them, or send them packages that hopefully bring up their spirits, reassure them. On top of everything going on in my life at that time, I had to constantly talk to our son and tell him that Ray was in Iraq at work, and that he loves him very much, that he would be home soon.

He would call whenever he could. The phone calls were short but reassuring. He was not on the front lines, and he barely left base, but it was still a war zone. Anything could happen. Along with going through the pregnancy, and dealing with the mood swings, I was always worrying that there was a possibility that he could not come back home alive and that he would never see our daughter. During his calls I could tell that he was down. This was his first child. (Brandon, our two-year-old, is his step-son.) He was very upset with the fact that he would miss the birth of his child. I was upset that he would not be there for it. But it was his duty to go. We both knew that, and we were proud of what he was doing.

Then, just when I was just getting comfortable with the idea that Ray would not be there for the birth or our daughter, we received great news about a week before she was due. My doctor told me of the *Freedom Calls* program. They are able to set up video feeds that let you see and talk to our troops overseas for some important events live. Luckily, they were able to hook us up with this technology. My doctors were able to induce me one day after my due date, so my husband would be able to be there with me the best way he could—through the computer screen!

Seeing him on-screen, after not seeing him for three months, and at one of the most important events in our lives, was wonderful, reassuring, a blessing, and awesome! He was able to see me, talk to me for seven hours up to Lorelai's birth, and I could talk and see him. Plus, they let him stay on the computer for two hours afterward. I had some complications with the birth and it helped me so much just knowing he was watching, knowing that he was there. Although he missed the first five-and-a-half months of our daughter's life, he was able to witness the miracle of her birth, and that is truly the best blessing in the world.

~NICOLE FETICK
Wife of LCPL Raymond Fetick (Marines)

♡

A woman is like a tea bag. You don't know how strong she is until you put her in hot water!
~BUMPER STICKER

The one important thing I've learned over the years is the difference between taking one's work seriously and one's self seriously.
The first is imperative; the second is disastrous.
~DAME MARGOT FONTEYN

Patience is the ability to idle your motor
when you feel like stripping your gears.
~BARBARA JOHNSON

Anyone who says he can see through women is missing a lot.
~GROUCHO MARX

Men go to meetings to meet. Women go to meetings to get something done!
~COKIE ROBERTS

Least favorite word: "Impossible"
~BARBRA STREISAND, INTERVIEWED ON SCREEN ACTOR'S GUILD

The most wasted of all days is that on which one has not laughed.
~UNKNOWN

To The Women in Uniform

Although being the wife of a man in the military has its challenges, being a woman, a wife, a mother, or even a grandmother in the military must be a completely different story.

Having been married to a twenty-six-year Active Duty naval officer for 20 years, I have seen firsthand the mothers in uniform saying goodbye to their children just before their ship deploys for months at a time. Nothing was harder to watch than to see her hold back her tears until her family had descended down the brow of the ship, and when that brow lifts, there is no turning back. One is officially severed from family. It was painful enough to be a wife left behind and left alone with small children, but I cannot imagine leaving my small children, or children of any age behind to set sail for enemy waters. The women who do this are a rare breed all of their own, and do indeed, deserve to be recognized and commended.

Since the mid 1980s, I have seen many changes in the military—especially the number of women in uniform. With each deployment, every ship christening, all the hail-and-farewell gatherings, retirement ceremonies, and the change-of-command events, what was most noticeable was the increasing number of females in attendance—in uniform.

Back then, our first correspondence with those who left usually took up to one month. There was no Internet, no email, no international cell phones, and no computer cameras to talk into, or with which to watch your children grow—just good old-fashioned letters and photos in the mail. I am sure technology makes it much easier for moms nowadays and for families in general but it is not the same as mom being home. I'm sure it helps but there is no substitute for a good-night hug and kiss.

For all the moms who crawl into a rack, a tent, a bunk, a cot, or a sleeping bag, all alone, missing their babies—little or grown; we send you our love and support from the comfort of our own warm and clean beds and thank you for your courage and dedication.

As an author and certified tea specialist, I write for the novice tea drinker and the neophyte spiritual seeker. I believe that combining the two—drinking tea and taking time for inner reflection—is a powerful experience and something we all need to do for ourselves on a regular basis. During these moments of surrender and serenity a calming takes place—both in the mind and for the body. This is something we all need. This is where our power comes from even when we have been led to believe we are powerless. That belief serves no one—we are all powerful beyond our own imagination. It is my gentle suggestion to quiet the mind and use this time of silence with a cup of tea as time for prayer, meditation, reflection, contemplation, gratitude, forgiveness or anything else one may need. I have written 101 healing prayers to enjoy while silently sipping tea. For the women in the military, I have chosen the following prayers for you. When the nights are long and home seems a million miles away, if you can, boil up some water, and steep yourself a cup of tea and let your mind take you back to a more pleasant time in your life and just feel the stress leave your shoulders and lighten your burden.

Fair winds and following seas, may your return be swift and safe, and may your family welcome you home with open arms and open hearts. You are women of great spirit and valor and we honor your heroism.

~DHARLENE MARIE FAHL-BRITTIAN

Author, Poet, Speaker, Tea Expert, Teen Motivator

www.TakeUpTheCup.com

www.LeanTeenSelfEsteem.org

Uniformi-Tea

I understand the common threads that unite us all.
Our ultimate unifier is God.
We are all woven together and connected as one.
In unity, I realize that God is all there is.
As we accept our sameness, our differences are not so great.
When asked for uniformity and conformity,
I choose to remember my uniqueness.
When I see others dressed like me,
it is more than their uniform I see.
I see each as an unparalleled version of God.
I am grateful for what unites us and
thankful for our individuality.
I look beyond the uniform, and the form, as well.
We are all God as far as I can tell.
I do not allow myself to get lost in uniformity
or choose to see things unilaterally.
Just as there are many sides to God,
I remember the versatility of humanity,
and the diversity of spirituality.
It is all good because it is all God,
and good is all it can be.
So I let that be and it is so.
Amen

~DHARLENE MARIE FAHL-BRITTIAN~
©2009

Liber—Tea

I remove all restraints. I set myself free.
This is emancipation day and I claim my liberty.
God is all I see; God is all there is.
Freedom opens me to see that we have always been one.
I no longer hold myself prisoner.
No one or no thing holds me captive.
For the first time I see that I am good—good enough, just as I am.
The blindfold and shackles have been removed.
Unchained, unconfined and
finally unconstrained,
I see God's pure light and my own bright light.
In jubilation and celebration I give thanks.
I am grateful for this divine liberation.
My soul is free; there is no intervention.
Relieved of ties, tears and tension, I soar freely.
I live wholly, and I am complete.
I rise up, I wise up; there is no defeat.
I go within and never go without.
In love I am healed; with grace I am free.
All is assured. There is no place for doubt.
I claim my freedom now. I live it, and so it is.
Amen

~DHARLENE MARIE FAHL-BRITTIAN~
©2009

From the Journals

Pot Pies and TV Dinners

Written in my journal at 30,000 feet!

Growing up an Air Force Brat has made me who I am today. Well, I'm still a brat—even though I'm now in my 50's—just ask my two older sisters and they'll tell you. I took my first international flight at age five, which might not be such a big deal today, but I'm talking about an era of prop planes, not jets. I still love to travel for business or pleasure. Actually, if I don't get on a plane once in awhile, I start to go into withdrawal.

Attending four different high schools in three different countries certainly makes for an interesting education. Today, I find myself relatively unfazed by change and can adapt to new places as easily as a chameleon changes color. I can feel at home wherever I go. Friendships come easily, too, although I recently realized that I saw all friendships as fleeting and *not* lifelong. Lifelong friendships weren't an option in the days before e-mail and the Internet, and moving as often as we did, often thousands of miles away.

At the end of a school year, or sometimes part way through the year, as you were all *shipped out* to all points of the compass—you would vow to your friends that you would write regularly. Unfortunately, a few letters would be exchanged and then you would get caught up in the adventure of a new place and making new friendships. If a few months passed, who knew where you old pals had moved on to, or if a letter would even find them.

It certainly wasn't a Donna Reed lifestyle, but with all the change, family was very important and even though there was camaraderie with the entire military family, the nuclear family was the only constant.

My sisters and I are still 3,000 miles apart, but are closer than we have ever been. With technology we stay connected through e-mail, the Internet

and regular *sister calls*—a three-way conference call. We often reminisce about our childhood years.

One of my favorite memories was when Mom and Dad went out for the night and, whether we had a babysitter or as we got older, when we were left on our own, there was always a *treat*. The treat was that we could cook dinner. Usually it was pot pies, and chicken was my favorite. I would peel off the crust and save bites for the end. Sometimes it was TV dinners and occasionally it was the "deluxe" dinners that came with dessert, too. Turkey, stuffing, cranberry sauce, mashed potatoes and gravy, peas, and . . . apple brown Betty. Yum!

I still find the time to appreciate the simple pleasure that life brings my way . . . and even occasionally eat a chicken pot pie!

~JUDY PEEBLES, THE JOURNALING JENIUS™
USAF "Brat" of TSgt Don A Peebles retired
www.TheJournalingJenius.com

You and I are American. I don't agree with what this country is doing to our families (Japanese-American Manzanar Internment Camp, WWII). But I do love this country. Long after we are no longer kept here, we will still be Americans. We are at war and I will do my part to defend my country. Man or woman, we all have our way, this is mine.

~NORM NOMURA
His mother recounted this childhood experience that changed her life

When we look for the bad in others, we shall surely find it. Look for the good in others—and in yourself.

~SHERYL ROUSH, SPEAKER, AUTHOR OF *SPARKLE-TUDES!*®

Off To War: Good-bye My Love

Would you, a final kiss for me
To hold me and to stroke my
auburn hair

Would you a final kiss
for our darling baby girl
and hold her and snuggle her
Fore'er and e'er

And while you are away
Would you gently caress my
Silken perfumed scarf
Of pure rose essence
And of warmth unfeigned
For wartime, kiss America 'Hello'
A throbbing kiss and
quaking long embrace

For me
An ominous
'Good-bye'

May these
not be
my
final words

~DOVETAIL~

© 2003 Norene Jensen

Point Man

Sharp-nailed thorns paw at my shoulder
Scratch my face, drawing blood.
Armed ebony shapes loom, menacing;
Dark octopi displaced and erect.
Night sky lighter still than they!
Should I fear? Should I welcome
The shelter afforded from smaller
Armed shapes, skulking, eyes piercing?

I push through brush long entangled,
Waiting, ears sharpened, alert to snap
Of twig, unseen, broken by human foot?
Or animal? Who goes there?
Cold steel leveled at cold steel.
Which shall discharge death?

Waiting, dry gulp of throat, heart hammering!
Charge! The foolish impulse—No! Wait!
Though waiting be more torture than
Reckless confrontation.
Ah! Hear you the sly footstep?
Has he discounted human presence?
Day! Where is your spotlight?
Flares! Your probing glare?
Breathing—close, unseen target!
Now! Finger tense, benumbed,
Involuntary pressure, resounding shot!
Crackle and thud of body falling!

continued

Should I move—or wait?
Is he solitary hunter?
Aching muscles clench,
Holding me still,
Crouched in granite.
Listen. He moves not; no comrades
Come to his aid. Endless time—
Humming quiet unbroken.
Cold now, accepting yonder peril,
Knee after knee.
Stop! Ears straining,
No answering brush sound.
(But where there is one may be many!)
Careful! Do voices murmur forward?
Turn! Retrace knee steps;
Think not of fallen prey.
Warning clamped behind bitten lips,
I reach others like me
And breathe at last!

~RUTH J. DECKER~
©Copyright 1969

Reprinted with permission by Ruth's son, Paul Decker, Sergeant E-5, Bravo Company, 2nd Battalion, 7th Regiment, 1st Cavalry Division, Vietnam (1968–1970)

Editor's notes: Point Man was penned in 1969, while she served as an infantryman with Bravo Company, U.S. 7th Cavalry in Vietnam 1968–1969. A number of Paul's fellow soldiers in Bravo Company have commented on how she "aced it." Point Man was published in a Senior Citizen's newsletter (Colorado) back in the early 1980's with a number of her other poems. There are a number of Internet web sites which display Point Man, including International War Veterans Poetry Archives: http://iwvpa.net/deckerrj/index.php

Gold Stars

When Your Doorbell Rings

My name is Miss Jackie, and I am 2Lt. Peter Burks' Momma. When my doorbell rang at approximately 6:30 P.M. on Wednesday, November 14, 2007, I transitioned, without my permission, into the world of a *Gold Star Mother*. To qualify for this title it meant that my beloved son, Pete, was killed in action (KIA) and called home to be with the Lord while serving our country in Iraq.

Allow me to hold your hand and walk you through the experience of *When Your Doorbell Rings* . . .

That Wednesday was just another routine day of a work and enjoying the company of my dearest friend, while preparing a wonderful dinner with country music playing in the background. All was well. I was happy and satisfied with my day's accomplishments. Then, my doorbell rang. My friend went to see who was at the door. He didn't return to the kitchen, so I looked around the corner to see what was taking him so long. Standing at my door were two uniformed soldiers just like you see in the movies. At first I thought they might be ROTC members.

As I slowly walked to the door, they asked, "Are you Jackie Merck?"

"Yes, I am. But you cannot be here for me." Then they informed me that beloved son had been KIA around 0800 Baghdad time that morning.

The best way to describe how I felt at that moment is to imagine that your life is like an exquisite crystal vase which is held by two hands. The hands holding the vase just let go, and the vase falls to the ground shattering into a million pieces. Each piece of brokenness is lying there crying out in disbelief and pain. There are not adequate words to describe the wretched ache within my soul. Humanly speaking it was *impossible* to put the millions pieces back together again. There I stood, stripped naked of *everything* that defined who I was and the world I knew. The very thought of my son, Peter, finished and done on this side of eternity was more than I could bear. What now?

You see, when the doorbell of life rings, the real you answers. You have a choice to make. Will you wage the "Why?" war in anger with God? Or will you surrender in your helplessness and brokenness, trust GOD in what you cannot understand, and BY FAITH cling to the only One who *heals the brokenhearted, and binds up their wounds*? (Psalm 147:3)

By faith, I made the choice to *TRUST* my God. I determined in my heart that I would wrestle God for what I call, *a little something more*. I remembered the truth that God promised in Romans 8:28 that He would cause all things to work together for good to those who love God, to those who are called according to His purpose. *ALL* things included Pete's "call home" to be with Him. I relentlessly cried out to my God UNTIL He answered and gave me *a little something more*—assurance that He heard my cries and saw my pain; confidence that *He knows the plans He has for me to give me a future and a hope* (Jeremiah 29:11); and a conviction that I have a *LIVING HOPE through the resurrection of Jesus Christ from the dead* (1 Peter 1:3).

You may wonder why I refer to death as a "call home." For those who have put their trust in Jesus Christ as their Savior, death is just the passageway for us to enter Eternal Life in Heaven. Peter, by his own profession of *FAITH*, declared, "Momma, IF I don't come home, you KNOW where I will be." Jesus says it best in John 11:25: *I am the resurrection and the life; he who believes in Me shall live even if he dies*" 2Lt. Peter Burks was *READY* to meet his God. Today, by Faith, I can rejoice that my son is alive and well with His Savior, Jesus Christ! One day, I shall see my son again, because I too am *READY.*

Dear one reading my story, *STOP* living every day like you a thousand tomorrows. Life can change without notice in a blink of an eye. Mine did. You have no guarantee for a tomorrow. *Yet you do not know what your life*

will be like tomorrow. You are just a vapor that appears for a little while and then vanishes away. (James 4:14)

Therefore, when the doorbell of life rings and death is standing at your door, will you be *READY*? If not, *TODAY* is the day of salvation. Look to Jesus and be saved, all the inhabitants of the earth; *For I am God, and there is no other.* (Isaiah 45:22). Anyone can look! It is adversity that gives you an opportunity to distinguish yourself as a warrior.

~JACKIE "MISS JACKIE" MERCK HLASTAN
Pete's Momma, NOW A Distinguished Warrior

Think of all the beauty still left around you and be happy.
~ANNE FRANK

The most important words you will ever hear are the words you say to yourself.
~MONA M. MOON

I think, at a child's birth, if a mother could ask a fairy godmother to endow it with the most useful gift, that gift would be curiosity.
~ELEANOR ROOSEVELT

Parents learn a lot from their children about coping with life.
~MURIEL SPARK

Children are the sum of what mothers contribute to their lives.
~UNKNOWN

A True American Hero!

September 11, 2001, changed so many of our lives. We got up like any other day and set off to work, to school, on errands. Then the unimaginable happened. We were attacked. Not just once or twice, but four times in a very short period of time.

My son, Justin, was sitting in his classroom watching in horror what was happening to our country. He did not say a word, but got up out of his desk and drove to the recruiting office, where on September 12, 2001, he enlisted in the U.S. Army. He left for Boot Camp shortly after his nineteenth birthday of that same year and then spent his twenty-first birthday in Iraq. No one should be in Iraq on their twenty-first birthday!

On December 31, 2003, we got a knock on our door. It was early morning and we truly had no idea, what was going on. We were informed that our son, Justin was killed! He wasn't killed in a firefight or hit with an improvised explosive device (IED). Justin was killed by friendly fire.

Our lives were changed! Can't remember the gal's name who was at my door, can't remember what I was wearing, can't remember most of that morning. Don't remember making any phone calls, but know that they got made. Don't remember who came by that day, but know that people did. All I truly remember is that my life had been changed forever.

Justin loved to go to school. He just did not like to go to class. He would meet up with his friends and they would head out to do "whatever" on most days. He loved to play football and baseball and to hang with his friends! Those were the things that motivated him to get going in the mornings. Justin loved his friends, he loved his family, he loved his community, and he loved his country. These memories will never be taken away from us.

The only thing that was taken was Justin's physical presence. There is not a day that goes by, that Justin's presence is not missed. No amount of time will change that! However, I can still hear his quiet voice, his "girly" giggle, his silly ways of trying to make everyone laugh! I also remember the way he

stood on his tiptoes in pictures to look taller than his younger brother, and the way he taught his little sister to ride her bike, and the way he took care of her so tenderly. These things will never be forgotten.

I am not in the military, but I now stand proud as an *American Gold Star* Mother. I try to take care of the newer moms who have paid the ultimate sacrifice for our country. I am also a Proud *Blue Star* Mom. My youngest son, Cameron, is now serving in the U.S. Navy as a *Riverine*. One of my greatest passions, and one of the things that keeps me going, is helping with *Operation Gratitude*. We send out care packages to our military still serving in harm's way overseas. We must not forget what they do for us everyday. They keep us safe and free. And this is just a small way of showing them how grateful we are to them for providing us the freedoms we take for granted.

I love the volunteer work I do; and, I love the wonderful people I have met along the way. Would I want my life changed back to before December 31, 2003? You bet! Am I a bitter old woman? No way! This is what I was dealt and this is the job that God has given me to do. I will stand up for my military proudly and try to serve them, and God, the best way I know how!

God has lit a fire inside of me to help others. Some days it's so surreal that Justin is not here on Earth with us. I know I will see him again in Heaven and that keeps me going. God has given me a *gift*! That *gift* is knowing I will once again be able to hug my beloved son, talk with him, tell him know how proud I am of him!

~SUE POLLARD

American Gold Star Mother of Spec. Justin W. Pollard, killed December 30, 2003.

Blue Star Mother of MASN Cameron M. Pollard, now serving as a Riverine

Mamas Like Me

A dedication to our nation's military and their families, past and present

On the porch with someone I thought was
someone I truly knew
I learned that friendships are not what they seem

When her question stunned me
and I found myself
staring at the floor.

Why, she asked, didn't you talk
and change your child's decision
from joining a force that'll send him to war
leaving you dry and crying.

Then with a pride not understood
by many privileged and free
and grace's patience guiding me through
I spoke to her with ease:

My child believes his calling is higher,
one among the few
led to serve his country,
lay down his life for our children,
for folks like me and you

continued

Our future to ensure and save
from an enemy who swears to destroy
the nation our fathers gave us
with their own generation's blood.

Sacrifice made to give you the right
to sit here free to speak
or worship as you see fit
without the threat of death.
Precious gifts you could very well lose
without children of Dads who privately cry
and Mamas just like me.

Then with not a word she walked away
believing I'd lost my mind
that 9/11 was just a dream
dust settled and forgotten

No grasp that her intellect, Hollywood
nor Wall Street highs
could save her precious freedoms
and leisurely way of life

But only the American Soldiers,
Airmen, Navy, & Marines
sons and daughters on a higher call
fighting enemies while she sleeps.

continued

The Mama's child who laid down all
and comrades she'll never forget
whose legacies will never die
as long as she has a breath.

Yes my child believed his calling was one
among the very few
to serve his country, protect, and die
for our children, me and you.

Our future to ensure and save
from an enemy who swears they'll destroy
the life our fathers gave us
with their own precious blood.

Yes Mamas like me and Daddys, too
lift up our children to serve
the higher call for freedom and life
for our children, for me and you.

~DEBORAH TAINSH~
Gold Star Mom
Sergeant Patrick Tainsh KIA 2/11/04 Baghdad

White Dresses

Gold Star Mothers

White Dresses . . . Gold Stars
Fallen soldiers . . . broken hearts
White roses . . . fill the air
HEROES . . . everywhere

In White Dresses . . . with Gold Stars
Folded flags . . . pressed to their hearts

★ ★ ★

One by one . . . they take their place
Silent pain . . . on every face
One by one . . . the mothers rise
As the name is read . . . of their child

One by one . . . they'll wear the pin
One by one . . . they'll rise again
And, One by one . . . on bended knees
They'll rub the names . . . in memory

★ ★ ★

continued

In White Dresses . . . with Gold Stars
Fallen soldiers . . . broken hearts
White roses . . . fill the air
"Gold Star Mothers" . . . from . . . everywhere!

★ ★ ★

And, they cry . . .

White Dresses . . . with Gold Stars
Fallen soldiers . . . broken hearts
White roses . . . fill the air

★ ★ ★

God Bless our . . . "Gold Star Mothers" . . . everywhere!

★ ★ ★

~SUSAN D. WISEMAN—"THE TRIBUTE LADY"~
www.WhiteDressesGoldStars.com (downloads are free)
©Copyright May 11, 2008 "Mother's Day"
Inspired by the Re-Dedication of 1st CAVs Memorial, Fort Hood, Texas
www.TheTributeLady.com

Honoring Our Veterans

Veterans Day

What does it really mean to honor or celebrate a Veteran? Veterans Day is an annual American holiday honoring military veterans who sacrificed their lives for the freedoms we enjoy today. There are those who have paid the ultimate price of giving their life—and those who spent part or some of their lives in service. There are spouses, children and other family members who have sacrificed, as well, by being family to a military member.

If you've never been in—or around the military—you may not realize the differences of a military way of life. The service member may be gone for months at a time, a year or eighteen months. You may take it for granted that you are able to get up and go to the bathroom in your own house—while a service member deployed to a tent city has to walk a long distance from their tent to a makeshift porta-pottie with no privacy.

We don't realize the sacrifices we make. We don't realize that our way of life is totally different from the mainstream world. We simply chose this life because we wanted to do something for our country. It became a way of life for many of us and a way to get started for others.

As I was writing this article, I looked up in the sky and saw a flock of geese flying overhead. The leader was "calling commands" to the others, and they all flew in tight formation. We are taught to trust our leaders and execute the orders given to us. We fall into formation and become one for the greater good. It's a life of discipline, integrity and total commitment.

No matter what you think about the war, thank the warrior for serving. We may not know what to say back as we rarely hear, "Thank you for your service," but it will touch our hearts.

~ELDONNA LEWIS FERNANDEZ, MASTER SERGEANT, USAF (RET.)

http://pinkbikerchic.com

Veterans: Forever in Our Hearts

In 1982, a group of Vietnam Veterans tumbled into my newspaper office, insisting on talking to me, the "Lady Vet" editor. They had heard I served in the Army, and that I had a soft spot for Veterans. The men were correct on both counts, although I would hardly compare my service to theirs. When I was nineteen, I joined the Women's Army Corps, intending to use my bennies wisely and eventually become the combat surgeon who pulled wounded soldiers back from the brink. I stayed in long enough to know that even though I loved the Army dearly; and I was best suited to loving it from the outside, looking in. I dropped my medical ambitions, and became a journalist specializing in national security. I had a soft spot for stories involving soldiers. I wound up immersed in issues surrounding PTSD—still wanting to pull wounded troops back from the brink, but by using my pen instead of a scalpel. I was still in the early stages of my journalism career that day in 1982, but somehow, the visiting Vets knew I would hear them out. They wanted to make a plea. They urged me to write an "enormously important" story about a new memorial to American troops who died in Southeast Asia.

The story was indeed important. But the Vietnam Veterans Memorial, slated for Washington, D.C., was a national story. It had no place on the pages of California's weekly *Dixon Tribune* newspaper. I barely had room for all the Dixon stories, let alone a national feature. I told the guys I couldn't help them. I expected an argument. Instead, the men turned away. Something in their manner—a sad acquiescence, so easily accepting of rejection—triggered an old memory. My father, a Korean War combat veteran, routinely went into paroxysms of rage over America's inexcusable mistreatment of Vietnam Veterans.

Once, my father and I were riding our horses when we encountered some "peace" bullies picking on a soldier in uniform. Incensed, I galloped my horse directly into the protesters. Afterward, I was grounded; but my father granted me custody of his treasured Combat Infantryman's Badge. The memory unleashed that old instinct, to stand up for the soldiers.

I called to the men leaving my office. "Wait!" I said. "You're local, right? I'll write about you, and what the memorial means to you." I did my interviews right there, on the spot. We continued for the next several weeks.

It soon emerged that the un-built memorial already radiated power, inspiring my Vets to express deep reservoirs of grief, love and pride. My veterans' excitement turned to angst. Some hated that the memorial— nicknamed the Wall—was set into the Earth. They were upset that the designer, Maya Lin, was an Asian woman. My gang of ex-soldiers turned against the Wall.

After the memorial opened just after Veterans Day 1982, though, my Vets were overcome with curiosity. Was the Wall a good thing, or a bad thing? Did it insult the Vets, or honor them?

None wanted to resolve those questions with a visit to Washington, D.C. The emotional risk was too great. Instead, they asked if I would examine the Wall on their behalf. They bought me a plane ticket. They tasked me with placing white roses before the panels containing the names of their dead comrades. I complied eagerly. I wanted to see this Wall, myself. But I was not prepared for what happened in Washington.

I had trouble finding the Vietnam Memorial. I wandered the Mall at length, toting my roses and growing steadily grumpier. I was about to give up when I nearly fell into a gorge that turned out to be the memorial. It was heartbreakingly beautiful. I was drawn in, mesmerized at seeing the real names of real soldiers who died while fighting for our country. Methodically, I began to deposit the roses.

I noticed a man standing beside me, entranced, as if in prayer. On impulse, I asked if he were a Vietnam Veteran. Defensively, he nodded yes. I blurted, "Thank you for serving." He seemed to hold his breath. Then he lunged forward and hugged me. He stood sobbing in the arms of a stranger. I, too, began to cry, in gratitude for this man's sacrifice, and from grief that an entire generation of our fine soldiers had been made to feel so thoroughly unappreciated.

Back at home, I told my Vets: "You have to see it." Eventually, most of them did.

When the last surviving Veteran from the Vietnam War has died, the Wall—which has become a cultural icon—will remain standing. Future generations will visit, and will be well served by the underlying message: *We as a nation honor, love and give thanks to our service members.*

This applies to Veterans who fought in all our wars, and who served our nation in peacetime. We all need to have a soft spot for Veterans. Mine has never once hardened over. Yes, I remain fascinated by national security and all its hard edges: espionage, warfare, machinery, and more. But, I never have lost my deep love for the individual soldiers. I continue to write about them, especially their struggles with PTSD, and will do so until I no longer am able to string words together on a page. They are forever in my heart.

~SUSAN KATZ KEATING

The decision to go to war is the most important decision that I can make as a representative in Congress. As a veteran, I see any potential military action first through the eyes of the young men and women who volunteered to wear the uniform and would carry out such a mission.

~MARK KIRK

The elections that have taken place in these countries are a reflection of the lure of Democracy, and the resilience of our men and women in uniform who helped bring freedom to many who never knew what the word truly meant.

~JIM SENSENBRENNER

My First Veteran's Funeral

I went to my first Veteran's funeral on a Monday right from work. I was in my uniform. I arrived at the funeral home about fifteen minutes prior to the service, just in time to accompany a friend up to say goodbye. I was glad they had a photo of her up there because she looked a little different than I remember. She did look peaceful though. Many of her older friends were present as well as her family, probably fifty people in all.

The funeral director closed her casket and completely unfolded the American flag that was draped over it. I was unaware she had served as a helicopter medic in the Army. The service started with the hymn *How Great Thou Art*. Then, her Pastor eloquently summarized her life. He emphasized her fervor for Jesus and that she knew where to place her hope. He also highlighted her passion for helping others and going on mission trips, including to Nicaragua. I bet her military training paid off there.

The Pastor delivered a powerful evangelistic message that had many of us wondering if we should go down front and re-dedicate our lives to the Lord. He also said that funerals make you face three things: your mortality, your priorities, and your faith.

Then, we queued up to drive to the gravesite and there must have been 20 cars. This was the first time I was an adult driver in a funeral precession and I wasn't prepared for how moved I would be when people on the other side of a divided highway pulled over out of respect. I have driven many an ambulance with the lights and sirens blaring and the person in front of me wouldn't pull over let alone people on the other side of the road! From now on, I will definitely spend the few minutes to do that knowing what that means to the people in the precession.

At the burial site, the Pastor recited the twenty-third Psalm, "The Lord is my shepherd . . . " I'm sure some people think the usual stuff gets old but to some of us it's all new and I really hadn't heard that Psalm in that context before. I'm glad he used that one and others seemed comforted by the familiarity of it. Next, the three Army Honor Guard members performed the Veterans portion of the service with the playing of *Taps* and the folding of the flag. *Taps* really got me. After all these years of hearing it at the end of the day to initiate "lights out," I really hadn't thought about what I would feel as I saluted a flag-draped casket. Not only about her service to our great nation but also about all of our country's Veterans. Being one, I sometimes assume I pay appropriate respect just because I put a uniform on, instead of actually saying "Thank you." That's what I did the entire time I held the salute.

Closing the service, the Honor Guardsmen retired the colors and they inserted a few spent M-16 rounds into the last triangular fold of the flag. They then presented it to Cindy's son, who was in his Army service dress uniform, and before the Sergeant could sit down a friend of the family (an Air Force Major in uniform) approached him and saluted him. The significance of an officer saluting an enlisted member might have been lost on the others, but not me. That is a special show of respect and love that civilians can't possibly comprehend, and was a fine way to end her beautiful ceremony. What a confirmation that the relationships formed around this Veteran during her time here will continue thereafter.

It is too bad people avoid funerals, I wouldn't have felt—or written—so much about a wedding.

~EILENE M. NIELSEN
Senior Master Sergeant, USAF, (Ret.)

~

War is God's way of teaching Americans geography.
~AMBROSE BIERCE

The USO—Taking Care of the Military

It was an emotional time for both. They were husband and wife, parents of three young children, and now they had a dilemma. Both Majors in the U.S. Army, he was being deployed far in advance of her deployment. For now, she'd remain home with their children, while he was assigned to a very long tour of combat duty. They worried not only about his safety, but whether their children would remember Daddy when he returned.

As always, the USO came to their rescue, through their innovative *United Through Reading* program. Before he shipped out, the USO video-taped Major "Daddy" reading some of his children's favorite books. Once he was sent off to duty, his children still had that comfort of Daddy reading to them every night before they were tucked in, month after month, until he finally returned home to a joyful reunion. That's one of the USO's thousands of ways to serve our military.

Most men and women serving our country today are not there because they were drafted into service. Most are volunteers who have given up their daily lives and suffered long absences from their families and friends to protect the United States. Many endure tremendous hardships, injuries, and more, to keep us safe every day.

The USO, formally known as the United Service Organizations, was formed in 1941. As the world prepared to go to war, President Franklin D. Roosevelt challenged the American people to show their appreciation for the military personnel who would soon be directly in "harm's way." For sixty-six years, USOs have provided entertainment, recreation and comfort lounges for traveling servicemen and women. Many of us remember the trips popularized by comedian-actor, Bob Hope, and his fellow entertainers, bringing joy and laughter to the troops overseas, and in the United States. Those trips still continue today, organized by World USO, headquartered in Washington, D.C.

The other segment is the *affiliates*, which run 137 *comfort centers* worldwide. Though the USO is chartered by the United States Congress, no government funding is provided, nor is taxpayer money used. The lounges are not-for-profit and totally self-funded, functioning on monies raised through fundraisers and the generosity of the communities they serve. Each USO is the link that connects the American public with our men and women in uniform.

Recently I had the pleasure of taking a donation (two new cell phones, with their own prepaid calling cards) to the Los Angeles/Ontario Airport USO based in Ontario, California. Each USO is staffed by male and female volunteers who formerly served and continue to serve in retirement. One cheery gentleman I spoke with was a World War II Tail-Gunner, another was a retired Army Sergeant.

The Ontario comfort lounge is located inside the retired airport terminal, which was converted to that use when two newer terminals were built. Like every other USO, this one is filled with as many creature comforts as possible for all active-duty and fully-retired military men, women and their immediate families traveling through the airport. Due to the available space in the retired terminal, it's also considered the largest military comfort center in the country.

Prior to this center's opening, troops in California's Inland Empire with flight layovers or ground transportation delays, had nowhere to wait other than the airport terminals. Due to security regulations, their access to food and beverages was very limited. Frequently, they could slept on hard benches inside, or on the grassy areas near the terminals.

The USO does not believe that this is the way we should treat those who defend our liberties and our way of life. Their primary mission, I soon learned, is "showing the military that we care about them by taking care of them."

Instead of sleeping in the airport terminals, military personnel are welcomed in the lounge. They receive a safe haven for several hours through a day or more, while they wait for their next transportation. In the 6,400-square-foot Los Angeles/Ontario facility, there are comfortable lounge chairs, televisions, and a computer access center for keeping in touch with family and friends. A canteen area provides beverages, sandwiches, snacks and quick meals during all open hours. Willing volunteers do the serving, and this isn't always an easy task when several hundreds of soldiers arrive at one time. No matter the circumstances, they are all efficiently served with welcoming smiles! Future donations are targeted for a shower room and sleeping area.

Families traveling with the military are also well-provided. A children's center provides cribs, rocking chairs, toys, books, games, and diapers; mothers can nurse their infants in a nearby private room. Library facilities and musical instruments are also available for use by military families, as well as, a ping-pong table, donated by the American Legion Post 426 in Yucaipa, California.

Military personnel and their families are transported between the Los Angeles/Ontario comfort centers, and the Los Angeles International Airport or Ontario Airport by airport courtesy shuttles. Military guests receive USO services free of any charge. Personnel traveling through the USOs require huge amounts of food, bottled water, and other supplies, so cash donations are always needed. It also takes a large volunteer staff to provide those services when troops and their families arrive.

Every USO in the country can greatly benefit through donations from individuals, businesses, and other non-profits. This is a marvelous way to show our gratitude for the extreme sacrifices these military personnel and their families make for us each day, every day.

When you read the touching stories of sacrifice, hardship, and deep love for our country, you will want to help. Contact www.USO.org to locate nearby facilities and determine what they need most. Volunteering or providing necessary items is a wonderful way to show those serving our country how much we truly care.

~KAY PRESTO, SPEAKER, AUTHOR, PRESTO PRODUCTIONS

© 2009 Kay Presto

Women Who Made a Difference

"Why do we need a women's memorial?" a fellow Reservist asked when I told her about WIMSA (Women in Military Service to America). "We've worked so hard to be treated equal to men, why would we want to have a separate memorial?" The answer is that we wouldn't have this equality if it weren't for the women who came before us.

I'd known about the memorial for years but hadn't bothered to register. I admit I felt ambivalence too. I didn't see the need. Until I met all those WWII Vets. One year, during three days of Veterans Day activities in Albany, Salem, and Portland, Oregon, I talked to many women who were WWII Veterans. I heard the pride in their voices and the concern that they wouldn't be remembered—that their sacrifices would be ignored. I realized then how little I know about the history of women in the military, and I realized how much I took for granted about my own military service and opportunities.

I knew that some women disguised themselves as men to fight in the Civil War. I didn't know that 400 women did so, including Loreta Valesques who raised, equipped, and commanded a Confederate battalion in battle before she was found out. I knew that we had some women involved in WWI, but I didn't know there were 34,000 of them. I'd certainly heard about Rosie the Riveter and her sisters, but I didn't know that she had 400,000 military counterparts, serving in the U.S. and overseas.

I don't think I'm the only ignorant one. As one speaker at WIMSA's dedication ceremonies in 1997 stated, this memorial will cure our "national amnesia" about the roles women have played throughout our history in the defense of our nation.

Women, then, were taught not to brag about what they do, so often they don't talk about their service at all. Many children of Veterans admitted that they didn't know anything about their mother's service—until now.

Lieutenant Colonel Rhonda Cornum spoke for many of us at the dedication when she said that she hadn't really realized "until these past two days" how much she took for granted. She's able to have a great career as an Army officer and have a family and child. The women who came before us couldn't do that.

For a long time, military women had to get out of the military if they became pregnant. Until the 1970's, women could not make up more than two-percent of the service and they could not progress past the rank of lieutenant colonel. For a long time, only a very few specialties were open to women. That has all changed because of the efforts of women throughout history.

Today so much more is open to women in the military. This year, we watched Ann Dunwoody become our first female four-Star General. Those of us who went through Basic Training with Ann always said she'd become a general some day. None of us dreamed that one of us would make four-Star!

I came into the Army in 1975 as a WAC—as part of the Women's Army Corps, a separate entity that disbanded in 1978. As I write this in 2009, I realize that much of what happened to us in my early military career would seem impossible to young women entering the military today.

Our uniforms weren't even conducive to work. The cords uniform wrinkled so badly that there were ironing boards and irons ready to go at all times, in all of the ladies rooms in our office buildings. You stopped in regularly to iron your skirt, so you could continue to look professional. Imagine being productive in a high-speed job with that kind of handicap!

As a brand new Second Lieutenant in Germany, I was thrilled to be wearing fatigues for work, a much more productive uniform, except for one strange thing—I noticed how all the enlisted soldiers, who were almost all men at the time, addressed me as Sir. I finally stopped one of them. "Okay, I know that fatigues aren't the most flattering of uniforms, but can you really not tell that I'm female?" I asked.

"Oh, no, Sir. I mean Ma'am," he replied, "In Basic Training they taught us to address ALL officers as Sir."

"Ha!" I thought to myself, "I bet they did that because it would be less likely to cause problems if they called a woman Sir than if they slipped and called a male officer Ma'am."

I chose to get off of Active Duty after three years, as I was getting married and the Army was going to assign my husband and I to two different posts—not the way we wanted to start our marriage. I joined the Army Reserves. As a First Lieutenant, I searched for a slot when my Active Duty husband was assigned to Fort Rucker, Alabama. I found a possible opening as a Platoon Leader of a Military Police platoon and interviewed for the assignment just as I would for a civilian job.

The interview took place on a weekend when the headquarters unit was drilling at the base. I had told the Colonel that my husband and I were on our way to Atlanta so I would not be in uniform and Greg would be with me.

"No problem," he said. I realized later he was probably thinking, "All the better." As we sat in front of him, this Colonel directed every question to my husband, not to me. "What do you think about her drilling all weekend with a unit of all male soldiers?"

"What do you think of her being gone one weekend a month and two weeks a year?" Greg responded, "She's good . . . she'll get the job done . . . no problem, Sir." I finally asked, "Sir, are you interviewing my husband or me?" Soon after I took the position, Army Reserve Magazine did an article on me, the first female platoon leader they'd ever had in a three-state Southern area.

Looking back now, it still amazes me that this shy, non-athletic, change-fearing girl ever chose to go into the military. Quite frankly, I did not do it out of patriotism. I did it because at the time, it was the best opportunity open to me. As I was graduating from college back then, all of the job interviews included the question, "Can you type?" Not what I'd spent four years of college to do.

The military forced me out of my comfort zone to tackle tough challenges and amazing levels of responsibility at a young age. I learned to express myself well in writing and in person, briefing senior individuals early on, and exhibiting self-confidence even when I didn't feel it. As a result, this introvert ended up in a career in public speaking and I've learned to relish adventures that come with change.

I worked hard to be as professional as possible, never wanting anyone to think they'd have been better off to have a man in the positions I held. Hopefully, my efforts are part of the bigger whole—of all women in the military—that continues to equalize military service for all women.

~KATHIE (HOTTER) HIGHTOWER, LTC, USAR (RET.)

www.militaryspousehelp.com

Editor's Note: If you are a female Veteran—or know of one—register at WIMSA, and check out www.womensmemorial.org. Your photo and memories of service will be entered into a computer, accessible to any visitor who comes to the Memorial who types in your name. When you visit Washington, D.C., visit the Memorial and be inspired by all those women who made a difference.

In World War II. it was said and it is probably true, that there was not a single American who did not know the name of somebody serving in uniform. Today, only 2 percent of the people know the name of someone serving in uniform. That means 2 percent of your listeners can actually conjure up the image of someone wearing the uniform of the military of the United States.

~OLIVER NORTH

When placed in command—take charge.

~NORMAN SCHWARZKOPF

Humor in Uniform

Light Weight

As a member of the Air Force, one is expected to do certain "additional duties as required" on a regular basis. Some of those "additional duties" are less than pleasant. The lower in rank you are, the worse the duties or "details" as they are called. In basic training, we all were assigned a detail. I was assigned to the stair-sweeping detail along with three others. That turned out to be a good time, as the guys' dorms were on the floor below us, so we got a chance to flirt with the guys while doing their portion of the stairs.

As a group in Basic, we had to mop and buff the floors in our 50-person open bay dorm, which included cleaning scuff marks with a toothbrush. That was an all day job, on a Sunday, to keep us occupied. As my career progressed, I was assigned to other tasks, such as trash detail around the base, yard detail at my unit in Florida (I operated the riding lawn mower and learned how to pop a wheelie on it!), landscaping detail at my unit in Texas, a painting and carpeting detail at my unit in England.

Then there was the dreaded detail that no one wanted—the urinalysis observer! The Air Force randomly tests military members for drug use on a regular basis. The member is selected at random by social security number. In my first twelve years in the military, I was never selected. In 1993, when I was at a base that was scheduled to close, I was selected twice in a six-month period. The second time, I was almost nine-months pregnant and couldn't see the cup to give the sample!

As required by regulation, an observer has to go into the bathroom with you and watch you from start to finish. The observer detail is usually an all day detail. You are required to watch dozens of women pee in a cup all day

long! Eventually, it came my turn for this less than desirable detail. My First Sergeant told me I was up for an observer detail in a couple of weeks. I did everything I could think of to get out of it, but we had very few women in our unit at that time and I was stuck with it. As the time got closer, I absolutely dreaded it and everyone in my unit knew about it.

I worked out regularly at the gym across the street from where my unit was located. About a week before the dreaded observer detail, I went for my normal lunchtime workout, and injured my back severely enough that someone had to drive me to the hospital. I was lifting weights, pulled wrong somehow and was in instant excruciating pain. I walked slowly and gingerly back to my unit, and one of my co-workers drove me to the base hospital where they immediately gave me Demerol to alleviate the pain. I'm a lightweight when it comes to medication so was instantly in la-la land from the injection. I'm real fuzzy about what happened after that, but it was recounted for me later.

I had to return to my office to give my Commander and First Sergeant the "Quarters" paperwork (the policy is the military member must deliver it in person) which released me from duty, and put me on "Quarters" at home to recuperate. Someone drove me home, and I spent the next several days in a fog from the pain medication. When I finally returned to work and went to check in with my Commander and First Sergeant, who sat across the hall from each other, one of them asked, "Do you have that disciplinary action paperwork ready for her?"

"Yes, I've got it all ready to go."

"Good, we have to get her for that insubordination that occurred."

"I know. We can't tolerate that behavior in this unit."

They seemed to have quite the banter going back and forth, and I was totally confused as to what they were talking about. They noticed the extremely puzzled look on my face, and asked why I looked so confused. I told them I had no idea what they were talking about; then they filled me in. Apparently, when I returned from the hospital all wired on the Demerol,

I walked into my Commander's office, threw the Quarters paperwork at him and said, "I jacked my back up, I'm on quarters for a few days, and don't have to do that stinkin' urinalysis detail! See ya!"

Of course there was no disciplinary action planned, they were just having fun and picking on me. They thought it was quite amusing how "out of it" I was from the medication. I think I would have rather had the pain of doing the detail instead of the pain from my back—but at least someone else had to do it—and I never got tagged for it again my entire military career!

~ELDONNA LEWIS FERNANDEZ, MASTER SERGEANT, USAF (RET.)

http://pinkbikerchic.com

Duty Woman

As junior female officers aboard a Coast Guard icebreaker, we were expected to attend formal functions in various ports of call. Those of us that rotated through the assignment were referred to as the "duty women." One evening in 1982, in Apia, Western Samoa, I was finishing up work, and told my officer buddies that I would catch up with them. As I left the ship several hours later, I had to pass a bus stop where a friendly Samoan greeted me.

He struck up a conversation, and although he didn't speak English well and I didn't speak Samoan (Polynesian) at all, his meaning became perfectly clear. I decided to pretend that I didn't understand him, which worked for about a minute. Getting a bit frustrated with me, he asked me in his very best English, "You-me, make baby?" I thanked him for his offer but told him that my friends were coming and I had another commitment. Fortunately, some shipmates were passing by at just the right time, so I bid my new friend a hasty farewell.

~JEANNE CASSIDY, CAPTAIN, USCGR (RET.)

Stripes

One day, a civilian supervisor was joking with two of his female military personnel. Looking at the ranks, on their sleeves he noticed they each had five stripes. "Gee, I can really tell how old someone is by the amount of strips they have on their sleeves, you guys are really old!" They looked at each other, and started laughing out loud. "If that's the case, you must be ancient!" one woman responded. He was wearing a pin-striped shirt.

~ELDONNA LEWIS FERNANDEZ, MASTER SERGEANT, USAF (RET.)

http://pinkbikerchic.com

There is no problem that cannot be solved by the use of high explosives.
~BUMPER STICKER

My most brilliant achievement was my ability to be able to persuade my wife to marry me.
~SIR WINSTON CHURCHILL

Real women don't have hot flashes. They have power surges.
~CHRISTINE MANSFIELD

Have fun in your command. Don't always run at a breakneck pace. Take leave when you've earned it, spend time with your families.
~COLIN POWELL

Experience is something you don't get until just after you need it.
~STEVEN WRIGHT

Stenographer Sends Enemy Communication

In 1942, at the young age of twenty-three, Loretta Cohn was working in Kansas City as a stenographer when she felt a patriotic urge to help the war effort. As a stenographer she would take notes in shorthand and then transcribe them on the typewriter. She was born in 1919 and was raised in Iowa, and had no brothers and two sisters. Since she had no brothers to get drafted, she felt she needed to do something so she entered the Women's Army Air Corp (WAAC) as a Second Lieutenant during World War II.

Her first assignment was Basic Training in Daytona Beach, Florida. Many of the women were put up in a local hotel and most of them had to dry their clothes on the roof of the building. Loretta was lying in bed one night and was worried that someone may steal her brand new underpants that were hanging out to dry on the roof. So, she took a flashlight in the middle of the night to the rooftop. She thought nothing of the event, but later, when she was assigned to her first unit at Lowry Field, in Denver, Colorado, she learned that it was recorded as a possible enemy communication!

She met Private First Class Harris at Lowry Field in 1944, married him three weeks later, and served until 1945. She was assigned to an Intelligence Squadron and she saw a file about strange lights on top of a hotel where they housed the WAACS in training. The report was inconclusive as to whether the lights were signaling the enemy. Loretta knew it must have been her that night searching for her underpants on the roof. Fearful that she may get thrown in jail, she did not say anything, but she was sure it was her on the rooftop getting her underpants!

This is the first time she has shared this story and she giggles about it to this day—as if it just happened last year!

~LORETTA COHN, STENOGRAPHER

2 Lt, Women's Army Air Corp (WAAC)

Tribute written by Angela Cody-Rouget, Woman of Mass Organization

www.MajorMom.biz

Flight Suits and Honey Pots

Reminds me of a saying I saw written on the inside flap of C-130 cargo plane urinal: "Men with short stacks or low manifold pressure; stand close." Of course, the guys pointed it out since I would have no reason to use the urinal. I did avoid the floor near the urinal though, since it always was a little sticky. Women have to use the honey pot, and as tradition goes, whoever uses it first has to dump it. So, all the guys would hold back until one of them would have to go #2. We women could always hold it if we needed to.

Speaking of the lovely honey pot, wow, I'm getting nostalgic. It literally was a metal can with a seat on it and a plastic trash liner to hold the contents. Good loadmasters used two bags for extra measure. I remember the can was elevated on a platform that was surrounded by a privacy curtain. But get this, the curtain was only halfway around just so that the front portion of the plane's occupants couldn't see you. The back area, where the cargo door is located, was *wide open and illuminated*! This meant you could see the silhouette of the person on the pot. This was good and bad. Good, because you could see if anyone was on it, wouldn't want to "Ooops!" anyone. Bad, because everyone could see your outline and tell how you approached the pot. I say *approached* because it was very much like an aircraft landing.

Let me explain. You had to get up on a little platform, about two feet off the ground, and then step up backwards to get into position. Then, you would unzip your flight suit and take it off your shoulders, and carefully tie the arms of the flight suit around your thighs. This seems strange, but if you didn't tie them, the arms of your flight suit could end up in the pot and it would only take one time of that for you to form a ritual of tying them around your legs. All of this is, of course, as you are bending over, still hovering trying to land on the seat.

Now, I must tell you that the C-130 Hercules is affectionately known as the 4-Fan Trash Can, after it's four propellers and the fact that it is used to haul just about anything. However, being a prop-job it usually flies lower to

the ground than other cargo aircraft and so the incidence of turbulence is
. . . well, *common*. So, you're busy hovering . . . tying . . . squatting . . . and
bump, you're face down on the floor with your flight suit arms tied around
your legs like a noose and your bare butt sticking up in the air for all to see.
I saw it happen several times actually. Quite funny! Oh . . . and no, it never
happened to me, although I had a few close calls! Luckily, I was never that
shy at *landing* in public!

Incidentally, the urinal vented directly to the outside, so it was in-flight
use only. Oh, you could use it on the ground, but then anyone outside the
plane would know someone was using it! Can someone say, "Yellow clouds?!"

~EILENE M. NIELSEN, SENIOR MASTER SERGEANT, USAF, (RET.)

We have women in the military, but they don't put us in the front lines.
They don't know if we can fight, if we can kill. I think we can. All the general
has to do is walk over to the women and say, "You see the enemy over there?
They say you look fat in those uniforms."

~ELAYNE BOOSLER, AMERICAN COMEDIAN AND ACTIVIST

When I joined Custer I donned the uniform of a soldier. It was a bit
awkward at first but I soon got to be perfectly at home in men's clothes.

~CALAMITY JANE

Laughter is a tranquilizer with no side effects.

~ARNOLD GLASOW

Sometimes the only sense you can make out of life is a sense of humor.

~UNKNOWN

Living the Dream

Proud to Wear the Uniform

In the fall of 1969, I was stationed at the Fifth Naval District Headquarters in Norfolk, Virginia working as a journalist in the Public Affairs office, after completing training at the Defense Information School—which was at that time at Fort Benjamin Harrison in Indianapolis, Indiana.

The Navy seemed a perfect fit for me right out of high school. At that time, the lure of the GI Bill to fund my future college years was very attractive; plus, I was a patriotic young woman. My dad had been a Lt. Commander in the Navy during the Korean conflict following World War II. The military cemetery in Hawaii, Punchbowl—or National Memorial Cemetery of the Pacific—where my parents are buried—has an impressive display of huge tile murals that depict key battles of the war, including Korea. A couple of years before he passed away, my dad—my parents lived in Honolulu at the time—showed me on one of those murals, the beach his ship landed on. He had a photo of himself taken the day of the landing. Somehow, standing looking at that mural, along with Dad's photo, and being right then on the island where the war began for the United States . . . that brought history to life for me.

I was proud to wear my uniform. However, very often I was mistaken for an airline stewardess. People would stop me in airports and ask what airline I worked for. I must have walked proudly, because on base, young Marines and Navy guys in bell-bottom dungarees would salute me. I found it amusing, but never saluted back because I was just a seaman.

My job in the public affairs office involved writing press releases about Navy news to send out to the area newspapers. I also wrote and called in a weekly Navy news radio report. Most of the time, the work was fun and interesting. But there were times, as when ships returned from Vietnam, that the job was difficult. Sometimes, I had to represent the office at a posthumous award ceremony, write up a news release and send it to the deceased's home town newspaper. This was always a sad job.

There were some highlights to being stationed in Norfolk, Virginia. One Easter Sunday, I attended dawn services on the flight deck of an aircraft carrier. On another occasion, I had to deliver a message to the captain of a destroyer. It was no easy task to climb up and down those ladders in heels and a tight skirt.

Being a Navy person had its advantages when the 50th anniversary of the end of WWII was celebrated in Honolulu, Hawaii in 1995. I was able to attend many of the ceremonies both on land and aboard ships. This occasion was the last time the late actor, Bob Hope, appeared; and, I watched along with many others in a Waikiki park as the aged actor made us all laugh. In the afternoon of that day, I got to ride on an aircraft carrier that stationed itself just off Waikiki, as a parade of international ships and planes went by . . . all celebrating the end of that terrible war. I was proud to be a Navy Wave.

~LINDA C. (LEE) SMITH, JOSN, UNITED STATES NAVY

linbistwo@sbcglobal.net

http://lindasbusiness.wordpress.com

Did You Know . . . ? At the time of Pearl Harbor, the top U.S. Navy command was called CINCUS (pronounced "sink us"), the shoulder patch of the US Army's 45th Infantry division was the Swastika, and Hitler's private train was named "Amerika." (All three were soon changed for PR purposes!)

~WWII HISTORY BUFF COL D. G. SWINFORD, USMC (RET.)

Finding Service

Tribute to Petty Officer Raquel Santiago, USN

Her life has been anything but easy. Born in a quaint, rural town in Puerto Rico to a working class single mother, Raquel learned at an early age how to care for herself and others. Most of her childhood was spent living in small houses, shared with other relatives to help make ends meet. She learned to survive off the land, trading fish with neighbors for fresh fruit. To earn extra money for bills the young fashionista took discarded telephones from her mother's work, manipulating the colorful wires into fashionable bracelets and selling them to tourist in Old San Juan.

Raquel surprised her family when she enlisted in the U.S. Navy. Looking to fulfill her sense of duty and adventure she traveled to Florida for boot camp and was recognized as the top of her class. Active Duty resulted in mundane back-to-back tours home in Puerto Rico despite countless requests for a more exotic location. The Reserves opened a door for excitement with the cargo handlers, this group was known for their *can do* attitude.

With time on her hands, Raquel moved to New York City to pursue her life long dream as a fashion designer. Sleeping on the couches of friends and family, she scratched and clawed her way into the fashion community. Her trend-setting designs caught the eye of critics. Soon enough *RSVanity* products and designs were born.

Everything was going according to plan until that fateful day of 9/11. It touched Raquel more intimately than most. Navigating through the ash-coated streets of Manhattan, she hurried to her apartment and readied her sea bag. The burnt smell of the attack stained everything she owned. Within hours she was ready but the call did not come. Impatiently she continued to wait, actively volunteering for deployments; still the call did not come. Over three years passed, and then the phone rang.

In 2004 a devastating tsunami in the Indian Ocean killed over 300,000 souls, leaving carnage and chaos in its wake. The U.S. was quick to respond, redirecting all ships in the region. A small contracting unit in Singapore was given the green light to buy everything. The plan was to utilize this facility to load large cargo ships. These ships would meet the aircraft carrier, frigates and cruisers circling off the coast of the tragedy. Once loaded, helicopters would fly inland to drop off supplies. On paper this was a logical plan, but the infrastructure was not there to support it.

Quickly, supplies piled up, yet replenishment ships departed Singapore half-full, at best. No one could account for what did and did not go out. Soon, the warehouse floors were flooded from broken water bottles, spoiling rice and ruining medical kits. Contracted labor buckled under the pressure, most calling in sick or quitting as scrutiny of their service increased. The Commanding Officer put out a plea for help, for U.S. Navy cargo handlers.

Flying to the other side of the world, Petty Officer Santiago began sorting and organizing the humanitarian relief aide within two hours of landing. I met her as I briefed the unit on the bus ride from the airport. A motley crew, predominately women, looked at me with blank stares as I explained everything they needed to know. I had been a liaison to the Navy for over a year but had not expected them to respond with the Reserves for such an important mission. Hopefully they would be up to the challenge ahead, if not hundreds of thousands would die.

Within a few hours a cargo ship would pull into Singapore. The group would have four hours to load the ship before it set sail, so it was imperative to have everything prepared. I was pleasantly surprised as they worked through the night. Circling by the warehouse periodically, I watched the Petty Officer leading by example and keeping her group moving at a steady pace. Fresh water, rice, rations and first aid kits were stacked and accounted for. Fork lifts readied, pallets placed. The team was on the brink of exhaustion but pleased with what they accomplished.

Jet lagged, they had only been in Singapore twelve hours. As the sun rose, she rallied her shipmates for a final push. The cargo ship's crew was thrilled to pull into port and see the Navy's cargo handlers standing pier-

side. A flurry of action followed as gallons of water, pounds of rice and individually packed first aid kits were loaded on to the ship. Forklifts and cranes operated in organized chaos. Orchestrating the action, the feisty Latina from New York inspired her weary team to continue. With entire nations depending on these supplies getting to their devastated homes it was the cargo handler's most important mission ever.

For the first time since the global disaster, a U.S. Navy cargo ship would leave Singapore at full capacity. Under Raquel's leadership, this was just the beginning. Soon, all cargo ships would be replenished here. Before the United Nations moved in to take over the relief efforts, the U.S. Navy cargo handlers would account for over 250,000 gallons of water, 700,000 pounds of rice, 300,000 rations and 500,000 first aid kits in just a few weeks time.

Returning to New York City, Raquel anxiously looked forward to relaxing in her bed. For the first time since 9/11 she did not look at her phone and curse not getting a call. Her duty complete, she knew what her team had accomplished regardless where the accolades fell. In a week she had a fashion show in Old San Juan. Up the hill from where she sold tri-colored bracelets to cruise ship tourists, her new jewelry line would be paired with notable clothing designers. Exhausted, months behind schedule, she knew what needed to be done. *RSVanity* was taking center stage, as her dream to become a fashion designer shifted to fulltime. Rest would have to wait; she had a job to do. No one would know her story; no one will know where she was the past few weeks. On the other side of the planet, families would give her thanks without knowing her name. Her quiet contribution saved their lives.

~CAPT. ADAM GRAVSETH, USMC

Editor's Note: Adam commented that they met towards the end of the tsunami recovery efforts and it was love at first sight. He already had to follow on orders to Iraq but they married just before he left. After a year in "the sandbox" Adam returned home and hung up his boots. They now live in Puerto Rico with a beautiful baby girl named after the Singapore town where they met, Nevinna.

Trust your hunches. They're usually based on facts filed away just below the conscious level.
~DR. JOYCE BROTHERS

Courage is rightly esteemed the first of human qualities,
because it is the quality that guarantees all others.
~SIR WINSTON S. CHURCHILL

Life is a daring adventure or nothing.
~HELEN KELLER

Above all, challenge yourself. You may well surprise yourself at what strengths you have, what you can accomplish.
~CECILE M. SPRINGER

I know God will not give me anything I can't handle.
I just wish he didn't trust me so much.
~MOTHER TERESA

Listen to your heart, because in the end it is your heart that matters.
~JENNIFER TYLER

When we seek to discover the best in others,
we somehow bring out the best in ourselves.
~WILLIAM ARTHUR WARD

The Challenge and Opportunity of a Lifetime

Captain Neil Williamson looked at the sea of faces in front of him. "You're first-place finishers and used to winning. I have a news flash for you, though. The jet you're about to strap into doesn't care about any of that. It's an equal-opportunity destroyer of careers, or lives, if you make a mistake." The students looked around at one another. Captain Williamson knew that they had already been through more than most could handle.

"Now comes the real test. Will you be able to master flying the supersonic T-38 to the standards set by the U.S. Air Force? Once you climb into the cockpit of a jet that can break the speed of sound, there is no doubt that some of you will fall by the wayside. Whether you make the cut will depend on how well you prepare, practice, perform, and pass your checkrides. You already know that Undergraduate Pilot Training is like fifty-two consecutive weeks of finals in college. You'll get to a point where you'll think that your mind and body have taken all they can, and then you'll simply have to demand more of yourself than you ever thought possible."

A jet flew directly overhead the briefing room, rattling the window blinds, punctuating Neil's statement. "Flying the T-38 requires the absolute mastery of a multitude of skills, some you haven't even imagined yet. You have to want this more than anything you've ever wanted in your life. It'll be the toughest thing you ever do—but also the most rewarding if you survive."

The excerpt above is from an *The Pilot—Learning Leadership*, which I co-authored with my husband and fellow pilot, Bill Hensley. The briefing is representative of what I heard 25 years ago when I was about to enter the advanced phase of Air Force Undergraduate Pilot Training (UPT). This phase of training tested every skill I possessed and revealed the essence of my character. It was both the challenge, and the opportunity, of a lifetime.

Our mission in pilot training was to learn to fly the supersonic Talon T-38, nicknamed the *White Rocket*. I knew that if I passed all of my evaluations, or "checkrides" as we called them, I would have the opportunity to fly a worldwide transport, four-engine jet aircraft called the C-141. During pilot training, I experienced an epiphany. It had less to do with learning to fly a jet, than it did with something that would affect the rest of my life in a profound way—I realized the military was the most level playing field that I could ever have imagined. Now, after decades of commercial airline flying and entrepreneurial business experience, I have yet to encounter an environment that compares. I can pinpoint a flight in which it all began to come together—one of the last I flew in pilot training, before I graduated and earned my *wings*. It was a formation flight of four T-38s. Formation involves two or more jets flying a mission together. In the T-38, such missions included everything from flying 500-miles-per-hour with merely three feet separating wingtips, to practicing air show-type aerobatic maneuvers.

On one particular day I was flying solo. Flying the number four position in something called *Echelon*—or line abreast—formation, I could look out and see three other needle-nosed T-38s, wingtip to wingtip, screaming through the air as we headed back to base at the end of our training mission. Four-ship formations were not common, so when they showed up overhead the airfield at an altitude of 1,500 feet and in excess of 300 miles per hour, it was quite a sight to behold. Upon arriving at a certain point above the runway, each jet "peeled-off" with an aggressive turn. The idea was to land with minimal spacing behind the preceding jet. I managed to touch down precisely in front of the runway control unit, or "mini control tower." The nose of my jet was raised high, just as my wheels smoothly contacted the runway. Over the radio, the controller remarked, "Nice touchdown number four."

It was at that point, that so much of what had taken place during my previous year of pilot training finally became clear. I understood that it was possible for a pilot's performance to be more significant than a pilot's gender. As time went on, I also came to understand that because of the seriousness of military missions, those involved focused on *what* was accomplished, rather than the gender of who accomplished it.

This attitude was verified repeatedly throughout my years of duty. For the most part, I was treated as a pilot, not as a *female*-pilot. When I flew worldwide missions in the C-141, from the Middle East to Europe, and to remote Pacific Island destinations, my crew didn't focus on my gender. Rather, they saw me as a pilot with whom they could entrust their lives. They saw me as a pilot who could handle any in-flight situation and land virtually anywhere on earth that our assigned missions would take us.

There is no group of people with which I have come into contact—before or after my military service—of which I am more proud. The term *family* is frequently used, often inappropriately, when referring to a business organization. In the military, that term has true applicability. There is something about the bonds that form when everyone in your organization is willing to give his or her life for the stated mission. There is something about the bonds that form among pilots who see not the gender of their fellow pilot, but rather the precise positioning of her jet as it flies alongside them in formation. There is something about the words made famous by General Douglas MacArthur during his farewell speech at West Point in 1962, when he said "Duty, Honor, Country—those three hallowed words reverently dictate what you want to be, what you can be, what you will be."

I express great gratitude to those who are currently engaged in the defense of our country and those who plan to serve. Our progress has been great and our country's future is bright because of the quality of our people.

Never pass up the opportunity to do the extraordinary, for you will be rewarded throughout the rest of your life for so doing. Nothing will ever match the sense of pride you will feel by being willing to put your life on the line for your country. I am honored to have been given the chance to serve, but I am the one who continues to reap the benefits of that opportunity.

~COLLEEN HENSLEY, AUTHOR OF *THE PILOT—LEARNING LEADERSHIP*
Former Captain, U.S. Air Force Reserve Pilot
www.thepilotbook.com
© 2009 Colleen Hensley

United we stand, divided we fall.
~AESOP

The day will come when man will recognize woman as his peer,
not only at the fireside, but in councils of the nation.
Then, and not until then, will there be the perfect comradeship,
the ideal union between the sexes that shall result in the
highest development of the race.
~SUSAN B. ANTHONY

All for one and one for all.
~MOTTO FROM *THE THREE MUSKETEEERS*, BY ALEXANDRE DUMAS

A candle loses nothing by lighting another candle.
~ERIN MAJORS

Never let the odds keep you from pursuing what you know in your heart you
were meant to do.
~SATCHEL PAIGE

The most beautiful adventures are not those we go to seek.
~ROBERT LOUIS STEVENSEN

Commitment is the igniter of momentum.
~PEG WOOD

Good Leaders are Good Followers

I was born to lead. Many have said this about me many times throughout my life. I love to be in charge and call the shots. I love the satisfaction of accomplishing a mission with a team of people. Slowly but surely, I was led to understand that being a good leader also means being a good follower. One day, not long ago, I was in church and a guest pastor did an entire sermon on honoring those above us even when we do not agree with them. He beautifully pointed out that the American culture has lost the art of honoring those in positions of authority. He also reminded us that God has put each person in each position and that dishonoring the individual is dishonoring to God. This pastor firmly stated that if we trust God, then we will have faith in His plan. Ouch! "Oh crap," I thought, "I am not a good follower." I am terrible at following. Oh, how I love to follow good, strong competent people. However, put a weak and incompetent leader in charge of me and I did not honor them.

Since I was born to lead, the military seemed like a good fit for me. As a young eighteen-year-old woman, I joined Air Force ROTC at Indiana University. As a freshman, the Air Force started to teach and train me about things a future officer would need to know in order to be a good leader and manager.

I started to discover that there was something deep down in my soul that craved order and systems, as well as, adventure and the unknown. Well, in spite of my lack of experience in honoring authority, I surely did excel in the military environment. The military is an environment where success is related to your ability to follow your leaders.

The Air Force taught me about all different types of missions and leaders. I started to discover that I had difficulty following and supporting managers and/or supervisors that seemed to be ill-fitted to lead. I really never thought that the military would have anything except perfect, storybook leaders. Well, I got my first dose of reality in ROTC when I realized that military officers are sometimes just humans in uniform! I also got a dose of leaders to die for and that I would follow to the end. I learned quickly that my least favorite type of leader was categorized as All Mission/No People. Wow, these kinds of leaders really saw us as a number and as a mechanism to achieve the mission. They did not give one the impression that they cared to deal with human issues at all. The other type of leader that I found very difficult to follow was the No Mission/All People. Oh, it is difficult to win battles if the leader is more concerned about the people than the mission. I struggled most of my career to support and follow these two kinds of leaders.

I entered Active Duty and spent my entire career in U.S. Space Command. In some units, we had a different leader every six months, and others it seemed like forever. Many times, I would analyze and fret over the decisions of my superiors and, sometimes, I would confront them when I really didn't understand their ways. As you can imagine, this never went well and they usually answered, "Just do it." Or, "Someday you'll understand." Or "You don't have a need to know."

You see no one ever taught me that good leaders are first good followers. I didn't know that I must first just do as I am told, as long as it is moral and ethical. This is something I discovered as I became a Captain, and then a Major. I clearly learned this when I took charge of my first flight, and made some changes to how things were operating, and they asked, "Why?" I thought to myself, "Because I know more than you, and I know what needs to happen!" Ah, yes, I was getting a dose of me . . . the not-so-good follower.

So, as I finally rose to leadership positions, I explained myself and my reasons, and got as much "buy-in" as possible. I was there to inspire and lead, not just manage. I carefully monitored myself and wanted to achieve the perfect balance between mission and people. I discovered that there were some instances where you had to be ALL MISSION and NO PEOPLE to prevent equipment damage or death, but in peace time one can usually lead with a balanced approach to the Mission and Its People stance. As a

woman, I could easily fall in to the All People/No Mission category because I am naturally motherly and nurturing.

I subscribe to the fact that leaders are born to lead and some can be trained to lead, but they must be taught early. Every leader is under someone else's lead, and therefore they must be good followers. They must show their troops that they follow the orders of their superiors.

I am so incredibly thankful for my four years in AFROTC, ten years Active Duty and four years in the Reserves. I resigned my commission after my second child was born. I exited as a Major in the USAF, and I am still learning how to be a good follower. I still struggle to follow a few of my leaders without questions or input, but I quickly pull out of old habits and salute smartly to their lead.

Since the Lord has not totally reformed me yet, I, of course, became an entrepreneur, and started my own company. I like to set the rules and call the shots. Lord, thank you for the numerous opportunities to lead, in spite of my weaknesses as a follower.

To my past supervisors and leaders: I apologize for bucking the system and not honoring you. Please forgive me. I so understand you just needed me to follow you.

~ANGELA CODY-ROUGET, MAJOR, USAF VETERAN
www.MajorMom.biz

Do your dream now! You'll find that once you commit to yourself, the Universe gives you unlimited support, and creates even more options for you. YOU CAN DO IT!

~CATHERINE ANN NARY "CAN DO"

Living Happily Ever After

Joining the Army changed my life. Yes, that's a bold statement. Yet, when I look at the life altering decisions I've made, joining the Army is top. You see, it took me out of an abusive household and allowed me to emerge as a leader, a woman of strength. It gave me confidence in myself, an ability to take risks, a feeling that I can do anything!

I grew up in a family of eight children, high school dropouts, drug and alcohol abusers, early pregnancies. I was physically abused; I had welts that lasted two weeks. Even more damaging emotionally, I was told by my step-mom that I was fat (I was a size 5) and ugly, and was just like my mother, who was mentally ill. And yet, there was a strength that was in me, a strength that allowed me to stay in that environment until I completed high school, while my brothers and sisters all dropped out and left.

My parents signed for me to join the Army at the age of 17, because they felt that I was a bad role model for my sisters. They thought I had been sexually active and they had me checked by a doctor who said I wasn't; they pronounced me both guilty and untouchable, despite my innocence. My sisters would not to talk to me. I left that environment behind and joined the Army. I scored high on the entrance exams and my recruiter told me I could do anything that was open to women. Because of my conditioning, my background, and what I thought I was limited to doing, I asked to be an Administrative Assistant 71L. I placed that limitation on myself.

I became an assistant Squad Leader in Basic Training. Everyone says to not volunteer in the Army, but when they asked for help, my hand went up. For the first time in my life, I was recognized as a leader. For the first time in my life, I felt attractive. I was sent to Germany, worked for the General at 32nd AADCOM, got all of my promotions early and started realizing that I had potential. I loved the Army. I traveled all over Europe, I danced, I dated, and then I started college. Neither traveling Europe nor starting college was a possibility for me without joining the Army.

I was invited to apply to Officer Candidate School (OCS), but I wanted to complete college, so my intention was to go through ROTC and go back in. I did complete college, thanks to the GI Bill, and went on to get my Master's from the University of Southern California. And I never returned to the Army. I chose the civilian life.

So yes, the Army changed my life. But I was left with a lot of anger from my upbringing. When I left home, I declared that *no one* would ever hit me again, nor would I allow anyone to hit my future children. I went through life with a chip on my shoulder, anger waiting to happen.

When I had children though, my modeling and how I was reared, kicked in. I got upset and hit my daughter leaving a handprint on her leg. I was appalled with myself. I had just done what I swore I would never do! The next day, I got a job, then my real estate license, which led me to the Landmark Forum. I was able to release my anger, which allowed me to make a true contribution to society. I have never hit my daughter since.

My Pastor says, "God doesn't intend for us to waste a hurt." We can become bitter or we can become better. I chose to become better, and help other women to grow. Now, my pet project—my heart—is working with women.

I had the privilege to stay home with my children, to volunteer in their classrooms for many years, as a Girl Scout Leader. My children acknowledge me for being an amazing mom, and for offering them opportunities that most children didn't have. I didn't realize that I was taking risks; as a single mom, I took my girls to all 50 states before my oldest was twelve.

I became a lay counselor at my church, and had the privilege of helping women to choose to create a healthy marriage, create healthy boundaries, or fall in love with their husbands again. I was a life coach for six years, five as a volunteer, and one year paid. Because of the experiences I shared, five couples stayed married, not just surviving in their marriage, but creating, and working toward the *happily ever after*.

I have taken groups of people (Girl Scouts, my small group from church, my Parents Without Partners group) into women's shelters especially on

Mother's Day. When the women are forgotten, I recognize them for being mothers, choosing a different lifestyle, or making a new life for themselves and their children. Many have left abusive situations or are trying to kick a drug or alcohol habit. I share my life story hoping my experiences will make a difference for them. I share my story to give them hope.

I've gone to dinner with a group of nine- to 17-year-old girls at Boys Town. When I told my story, it allowed them to open up and share things that they had never shared. I left them with the concept that they do not have to be constrained by their past, that they can make choices for excellence. I acknowledged each of them for the hard work they were putting into making their lives whole and complete. I've also collected clothing for Working Wardrobes, who hosts a *Day of Self Esteem* for women in shelters. In the *Day of Self Esteem*, women select two outfits, receive coaching for job interviews; they get their hair and make-up done and they participate in a fashion show at the end of the day to boost their self-confidence.

All of my education has led me to become a real estate investor. I love helping anyone learn to invest, and my focus is on women. A woman can buy a cash-flowing house and create more income than she can from a part-time job. This allows her to have a choice to stay home with her children if that is her desire.

My goal, as I create even more success in investing, is to underwrite a *Day of Self Esteem* each month. My vision is to take it even further: to enroll a few coaches, to work with the women, contribute to their lives for a month and help them form new habits.

I have an amazing life. My life is so very different from that of my brothers and sisters. And I credit my Army experience, acquiring the discipline, accepting risk, feeling successful. My life was forever altered because of my decision to join the Army; and, I'm forever grateful for the life skills I acquired while in the service.

~CINDY LOGAN, SPEC 5, U.S. ARMY

www.Investthebestway.com

The Honor Guard

In 1984, I was assigned to Bergstrom AFB in Austin, Texas. I remained there for nine years until the Base closed in 1993. I had my two kids there, and received my Bachelor's Degree in Business Management from Park University while attending night school. I was also a member of the Base Honor Guard as an additional duty, for five of the nine years I was assigned there.

The Honor Guard is about precision in rendering military honors at funerals, leading off local parades, and posting the colors at change of command ceremonies, special events, or dignitary arrivals. We led off many big parades in Austin, and the surrounding area, and at private events like the Special Olympics. We were filmed and interviewed on several news programs, and always in the Base paper or local city and community papers where we performed.

The Base had visits from Queen Elizabeth, Prince Charles, the President of Mexico and many others. One of the "jobs" of the Honor Guard, is Color Guard. As a member of the Color Guard, we would be posted out on the runway to greet the dignitary's plane as it arrived. We carried the colors in harnesses up high for these events, usually standing four-abreast with the Air Force Flag and the United States Flag. The Color Guard Commander carried the United States Flag. I was usually always the Color Guard Commander. There would be an extra flag for the visiting dignitary's country, which would increase to five-abreast.

On one occasion, we were set up and ready as the large jet, about the size of Air Force One, rolled in with Prince Charles. The wind caught the flags and they started flapping ferociously. I started to be taken by the wind, and the only thing that saved me from toppling over backwards were the two members on either side of me putting their shoulders in my back so I didn't blow over! I stood there flapping back-and-forth with the flag until the pilot cut the engines and the wind died down. Improvising was a big factor in Honor Guard details.

One annual event was the Military Ball, where I was Color Guard Commander for a multi-service (Air Force, Army, Navy, Marines) Color Guard one year. The event was in a large hotel, and filled to capacity with 500+ in attendance. I stand only 5'5" and am petite. When the other service members (who were all men) saw me, they started making comments. "I hope you can call commands loud enough for people to hear." "Do you really think you can handle this big room?" The Marine was especially doubtful, and unimpressed with this small, female Air Force Staff Sergeant who was in charge of the detail. "I'll show them," I thought. We set up to practice, and walked the aisle several times in formation. It required the Color Guard to march down the center aisle, stop and then the two flag bearers (me and the Marine) to march to separate ends of the stage and post the colors. The Color Guard Commander (me) had to call the commands, "Present Arms!" and "Order Arms."

When the time came for the official posting of the colors we marched up the aisle with perfect precision. Five hundred sets of eyes were watching in total silence as we marched up. As the two of us carrying the colors faced, and marched off to the opposite ends of the enormous stage, I kept thinking to myself, "just let my voice carry across the room." We reached the flag stands at exactly the same time and with perfect precision faced, placed the flags in the stands and took a step back. I took a deep breath and out came the most resounding "PRESENT ARMS!" I had ever called.

As we stood silently through the National Anthem, I couldn't help but crack a grin. I called an "ORDER ARMS!" that must have been heard two blocks away from the hotel—and again with perfect precision—we marched back to the center, faced, stepped back into formation and I marched us out. Once outside of the room with the doors closed, there was a look of shock on everyone else's faces on the Color Guard but mine. I had a slight smirk, slight grin and a total "yeah, I'm bad to the bone" countenance as I stood there, and looked at the other three members of the Color Guard team. The Marine spoke up, "Wow, I'm totally impressed. I must admit I didn't think you could do it; I was wrong. Good job, Sergeant!" The others chimed in with kudos, as well. Just goes to show you not to underestimate a woman just because she's small in stature!

I served many more times on the Honor Guard for special events. Many times, I was requested by name for my precision and leadership ability. On one occasion, with the entire floor of the University of Texas arena packed to capacity for a special military banquet, the Color Guard had to march down a long aisle the length of the concrete arena floor. I wore large horseshoe taps on the heels of my boots and had to put tape over them to keep from slipping. The flag bearers (myself and another member) had to march to the end of the giant stage, march up a flight of six metal stairs, and to the flag stands positioned on the stage. It seemed like a daunting task. Each step taken on the stairs and the stage echoed across the entire arena. One wrong step on either of our parts, and the whole place would know it immediately.

When it was time for the banquet to begin, we assembled at the back of the arena and waited for our queue. The MS announced, "Post the colors!" I called the group to attention, and called, "Forward March!" The sound of my tape-covered taps kept the cadence as we marched up the long aisle. "Detail, Halt! Post!" The two of us carrying the flags, stepped out, faced opposite directions and stepped off. The thing that makes this so complex is being in precision while not even looking at the other person. It has to be done by instinct.

We marched to the opposite ends of the stage, stopped, did a facing movement, paused, then, stepped up to the set of stairs. One-by-one with perfect precision—as if only one person was stepping—we marched up each step perfectly and came to a stop at the top—faced towards each other—a couple steps more—faced the flag stands—and marched several steps to the flag stands, posted the colors, stepped back and I called out, "PRESENT ARMS!"

We stood, saluting at attention, through the National Anthem and I called, "ORDER ARMS." We went back through the motions the same way we went up—in perfect precision, formed back up and marched out. This was a show-case moment for us and we received many kudos and letters of appreciation.

My entire experience on the Honor Guard is one I'll cherish for a lifetime, and I am grateful for my long standing participation and the memories.

~ELDONNA LEWIS FERNANDEZ, MASTER SERGEANT, USAF (RET.)
http://pinkbikerchic.com

It's never too late to become the person you might have been.
~GEORGE ELLIOTT

You can never go wrong by doing right.
~SUE SHEFFLER

*The more you praise and celebrate your life,
 the more there is in life to celebrate.*
~OPRAH WINFREY

*If there is light in the soul, there will be beauty in the person.
If there is beauty in the person, there will be harmony in the house.
If there is harmony is the house, there will be order in the nation.
If there is order in the nation, there will be peace in the world.*
~CHINESE PROVERB

Military Brats

An Air Force Brat

I'm an "Air Force Brat" and proud of it, too.
My favorite colors are red, white, and blue!

My Dad served our country for over 30 years,
In the United States Air Force and the U.S. Army Air Corps.

My Mom made sure it was a team effort for all of us, too,
keeping a positive attitude with every new move.
As soon as she'd hung just a picture or two,
it was suddenly "home" and we knew what to do.

What's it been like for all of my life?
It's a privileged adventure, a constant safari.

You learn about kids all over the land, what they are made of, happy or sad.
We were stationed in California (three times),
Alabama, Guam, Georgia, Kansas, and Nebraska (twice).
Twelve different schools in 16 years—what an adventure—what a career!

Over and over, I've been the new kid at school,
Trying to fit with a group that is cool.

Sometimes I'm a loner, waiting to find
some other new kids who are also my kind.

First day of school, often scary or funny.
What will they wear? How will they sound?
Southern accents? Yankee clips?
Midwestern twangs? California quips?

Be invisible; get the lay of the land.
What's out there to greet you?
Town kids or other "service brats?"

City kids often lock the door,
They might try to make you feel different or even poor.

But after a little while, not very long,
you look around to find you really belong.
The group or the church kids or the ones from school
have opened a tiny door and you've earned your way in.

So now you can see, in so many ways,
I've learned to live *anywhere*,
That's the great joy of being an Air Force Brat!

~EMILY DESHAZO~
©2009

Parents can only give good advice or put [their children] on the right paths,
but the final forming of a person's character lies in their own hands.
~ANNE FRANK

A Military Brat

I grew up as a military brat, as the term goes. My grandfather served in World War II and my uncle's career was in Army Intelligence, as well. My mom remarried an Air Force officer when I was six-years-old, and she was 24.

I remember leaving my grandparents' house unexpectedly one night and riding in the back window ledge of a 1946 Ford from Los Angeles, California to Bangor, Maine. The trip for me was looking out the window at the stars and wondering where I was off to. My life had changed. It was the beginning of many adventures and trips across the States, and although I did not ride in the back window, I did roll the window down and snuggle under a blanket and feel the cold air on my face.

We moved to Sumter, South Carolina, for six months and then on to Biloxi, Mississippi, where we stayed for two years, and where my brother was born. I loved Biloxi: the gulf, fishing for catfish and swinging on a tire across the ravine close to home. We ran and played and explored without worry. I ate fresh sugar cane and picked up a Southern "y'all" drawl in my language. My dad adopted me while we were in Biloxi. As we moved from place to place, my mom was able to stay at home. She was the stability and the one who welcomed me home at the end of my school days. She taught me to Jitterbug, sew, and play Canasta.

We were transferred to Nellis Air Force Base in Las Vegas for a few months where we lived on the edge of the desert, and I learned to go door-to-door asking if they had anyone who could play with me. My dad trained for war. For friendly me, moving so much meant I learned to meet people easily and strike up friendships. They might be shorter, but still important to my happiness. The other kids were like me. I grew confident and learned to reach out.

My dad was an Air Force pilot. The Korean War was on, and he was sent to duty. He named his plane after my Mom, Brother and me, *Jakachi*. It had bullet punctures all over it that they would patch up when he returned from maneuvers. He was emaciated when he came back to the States toward the end of the War. I could tell even as a kid the big price he paid for the stress of war and fighting.

We had stayed in Los Angeles, close to my grandparents. We were sent back to Las Vegas for another tour. They had a very active social life with other families, and it was fun for me. I was free and safe to play on Base and learned to love the desert and its creatures in our back yard. There was a lot of Cold War pressure, and I was taught to respond to emergencies without questions. I watched the A-bomb tests twice while there. I learned the world had danger in it.

A couple of years later we were sent to Washington, D.C., as my parents attended protocol and language school and then by ship, we were on to Rome, Italy, where we lived in the city for four wonderful years. We were taught to be good representatives of our Country, not "ugly Americans." We were taught to respect the culture and the Italian people. My father's job was to help the Italians rebuild their Air Force and teach them to fly again. In Italian! I know that for a boy from Texas there were many challenges for him, but he met them all and did his job well.

He was very proud of what he did. Claire Booth Luce was the Ambassador. My mom and dad had a very busy social life and it was truly La Dolce Vita for me, too. I grew sophisticated living in Rome, and going to school with other kids from many countries who traveled the world with their parents. I was fluent in Italian within three years. I have many, many good memories of those days and was very fortunate to have lived there throughout my teen years and receive the education I did. When I was almost 18, we were posted to Everett, Washington, where I completed my senior year in high school and went on to college.

I learned to be a proud American and to feel patriotism. I grew up in an era of The Cold War. My dad was on stand-by for the *Bay of Pigs*. He fought in the Korean War. There were many moments of real concern for my mom

as he was a defender and a protector of our Country and its values. They lost some friends to war and accidents. I still get real warmth in my heart and tears in my eyes at the playing of the *Star-Spangled Banner* and *Taps*. I say the Pledge of Allegiance and mean it. I am a military brat.

My dad died a few months ago and received full military honors as he was buried here in San Diego. My mom still plays cards with other military wives at the local base. It is a community, and once you are a part of it, you always carry it in your heart with pride. I am grateful for the life I had. It was fascinating, and I met fascinating people. I am proud I was a military brat.

I married at college, and my folks came through the town I lived in on their way to another posting. As they drove away, I ran calling after the car, "Wait for me! Wait for me!" Tears were running down my face. I saw my brother looking out the back window as they were on their way to their next adventure in Wichita, Kansas. I wanted to be in that car, snuggled under the blanket with the cold air on my face and on to the next adventure with them.

I loved being a military brat.

~KATHY MAYO NELSON

Daughter of Major John B. Mayo, III and Jacqueline M. Mayo

Never help a child with a task at which he feels he can succeed.
~JUDY GARLAND

Do not teach your children, for they will not understand.
Rather show them how you live and they will follow you.
~JACQUELINE WATTS

Sand Dunes and Helicopters

Dad flew nearly 2000 missions to rescue downed pilots and others. After his retirement from the Navy, he was asked by President Jimmy Carter to do one last rescue attempt from Iran. He was a high-ranking officer in the Navy. My husband was an E6 when we married. You can imagine what kind of event my wedding was! But I'll save that story for another day. What I remember as being humorous about having a Navy pilot for a dad seemed normal to me as a young girl. Later, I realized how different our lives were from "regular kids." My friends' fathers didn't fly helicopter rescue missions into North Vietnam!

Not only was Dad a *rotor head* but he flew fixed-wing aircraft on carriers, as well, and made carrier landings on the U.S.S. Midway. I still have some landing photos for the now floating aircraft carrier museum in San Diego. My dad was the ultimate adrenalin junkie. I believe this is an inherited gene which has cursed each of us kids. My brothers, when not killing bad guys in Iraq or Afghanistan, were busy bungee jumping, hang gliding, parachuting or just riding their motorcycles way too fast.

One summer when my dad was home on leave from Vietnam, he took us out to drive in the sand dunes. He managed to get the car stuck in the sand on several occasions. We lived in the desert back then, and were stationed in Fallon, Nevada. Dad hitchhiked to the base and flew back to where we were stranded. He got a Sikorski helicopter and some webbing. He landed and quickly had the car covered with thick, green webbing. We watched as he picked up the car with the helicopter and put it back on the road. Mom drove it back to the base, and picked him up after he returned the helicopter. I had no idea how much sand one of those things would kick up, nor did I realize how noisy they would be! This seemed to be something we did as a family on several occasions. I never saw Dad use a jack or a shovel to get our car out of the sand, just a helicopter!

I didn't realize until I was in high school that this was not a normal way to get a car out of the sand. During a high school science club campout, the axle of the van we rode in was stuck in the sand. The teacher got shovels, a piece of carpet, and a jack to try and get the van axle unstuck. He had all the students pushing. Nothing worked. I was laughing at their antics, because I knew the *proper* way to get a car out of the sand. "Why aren't you helping us, Patty?" the teacher asked. "You're doing it all wrong," I replied. "We need a helicopter!" I shared with them my childhood memories of Dad rescuing our car from the sand with a helicopter, as they looked at me as if I were from another planet. My father would have come in handy had he been on this trip.

~PATTY ANDERSON
Member Women in Defense, National Defense Industrial Association

God,
I read the bible. What does begat mean? Nobody will tell me.
Love, Alison

Dear God,
Do you draw the lines around the countries?
If you don't, who does?
—Nan

Dear Mr. God,
I wish you would not make it so easy for people to come apart.
I had to have 3 stitches and a shot.
—Janet

~KID'S THEOLOGY

Wait Until Your Father Comes Home

I was a military brat growing up. My dad, an Air Force Pilot, flew all over the world. He was gone months and years at a time, leaving my mother home to raise us. He missed birthdays, Christmas, dance recitals, and school events. Looking back, it was like my mother was a single mother most of the time. As children, we accepted that this is just how all kids grew up. However, it must have been difficult for my mom to have the man she loved gone so much of the time.

Many times if she was frustrated with us, Mom would say "Wait until your father comes home . . . ." When we were young, this was a threat we took seriously, as we did not want our dad upset with us. Even after all these years, I can still feel the fear her scolding could evoke. Of course, by the time Dad came home Mom usually had forgotten why she was mad and Dad only wanted to have fun with us. He was more like a part-time "Disneyland Dad," while Mom took care of the daily routine of child-rearing.

Even though we moved many times to Air Force bases throughout the United States, Dad was stationed around the world in the various countries. Whenever he came home, it was like Christmas. He bought us countless gifts over the years. We would get hula skirts from Hawaii, jewelry boxes and dolls from Japan, China sets from England. And we would always have fun vacations. We had water skiing boats, house trailers and fishing boats so we could enjoy camping in wonderful places throughout Canada and the United States. Dad made sure we visited Washington D.C., introduced us to live theater productions, and taught us to play bridge, poker and chess!

Despite living with the sacrifices, I always felt pride and respect for what my father has done for our country. He fought in Africa and Europe during World War II, flew in the Korean War and was a pilot and commanding officer in Vietnam. Since so many of his fellow officers and friends did not return, we are forever thankful that he came home to us.

~LYN R. WHITE

Airport Package

I'm a military brat; I grew up with both of my parents in the Air Force. When 9/11 happened, the world I knew slowly came to an end. My mom was working crazy hours practicing "war games" and always had her bags packed—because she was getting told she was going to be deployed—but they ended up being false orders. Finally the news came that she was actually getting deployed to the Middle East for a 90-day-period which ended up being almost 120 days. That may not sound too bad compared to the six-month tours many soldiers are going on; but for an 11-year-old girl with a nine-year-old little brother, that was the worst possible situation. I don't quite remember her leaving, you know, the whole airport scene, but what I do remember is her being gone.

While she was gone, my dad ended up getting deployed to Korea for a year. My brother and I had to live with our aunt and neighbors with no parents. My mom was gone on a "top secret" deployment, so we didn't know exactly where she was. Both of my parents were very hard to contact. We would write and receive letters but it would be weeks at a time with no contact to either of them. It was a very hard time in my life. Having both of my parents gone took a toll in all aspects of my life. I gave up in school and I didn't care about my grades or my social life. I had a best friend who I could talk to about everything, but other than that I was quiet and sad.

The time finally came; my mom's tour was over and she would be coming back. We lived in the smallest little town in New Mexico, so to go to the airport, you had to drive about 90 miles. My aunt and her boyfriend decided to take me and my brother out for a day of fun in El Paso, Texas (where the closest airport was). On our way home they said we had to stop by the airport to pick something up. I remember sitting in the airport thinking to myself, "I'm gonna be here in a week to get my mom." Little did I know, that's why we were there.

My mom ended up coming home a week early! I remember sitting in the airport just looking around—not paying attention to anything at all-and I turned my head and I see my mom. I was like, "Oh, hey; it's my mom." Just like it was no big deal. Then I had to do a double take and I jumped up out of the seat and said, "It's my mom!" Both me and my brother jumped up, ran and tackled her.

It's a different life being a military brat. You have to sacrifice things that non-military kids don't even know about—or understand—and you gain an understanding about the importance of sacrifice. I have considered going into the Air Force myself and my brother is planning on joining when he graduates High School. Maybe when we have children both of our kids will turn out to be military brats and continue the tradition too!

~MARISSA FERNANDEZ

Proud daughter of Eldonna Lewis Fernandez, co-author of Heart of a Military Woman

Please know that I am aware of the hazards. I want to do it because I want to do it. Women must try to do things as men have tried. When they fail, their failure must be a challenge to others.

~AMELIA EARHART

I've definitely never had to look very far outside my family for inspiration. I'm surrounded by unbelievable strength and courage. Even in very difficult times, there's always been a lot of humor and laughter.

~MARIA SHRIVER, INTERVIEWED IN *MORE* MAGAZINE, MAY 2004.

Military Moms

Single Mom Support

I became a single mom in 1997 and had six years of Active Duty time as a single mom. As a single mom, or even dual military married couple with a family, we are required to have a power of attorney and other documents in order with a plan to turn our kids over to a civilian caretaker should we be deployed. Being a single mom is tough in itself, but being a single mom in the military presents some other challenges that most people in the "civilian world" wouldn't ordinarily experience.

I deployed to the Middle East in support of Operation Enduring Freedom after 9/11. I was deployed for four months and had to leave my kids behind. Other times I was sent on temporary duty for one day to six weeks. I've often been asked by those unfamiliar with the military, "How could you leave your kids behind?" To be honest, it was the hardest thing I ever had to do. However, I took an oath to support and defend the Constitution of the United States against all enemies foreign and domestic. I felt wounded by what happened to our country on 9/11 and wanted to do my part to support it.

The military community is like one big family and when you arrive at a base, you are immediately welcomed into the community and given support. When I was stationed at each new base, I was provided a sponsor to help me get settled. When I arrived at my base in New Mexico with my kids, my sponsor picked us up at the airport and took us to our hotel on the base which was a small apartment fully furnished with a kitchen. I moved into a house on the base, and the day my household goods arrived I came down with a severe bout of stomach flu, and had to go to the hospital. The new neighbor I had just met sat outside with the movers and checked off the boxes as they were brought into the house. We lived in a duplex on base with connected carports and patios.

A couple of months later, my neighbor moved out and a family with two kids moved in next door. The husband was active duty and the wife was prior military. Around the same time, another single mom arrived in my squadron who had three kids, two of which were the same age as my two. We became an instant support system for each other, and my neighbors would pick my kids up from school or the youth center if I was delayed at work or working an exercise.

During exercises, we worked 12-hour shifts and simulated being deployed to a war zone. We had long days of chemical warfare training, wearing the gas mask for hours and performing first aid and perimeter sweeps after an "attack." The other single mom and I would move into one house with all the kids and arrange to have opposite shifts so were able to have round-the-clock coverage and care for our kids. In essence, we became parents of five kids for a few days and worked together as a team to ensure we fulfilled our military requirements, as well as, our mommy roles. Being in the military as a single mom is difficult in many aspects; however, the relationships we develop turn into a support system and family unit that are there for you whenever you need them. I always knew I could count on my military family to be there for me when I needed them most. It's the military way of life.

~ELDONNA LEWIS FERNANDEZ, MASTER SERGEANT, USAF (RET.)
http://pinkbikerchic.com

A woman is always younger than a man of equal years.
~ELIZABETH BARRETT BROWNING

The Price to Pay

I am a mother, wife, nurse, and an Army Master Sergeant. In February 2003, as a Reservist, I was mobilized to serve my country when my daughter was only three years old. If I had to think of the hardest event in my life, it would have to be the day I left. The frontpage of the *Dallas Morning News* said it all in a picture. It showed my daughter being ripped from my arms as I boarded the bus to leave. I have a love for my country and if everyone said, "Military life is not for me," there would be no one to keep us safe at home. That heartache you never really get over it— and your child never forgets it.

It became a way of life for my daughter to have her mother leave. At age five, in December 2004, I was mobilized again. The sadness I felt was relived all over. This time my daughter was more understanding. In her Kindergarten class she would say, "My mom is serving our country so we can live here free." I do not know if she truly understood what she was saying, because it was so far beyond her years. But living the life as a military child teaches our children values others never really achieve.

I trained soldier medics, who were on their way to Iraq, the skills they must possess to stay alive and help others who were in need of medical help on the battlefield. The pride I felt—and still feel—to get an email back saying lives were saved from what I taught is beyond words.

As a woman and a mother of three, I have a fear after 15 years of serving my country, I will get that call again. But it is a price I must pay to make ensure my children will have a save place in which to grow old.

~ANGELA PEREZ, MASTER SERGEANT, USAR

It's not the load that breaks you down, it's the way you carry it.
~LENA HORNE

Is It Worth It?

Sacrifice. No one knows that word better than a Soldier. Well, except maybe a Soldier who happens to be a woman. Looking back over my last 15 years in the Army, I've seen a life full of sacrifice, but I can honestly say I have no regrets.

Young people talk with me about joining the military all the time, and I always let them know that the Army has been good to me. My career has afforded me the opportunity to see lands I'd only read about. I've encouraged young soldiers to chase their dreams. I've met some of my heroes, and met people who would become my heroes. And in a few months, I will have attained my Master's Degree in Human Relations, thanks, in part, to the military's tuition assistance program—and I'll be able to turn my Montgomery GI Bill over to my daughter when she starts college.

My career hasn't been easy. Things haven't always worked the way I would have liked. Yet, I couldn't imagine my life any other way. As I boarded the plane headed toward yet another remote assignment, my mind wandered to the sacrifice I'd endured in just the few days leading up to my trip to Korea. I had left my daughter in the care of my mother for the third time in five years. My fiancé, a civilian, ended our engagement, unwilling to maintain a relationship across the waters, and even less willing to give up his career to follow me once I returned. Although I knew my time in the States wouldn't last forever, I couldn't help but lament all the things that had grown dear to me, my home, my church, my friends, in the short two years I'd been back from the desert.

Had it all been worth it? Some would say I was fortunate to have gotten two years with my family. There were many women in the Army who had less time with their children before returning to the desert. Some were lucky to get a year. Yet, they continued to find a way to make it work.

Each day, women struggle with the decision to be a career soldier, or a wife and mother. While many have been successful at both, the sacrifice that comes with that success is more than many can bear.

Women in the military are some of the strongest people I've ever met. Who else can endure twelve or more hours on the job, many times enduring discrimination, sexual harassment, and control issues, only to come home and slip into wife and mother role, cooking dinner, helping the kids with their homework, putting them to bed, and then starting the entire cycle over again? On top of that, the threat of frequent deployments, broken relationships, and family struggles compete with the desire to finish college and participate in their communities.

Deployments don't stop these fireballs. After working all day, they remember to call back home to the States so they can be the first voice their child hears before rushing off to school. They then wake up in the early hours of the morning to read their babies bedtime stories before they drift off to sleep. They spend their weekends refereeing fights over the phone, sometimes trying to keep their kids from running away from their guardians' strict rules. They even find time to find creative ways to maintain intimacy with their husbands or significant others.

I hold women like them in high esteem. They are the true role models. I drew from their strength as I went through my two-year assignment in Korea. Well, that and a lot of prayer. I returned to the States greeted by a well-adjusted nine-year-old daughter who, although I've spent more birthdays away from her than with her, feels her mommy can do no wrong. She doesn't like the fact that Mommy has to leave all the time, but she understands that Mommy is a United States soldier. And that is what makes what I do worth it.

To repay her, I ensure that my leaving is worth it to her. This is why I work so hard in school. I must lead by example if I expect her to see the importance in education. Although I get tired and discouraged when things don't go my way I work, I continue to give it my all to show my daughter that hard work does pay off. We can't just quit when it gets uncomfortable for us. And as a single parent, full-time soldier and part-time student who has authored three published novels, I understand that quality time can be a premium, so I make the most out of the little time we have together.

As I think about it, the heart of a military mother isn't that different from that of a civilian mother. We both teeter on the fine line between career and family. As single parents, that line becomes even thinner. Yet, we keep finding a way to make it work. And, as our patience grows thinner and our energy depletes, we still remember our priorities: our children. They are the picture we keep in mind when we trudge through the work day, demanding respect and battling stereotypes.

So has the Army been good to me? I would have to say yes, without a doubt. Has sacrificing time with my daughter and remaining single as I strive for career been worth it? I don't know. Has my daughter's quality of life been worth the sacrifice? Sometimes I think so. She's happy. She's smart. But when she comes into the room just to say "I love you, Mommy," I'm sure.

~RHONDA M. LAWSON

Submitted on her behalf by Kevin Avery

The most beautiful people we have known are those who have known defeat, known suffering, known struggle, known loss, and have found their way out of the depths. These persons have an appreciation, a sensitivity, and an understanding of life that fills them with compassion, gentleness, and a deep loving concern. Beautiful people do not just happen.

~ELIZABETH KUBLER-ROSS, AUTHOR

In the sheltered simplicity of the first days after a baby is born, one sees again the magical closed circle, the miraculous sense of two people existing only for each other.

~ANNE MORROW LINDBERGH

"Three Star" Military Mother

I am a *Three Star* military mother, with three sons currently serving in the U.S. Armed Forces. Their late father, Robert and I are both U.S. Navy Veterans. Being their mother, I am very proud of my children, and the jobs they are doing to serve and protect our country. Having family members in harm's way is a very stressful and worrisome time. I am overwhelmed with fear; I miss my children and worry for their safety. With my boys being an ocean or two away, I find myself trying to keep my home together, staying positive, focused and busy knowing that my home doesn't exactly feel like a home, and won't, until we are all together again.

An Ocean or Two Away

Our oldest son Michael, 28, is in the U.S. Army. He is a M1A1 Abrams Tank Crewman, currently stationed in Villseck, Germany, with a Stryker Tank Brigade. Jason is 22, in the U.S. Air Force, based at Tinker Air Force Base, in Oklahoma, and is a Ground Radar System Apprentice. He is currently serving in Kabul, Afghanistan. Our youngest son, Eric, is in the U.S. Army at age 19. He is attached to the 82nd Airborne Battalion, based in Fort Bragg, North Carolina. Eric is a Field Artillery Fire Finder Radar Operator/Paratrooper, currently serving in Baghdad, Iraq.

I know I am not alone, because there are so many families that are experiencing the same loneliness and fear as me. We share concerns, support, pride and most of all our devotion to our family members. I know people handle these deployments and separations differently than I do, but this is what I have been experiencing and I also know that we need to keep ourselves busy, continuing with our daily routines to pass the time away, until our loved ones return home safe to us. To all of our men and women serving in the United States Armed Forces *we thank you for your service*! God bless you!

~ROSE DOMMER
www.RoseDommer.com

My Prayer

Dear Universe, All That Is, Source, God, Angels, Guides and Masters,
Help me remember that my son is a complete Godkit
with his very own personal connection to Source.

Help me remember that he has his very own Internal Guidance System
which he knows how to follow naturally.

Help me remember that he is the sole Creator of his Life;
that Source is responding to his desire for his safety, effectiveness,
service and a long, healthy life with a dream of children of his own.

Help me remember that everything is within God, even war.

Help me to remember that All is Well
and that Well Being is all that is Real

Help me to remember that my job is to stay in Well Being myself;
and this is how I can best serve and support him.

Help me to remember that there is nothing to fear;
and nothing to worry about, ever.

Help me to hold the Space of Well Being
so that others may find it, too.

Help me to envision him only as safe, happy and productive,
being the beautiful Light Being he is even on deployment.
Maybe, especially there.

continued

Help me to feel the bond of love that I have with him
and send nothing but more Love
over the airwaves via my heart and my thoughts.

Help me to send Love to everyone,
including those we are "at war" with.
Help me remember that there is no death,
but only this eternal adventure of Life.

Help me thus to be a Light in the World
by assisting our collective evolution into Oneness,
the Christ Consciousness, where there is no separation
and at last we are living Heaven on Earth
Thanks All, Judd's Mom

~KATHY K. KIRK~

http://www.appliedspirituality.com

It makes sense that there is no sense without God.
~EDITH SCHAEFFER

Be faithful in small things because it is in them that your strength lies.
~MOTHER TERESA

A mother understands what a child does not say.
~UNKNOWN

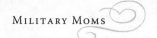

Bye-Bye, Mommy, Bye-Bye

Tear stained cheeks at a chain link fence
Were the last thing she saw that day,
As she slowly boarded the plane,
That would take her so far away.

She felt trim and smart in her uniform,
And her boy and girl were so proud,
They stood tall and straight at the airport gate,
While they waved to their mom from the crowd.

"I won't cry, Mommy," promised her girl,
As they hugged each other good-bye,
"I'm a big boy now," bragged her son,
Who vowed, "Mommy, neither will I."

Yet tears did squeeze out of their tightly closed eyes,
Forming streaks down their soft baby cheeks,
Then chubby, pink hands quickly wiped them away,
So poor Mommy would not see them weep.

She looked out of the transport's cramped window,
And dabbed at her own tearing eyes,
She saw two brave, little souls at that fence,
Mouthing, "Bye-Bye, Mommy. Bye-bye."

For a moment guilt flooded her conscience,
How could she ever leave such sweet kids?
God bless her babies; she loved them so much,
But now too late to undo what she did.

continued

Her country had put out a call,
They sought women with special skills,
Her qualifications matched their needs,
And she perfectly filled their bill.

Torn between family and country,
The dilemma was carefully weighed,
Then, as one, the whole family agreed
She must go; her decision was made.

Far too many soldiers were dying,
In unknown lands across the sea,
If she could help just one to survive,
How worthwhile her actions would be.

So now she was going to war,
And sadly leaving her loved ones behind,
Yet taking each soul in her heart,
Along with visions of all in her mind.

She knew this thing was right to do,
No matter how painful it seemed,
Now was the time to sacrifice,
To put on hold her prior dreams.

The children at the fence grew smaller,
As the plane turned and taxied away,
"Brave little cherubs," she thought aloud,
"I hope they'll remember this day."

continued

"That they will recall a mother,
Who one day went away to a war,
Because she loved her country a lot,
But loved her kids even more."

~VIRGINIA (GINNY) ELLIS~

© January 2009

The Babies in the Airport

I still feel a sense of pride—of protective motherhood—of territoriality—of relationship—when I see a short-haired, tight-faced, erect-standing serviceman. This title does the boy I currently watch no justice, though, for he is neither an Airman, nor Sailor, nor Soldier. He is a "baby" Marine—my "baby" Marine, though I have never spoken with nor made even eye contact with the young man. We are connected with a bond few people will ever understand.

"They're home from training," I say. I know this because, although it's been 8 years since I've been in their shoes, I remember the feeling clear as day. Walking through an airport in a uniform is a reassuring feeling.

"How do you know the young men are Marines?" Ironically I search for any answer besides the truth, which is "Because I'm a Marine." Knowing a secret is sometimes more elating than announcing a label of prestige. After all, these feelings are mine—the unspoken connection, the pride—and I care not to speak my title to anyone. They can't understand, and they will never be capable of relating, though their effort is superficially appreciated.

The "babies" have left the terminal. They are meeting their families, I'm sure: embracing their mothers with a new-found sense of worth; their shoulders absorbing tears of joy.

~ANTOINETTE (AMI) IZZO, MHT, MNLP

Mommy's Deployed

My first birthday
Had it all.
A pony, two clowns
And a bouncy ball.
Grandma was there.
Everything just right,
Except for Mommy
Who kept squeezing me tight.
Since the party
Grandma came by more.
I thought I was spoiled,
No idea what was in store.
Late one night
I felt Mommy near.
She touched my head.
Said "I love you dear."
The next morning I woke,
It was just Grandma.
I felt something was wrong
Cried out "MA-MA!"
Grandma hugged me and said
"Mommy went to war . . .
She's on a plane
For a distant shore."

She had Mama's picture
So I'd remember her face
But I really longed
For her warm embrace.
A year for me
Felt like eternity.
Though I heard her voice
I was filled with uncertainty.
Grandma crossed the days.
We got closer to the star.
Finally on the day,
Arrived a mysterious car.
With a scary lady,
A scar on her face.
She came to my door
So I found a hiding place.
Her voice sounded like Mommy,
Dressed up in green.
Tears in her eyes,
She was not mean.
"Mama, it's you?"
She dropped to her knee.
Her arms reached out
"Yes, my love . . . It's me."

~RAQUEL SANTIAGO, U.S. NAVY (1994–2005)~

"Mommy, I Love You"

A distant cry of pain is heard of a mother, father, child
One that is so disturbing the jets above seem mild.
A loved ones heart is breaking, every single day
Awaiting for those to return that are here so far away.
While here a mother sits on a cot a picture of child in hand
And wishes she was with that child not in this distant land.
A husband lays awake at night longing to hold his wife
He prays everyday to return back home to his normal life.
Now the mother with the picture has begun to cry
We don't even bother asking, because we all know why.
We can see it in her face that the pain is now so real
Even those without a child knows just how she feels.
The loneliness of the man that lies awake at night
Is a feeling we all have no matter how hard we fight.
Though it may not be a child or love that we left that day
That someone special keeps us going while we are away.
So when you feel that your days here have been on day to long
Just remember you're here fro them and that will keep you strong.
Here as night unfolds we all begin to dream
And those who are so far away are not as distant as they seem.
A mother can hold her child again and hear "Mommy I love you"
A man can hold his wife and hear "I love you" too.
As we lay in bed tonight and into our dreams deploy
Those distant cries of pain we heard are now the cries of joy.

~ANONYMOUS~

This poem was inspired by the women in my tent;
all of them are married and most have children.

February 28, 1998

Dawn Vogel

Missions

Sweethearts for Soldiers

Cory and I met on the Island of Bahrain located in the Persian Gulf. It was July 2001 and I was on a tour entertaining our troops around the Middle East. While on a day off, I went to a shopping area and as I stepped out of a shop, I bumped into this young handsome American, who turned out to be a true gentleman. We became instant friends and while I was leaving in just a few hours, he would be staying another 5 months. Over those next 5 months we talked many hours on the phone, wrote letters and emails to learn all we could about each other and came to realized that we had a great deal in common. I flew to meet his parents over Thanksgiving and learned this was a special family. With much anticipation, Cory was due back in the States and on December 15 flew to Phoenix to see me and meet my family. He received their approval and with that we were off to spend the Christmas Holidays with his large extended family in Wisconsin.

In 2002 we got engaged and in 2003 we were married and moving to Maryland into our first house. After moving I tried out for—and made—the Washington Redskins Cheerleading Squad. Once again, I was able to go on tours to entertain our troops. Cory always supported me going on these trips as he remembered how much it meant to him as well to his fellow troops. In 2006, Cory was up for orders and lead to us moving to San Diego that November. While on a training mission early 2007, his helicopter crashed into the Pacific Ocean and all four crew members were killed. I lost my very best friend, soul mate and husband that day along with three other spouses, whom now I have a very special relationship and bond with.

I am so thankful to have been able to form an organization with one of my best friends around the same time I moved to San Diego. We formed a charity called Sweethearts for Soldiers, a group of former NFL/NBA cheerleaders and dancers. We produce a military charity calendar, perform a Variety Show overseas, and hold Military Youth Cheer clinics. We have ladies who sing, dance and entertain the troops abroad and at various military functions here in the States. In 2009, we applied for our Non-Profit 501(c)(3) status and also creating a grant to be in Cory's memory called "So Others May Play" which fits both his SAR values "So Others May Live" and his passion for golf. This grant will be awarded to children of fallen soldiers who have the same determination for the game of golf, and in efforts through the Snowball Express Organization.

I feel so fortunate to have something in remembrance of Cory and that I am so passionate about. I have also met another angel that will accompany me through the journey of life. My mission is to "Sweeten the Lives of Troops Everyday" and I hope it can be your mission to thank your service members every chance you get. I leave you with a quote I feel represents our service members and their mission.

Freedom is never more than one generation away from extinction. We didn't pass it to our children in the bloodstream. It must be fought for, protected, and handed on for them to do the same, or one day we will spend our sunset years telling our children and our children's children what it was once like in the United States where men were free.—Ronald Wilson Reagan

~TONYA HELMAN

Surviving Spouse of AW1 Cory J. Helman

USNCo-Founder of www.SweetheartsforSoldiers.org

I've often thought that when something is hard for you, whether it's going to law school or anything else that challenges you, that's probably what you should do.

~HILLARY RODHAM CLINTON

Operation Babylift

During the final months of the Vietnam War, the plight of thousands of Vietnamese War orphans was of great concern to many who had served in Vietnam as well as the orphans civilian and volunteer orphanage caretakers.

Their plight was brought to the attention of President Gerald R. Ford, an adoptee himself, when a maverick flight landed in Oakland, California on April 2, 1975 with 57 Vietnamese War orphans on board. This humanitarian effort galvanized the public and the next day, President Ford signed the *Operation Babylift* (OBL) Executive Order, stipulating that American military personnel would undertake a massive evacuation of the orphans.

Tragically, the first OBL military airplane, a C-5A Galaxy, crashed twelve minutes after departing Tan Son Nhut Airport. Among the casualties was USAF Captain Mary Klinker, one of only eight women "on the Memorial Wall" in Washington, D.C.

One of the survivors is Retired USAF Colonel Regina Aune, who, although severely injured, helped pull children from the wreckage until she was able to request relief from a rescue officer. Of the 54 American civilian women who died during the entire Vietnam War, 37 died in the OBL crash.

All of the Military and Civilian Defense Attache Officewomen were recognized on Veterans Day, November, 11, 2008 during the 15th Anniversary Ceremony at the Vietnam Women's Memorial in Washington, D.C. where they received the *Posthumous Heather Constance Noone Memorial Award* for their sacrifice and heroism during OBL. The award was presented by Lana Noone together with a representative from the Defense Attache Office (Vietnam, April, 1975) and USAF Sergeant Philip Wise (Ret.), a survivor of the crash. The award reads, in part, "You are the full measure of American courage and patriotism" and each woman's name is inscribed on the award plaque.

Several family members of the deceased women were in attendance, as well as, a large audience of Americans who wanted to pay tribute to the women. On behalf of the OBL adoptive families I'm honored to recognize the heroism of all involved in OBL. During the final weeks of the Vietnam War, their heroic efforts enabled 2,548 Vietnamese War orphans to be evacuated to their new homes in the United States.

We will never forget you and all you did for the adoptees. I pray the deceased know they are always in our thoughts and prayers.

The *Posthumous Heather Constance Noone Memorial Award* presented to the military and civilian women casualties of the OBL C-5A plane crash on April 4, 1975, was accepted on Veterans Day, 2008 at the 15th Anniversary of the Vietnam Women's Memorial by Diane Carlson-Evans, President of the *Vietnam Women's Memorial* Foundation.

~LANA NOONE
www.Vietnambabylift.org
September 8, 2009

We will not be intimidated or pushed off the world stage by people who do not like what we stand for, and that is: freedom, democracy, and the fight against disease, poverty, and terrorism.
~MADELEINE ALBRIGHT

Courage is the ladder on which all the other virtues mount.
~CLARE BOOTH LUCE

Welcome Home Our Sisters

*Written to Honor the 10th Anniversary
of the Women's Memorial*

We are standing here behind the WALL on the other side of life. It has been a long time since we have seen you. We are here today to say "thank you" once again. It is your time today that we stand here waving, cheering, and so proud that you came. The time is short so some of us have been selected to say what we all feel. Thank you for caring and loving us and most of all for just being there.

"My name is Mike; I was a Marine, stepped on a mine, during Operation Allenbrook. I lost both legs. You were my nurse who told me I was going home. You bathed me, kept me out of pain; you talked to me about beginning a new. It was not easy but you gave me hope. Today, I just retired; I have thought of you often. I don't even remember your name. I remember your face . . . thank you for being there for me, giving me that hope."

"My name is Roger; I was killed during a mortar attack, in Plieku. You worked in graves registration. You made sure all my personal effects made it home to my wife. I was there at night when you cried over all of us. I know it is hard my sister. Thanks for the prayer for my family and me. Yes, God does care and He remembers you."

"My name is Tan, I was a little child in Ban Me Thout, and you cared for me and helped me. I have leprosy. I was there when they took you away in the middle of the night. I missed your singing to me. You were my missionary. My daughter has your name."

"My name is Tony; my helicopter was shot down in the Plain of Reeds. I was on your burn ward. You were the Red Cross worker that wrote letters home for me. I told you that I loved you and you said all the guys said that

to you. You don't understand I still do. It was love at first sight. I didn't mean to die in my sleep. I miss your smile."

"My name is Wayne; I was killed when our base camp got overrun at Bihn Phouc. I remember the times when you came to play games with us. You were our Donut Dolly. You took my mind off the war, you made me forget. I was from Indiana. I told you that you reminded me of my girlfriend."

"My name is Susan, I was a nurse on Operation Baby lift and we are still caring for the Children. Thank you for your help in getting the children out and caring for them. I tried to save them; they took two little ones out of my arms who made it. I am So Thankful."

"My name is Johnny, they called me "lucky" 'cause you pointed to me to come dance with you on stage of the Bob Hope Show in Dong Tam. Thanks Ann Margaret, thanks for letting me be your leading man. I died during a firefight in the Delta with the Mobile Riverine Force. Thanks for the kiss on the cheek."

"My name is Joe, and I am from Memphis. I rode on your plane coming over to the Nam. You told me it was okay to be scared and you were going to pray for all of us. You took my last letter I wrote to my mom and mailed it for me. I remember your perfume and your beautiful green eyes. I was killed by a mine that blew up my truck my first day."

"My name is Sharon; I am from Ohio. I was a nurse at the 312th Evac. Mom, it's okay. I have missed you all. Thank you for helping build the Clinic in Vietnam. The people are needy and they don't hate us. I did the right thing and I am so proud of you. Daddy is here and he misses you so very much."

"My name is Jimmy, I was a medic and taken as a POW, you were the unit clerk that typed up the letter telling my parents that I was *Missing In Action* and told them that all that could be done was being done. I died 12 years later in Laos. No medicine, there were others. I know you think of all of us but just know; some of us are still alive and waiting to be found. Please keep searching."

"My name is Stan and I flew Tomcats. I was shot down over Hanoi. You were the Air Traffic Controller who marked my location and sent in the teams to get me out. But the NVA shot and killed me. It is not your fault—I took the risk . . . it was worth it."

"Hello, Dusty, my name is David. I never got to tell you thanks for being there for me. For holding my hand and telling me I was going to be okay. Thanks for writing the letter to my mom; she told me she so appreciated it when she got up here last year. Dusty, thank you for staying with me when I passed over. It is so beautiful here. I will be there for you when it is your time to come. I will call your name and I will hold your hand. I love you."

So our sisters, one and all, you all did a job well done. Please be easy on yourselves. Do you realized how many of us you saved, do you realize how many of us still have legs and arms that should have been removed. You helped ease our pain. You took our minds off the war. Do you realize that you are the best and we appreciate all that you did? We love you so very much . . . thank you, WELCOME HOME OUR SISTERS.

~KERRY "DOC" PARDUE

©Copyright November 2, 2003

www.kerrypardue247.com

It is one of the most beautiful compensations of this life, that no man can sincerely try to help another without helping himself.
~EMERSON

You give little when you give of your possessions.
It is when you give of yourself that you truly give.
~KAHLIL GIBRAN

Doolittle Air Force

I am a military woman telling you straight from my heart
My experience in the U.S. Air Force played in my life a big part
It taught me leadership and launched my career off to a great start
I entered the United States Air Force as Lieutenant Karen Doolittle
To follow the footsteps of my relation General James H. Doolittle
In case you have not heard of this famous name before
He led the raid over Tokyo in the Second World War
In the film Thirty Seconds Over Tokyo, Spencer Tracy portrayed him
Honored again in the Pearl Harbor movie starring Alec Baldwin
Now I did not skydive or fly a fighter airplane
Nor did I launch missiles or shoot M-16s in the rain
But I was proud to serve my country as a Registered Dietitian
After obtaining a Bachelor of Science degree in Nutrition
Eight of us dietetic interns obtained our military commission
And joined a group of doctors and nurses ready to serve our mission
We received our medical service officer military indoctrination
So that we could be better prepared to serve our free nation
It was not quite a boot camp
But more like a salute camp
Two and a half weeks of lectures, drills and fun
In the Wichita Falls, Texas sun
105-degree sunny weather with very high humidity
Protecting our bodies that were now government property
Wearing our BDU's and loads of sunscreen
Learning how to keep our boots shiny and clean
Obstacle course drills for physically fit students
Two days without showers after sleeping in tents
Watching the doctors attempt to march and me concealing my laugh
Trying not to breathe in through my nose when exposed to tear gas
Dragging a three hundred pound doctor on a stretcher under barbed wire

Navigating to camp with a compass and training on an M-16 that I did misfire
Eating MRE's accidentally reconstituted with Gatorade
My flight was a highly impressive military brigade
About an impending uniform inspection we got the news
We used up an entire can of starch trying to iron our blues
It looked like we had coated our shirts with cotton candy
Perhaps another can of starch would have come in handy
The night before we ironed our blues and starched our shirt
We had a toga party to break in our boots so they would not hurt
Before the inspection they played "Don't Worry, Be Happy" to calm our nerves
Then the inspector gave us the praise that we so deserved
With the orientation complete we headed to Andrews Air Force Base
To begin our dietetic internship, after barely unpacking our suitcase
We trained in the hospital all day and all night
They told us for nine months we would not see daylight
And they were right
We completed clinical rotations for patients with therapeutic needs
For diabetics, and heart patients and lactating women who breast-feed
We also completed foodservice rotations on how to best feed the troops
We created cycle menu plans with nutritious entrees and soups
I hosted a Black History Month theme meal with live gospel singing groups
They groomed us as leaders with integrity, loyalty, and decisiveness
And strengthened our value for commitment, energy, and selflessness
When the internship was complete we were assigned to our own base
When I found out my place
You could see the shock on my face
As far as hardship assignments go, I felt I had met my quota
When I was told I would be based in Minot, North Dakota
I must admit while I was driving there I grew nervous and began to cry
When I arrived I learned there were only two seasons—Winter and 4th of July
So upon arriving in July I was issued a thick and fuzzy coat
With a city population of 10,000 this base was somewhat remote

We put block heaters on our car engines so they would not freeze from ice
What I liked most about the base was that the people were quite nice
As the Director of Nutritional Medicine Service I wore many a hat
Although it was highly unlikely for a dietitian to fight in combat
I made recommendations to the hospital as the Regional Consulting Dietitian
During site visits I certified techs to teach classes on weight loss and nutrition
As the Assistant Health Promotions Coordinator I made wellness my theme
For disaster preparedness I supervised the Hospital Disaster Shelter Team
My main job remained as the dietitian for Minot Air Force Base
The goal was to turn my department into a better place, a showcase
I inherited a department with significant management concerns
With personnel shortages, financial losses and food quality concerns
My initial task at hand was to listen to my boss
He told me to first correct the financial loss
Next I created a strategic plan based on the hospital commander's goals
I wrote policies and procedures to establish new operating controls
When this was done I knew just what to do
To implement an improved four-week cycle menu
Then pilots and missiliers visited my hospital for a great meal
And our specialized therapeutic diets allowed the patients to heal
Then I branched out to the community
Was interviewed about nutrition on TV
Nutrition articles and public speaking to officer's wives clubs and pre-schools
Commissary tours to teach healthy food shopping and provide helpful tools
With meetings and trainings my team knew what to work towards
Then four of my staff received employee-of-the-quarter awards
So here's to my serving in the Air Force from 1989 to 1991
Some days hard work, some days filled with fun
After just three short years my tour was done
As far as regrets, I must say I have none!

~CAPTAIN KAREN DOOLITTLE, USAF

www.DoolittleCooking.com

On the Home Front

Cardboard Boxes and Blank Walls

The Challenge of Every Military Wife

What do you mean we have to be across the country next week? How can the kids be pulled out of sports, school and the arms of their best friends again? Good thing we still have some of the cardboard boxes left from the last move. We never got around to unpacking them, so that is even better. At least the contents are written on the outside of the box. The majority of the boxes ended up with labels of kitchen, miscellaneous, bathroom or "I Hate This Crap-I Don't Want to Move-signed by The Indentured Servant Who Wanted to Go to The Mall Today."

One would think after twelve moves in fifteen years, a smart family would begin to simplify their possessions. A smart family would rid themselves of old yearbooks, unused cookbooks, scruffy stuffed animals and pans with no lids. A smart family would just look for the nail in the walls and hang their pictures on them, regardless of placement. By the time we found the separate boxes holding the hammer, level, hooks and pictures, it was almost time to move again.

No, we weren't the smartest family in the military, but we were one of the most grateful. We were filled with gratitude for each other, the ability to see the country and to make new friends and grateful for the experiences along the way. One particular pivotal experience was moving into military housing on Vandenberg Air Force Base in Lompoc, California. As Dwain and I were unloading boxes, the children ran into the backyard to explore. They came rushing back to tell us about the strange "thistles" all over the place.

Always the teacher, I called everyone around to tell them about artichokes. I explained how delicious they were and that we would savor them at a coming meal. I also used the teaching moment to say that the people who had lived here before had planted the artichokes, knowing that they may never see the fruits of their labor. Given that it takes artichokes two years to produce, they were leaving a gift for us.

We talked about how we must follow their example and plant seeds everywhere we went. We would plant vegetable seeds, flower seeds, but most of all we would plant the seeds of kindness. We may never see the fruits of our labors just like the family before us, but we would do it anyway.

As we sat on cardboard boxes and looked at blank walls, we feasted on artichokes and butter and praised those who had given us this gift. Our daughter Deb remarked that the artichoke was like some of the families I work with as a parent educator; the outer edges are tough, closed off and have prickly parts that can hurt if you get too close. It is only through time, warmth and patience that we can find the outer leaves peeling off more easily and we reach the real treasure—the heart.

The artichoke is now my logo and stands as a symbol of finding the heart of the story in the journey of life. Our journey with cardboard boxes, blank walls and a military life may be a thing of the past, but the life lessons and forever friends will always remain in our hearts.

~JUDY H. WRIGHT, SPEAKER, AUTHOR

www.ArtichokePress.com

© 2009

There are no short cuts to any place worth going.
~BEVERLY SILLS

Proper Mrs. Lieutenants in 1970

On my third date in late winter of 1967, the young man who would later become my husband Mitch, said, "I'm going to Vietnam." At that moment, *Duke of Earl* was playing in the background of the party we were attending with other members of the staff of the *State News*, Michigan State University's daily newspaper. Over 40 years ago, and I still remember it like yesterday.

At that time, the Vietnam War was raging—battlefield casualties were shown on the nightly news, in only black and white. And the anti-Vietnam protesters were raging, too. No voluntary army then, but a draft, although the first draft lottery in December of 1969 had not yet taken place. Mitch was a junior, two years ahead of me, and he was in Army ROTC.

The summer of 1968, a year later, Mitch was commissioned a second lieutenant in infantry. That summer he attended ROTC summer camp at Fort Riley, Kansas; a hell-hole in the days before air conditioning. Of the four of six weekends that the men got off, they drove to a motel and slept four each in an air-conditioned room. The cookies my mother sent Mitch from Elgin, Illinois, melted in his locker, and he reported that at 3 A.M. the temperature was still unbelievably high. At Fort Riley, Mitch's hay fever was so bad that he was in the infirmary for three days with pneumonia. He got out of sick bay for the night compass course because, if he had missed that exercise, he would have had to repeat summer camp.

Before Mitch went off to summer camp, he insisted he didn't want to get married until after he had served his ROTC two-year commitment. Upon his return from Fort Riley, he changed his mind. We set our wedding date for September 7, 1969, as Mitch had a year's active duty deferment to get a Master's Degree at MSU.

During the year that Mitch got his Master's Degree in Communication, and I finished my undergraduate Journalism degree in three years, I typed on a manual typewriter numerous copies of Mitch's request for a branch transfer to military intelligence, while he took an Army correspondence course in psychological warfare.

We were married as planned, and when we returned from our honeymoon, Mitch was scheduled to report to Fort Benning, Georgia, for Infantry Officers Basic Training. Mitch called an Army clerk in St. Louis, Missouri, to ask about his branch transfer. She told him not to report to Fort Benning; she would put his orders on hold until he heard about his branch transfer request. This delay, and the eventual granting of the branch transfer, put us on the road to Fort Knox, Kentucky, for Armor Officers' Basic Training (Military Intelligence officers had to first take a combat officers' training course) in May of 1970, a few days after the Ohio National Guard shot and killed four students at Kent State University. The students were protesting against President Nixon's incursion into Cambodia.

Even though the Army hadn't said officers attending Armor Officers Basic (AOB) could bring their wives, I insisted on going with my husband. The Fort Knox housing office had a list of available off-post housing, and we found a one-bedroom apartment in Muldraugh, Kentucky.

Mitch started AOB, and suggested to a classmate from the South who lived near us, that the two men carpool and their wives share the other car. Suddenly, I was spending my days with someone who until now hadn't known a Jew (me), let alone been friends with a Northerner.

And, then the ironic surprise: even though the Army hadn't said AOB wives could come, there was a training program for us to learn how to be proper Mrs. Lieutenants. I raised my hand to be Chair of the Entertainment Committee for the Wives' Graduation Luncheon. Of course, my carpool partner had to be on my committee because we shared a car.

Somehow, we got three other AOB wives on our committee: a Black (the correct term in those days), a Puerto Rican who spoke English and was the daughter of a career-enlisted man, and a Puerto Rican who didn't speak English. And then, the five of us had to adjust to our racial, religious and class differences in order to get along. This coming together of different women

because our husbands went on active duty at the same time together made a lasting impression on me. I soon realized that, as different as the five of us were, our husbands' well-being was the most important thing to each of us. And that in this shared concern we were all proper Mrs. Lieutenants. 38 years after my time as a new Mrs. Lieutenant, I published my novel *Mrs. Lieutenant*, to tell a fictional story of this experience and its impact on my life.

~PHYLLIS ZIMBLER MILLER, FORMER MRS. LIEUTENANT

www.MrsLieutenant.com

www.InSupportOfOurTroops.com

BlogTalk Radio Show YourMilitaryLife.com

Really Home

My face against your back in that just before sleep
deep breath of aura air, a little soap scent
and something untamable
that rises from every pore and follicle
something herbal, medicinal, clearing
My head empties to a memory
I am walking toward baggage claim after two weeks away
fast furious little muscles and bouncing ringlets barrel into me
I drop to my knees and try to contain the jerky kisses
and hugs from all directions,
I balance and snuggle, bob, weave and nuzzle
just can not get enough of them
still knowing, I won't really be home
until I move that few more feet to you, zoom in, lock down,
cheek to shirt collar, nose to neck and inhale

~COL PEGGY GIGSTAD, U.S. ARMY (RET.)~

Lives Forever Changed!

The proud Marine I love so much his pain he cannot share,
He came home from Vietnam yet he still is over there.
In haunting nightmare after nightmare he sees his brothers fall,
Over and over and over again he hears their anguished calls.
They call out to their mothers, fathers, girlfriends and their wives,
So proud to serve their country, they honorably gave their lives.
Lives Forever Changed!

Booby traps detonated as wounded brothers cry out in pain,
You are brothers in arms forever who will never be the same.
Sadness, guilt and grief are mirrored in your eyes,
Honey, I can't reach you no matter how hard I try.
Alone you came home to face the disdain of the Americans you had defended,
Thirty-four years with no peace of mind so your tour in Nam has not ended.
Lives Forever Changed!

The invisible, defensive perimeter around you is keeping us apart,
Flashbacks, hostile fire and silent rage have hardened your wounded heart.
Overwhelming painful memories you try to hide with the morning light,
They are burned into your heart and soul to torture you each night.
Take my love and dedication and let them help you to cope,
Put them with your courage and determination to give you much needed hope.
Lives Forever Changed!

Often you say I don't understand you and Honey that might be true,
I've never fought in a war or experienced what you've been through.
You say you don't fit in anywhere and you just want to die,
Don't give up Sweetheart, don't give in and please continue to try.
Death, disability, heartache and pain make the cost of freedom high,
You are my hero who served our country with honor, courage and with pride.
Lives Forever Changed!

continued

Leave your haunting memories back in Vietnam along with all your sorrow,
Living each day in the present will bring healing for a better tomorrow.
Remember Dorsey, Shepherd and Lieutenant Gaines as they stood proud and tall,
Let your fallen brothers rest in eternal honor on the far side of The Wall.
I believe in you Marine and need you to come back home,
Safe in the arms of your loving wife and you'll never be alone.
Lives Forever Changed!

~JUDITH DURAN, MAY 20, 2000

Dedicated to my husband, Ronnie L. Duran, USMC, and to the families of
2Lt. Charles J. Gaines, Sgt. Harry J. Shepherd Jr., and Cpl. William B. Dorsey.

How do you focus on your career when you know your husband's job is putting him in danger?
One of the reasons I can make it through deployments is because I focus my energy on my physical therapy work which I am dedicated to and love. I work with families over a long period of time who are going through similar situations and I find it really helps to share and compare our experiences.

What words best sum up your marriage-to-the-military?
Expect change. Plan, but be prepared to adjust your plan.

~MONICA SHEPPARD, PEDIATRIC PHYSICAL THERAPIST

Wife of Navy Lieutenant Geoff Sheppard, Operations Officer/Speechwriter for
Naval Surface Forces

As interviewed by Life Coach (and Aunt), Laurie Sheppard

Expecting the Unexpected

Being a military wife gives you experiences you don't expect. I grew up in the suburbs of Orange County, California. My husband grew up in Aberdeen, a small logging and fishing town in Washington State. Rick joined the U.S. Air Force, and I became a military wife and new mother in short order. His first tour of duty was in Germany. I had lived in Holland for a year. Rick had never been out of the country.

Our two middle children were born in Germany, which was different enough, but they were born under completely different conditions—one on a U.S. military base during peacetime and one in a German hospital during *Operation Desert Storm* at the beginning of the Persian Gulf War.

Rick, baby Michael, and I moved into a small apartment in a tiny village called Hefersweiler near Saarbrucken, Germany. I was 19 and pregnant again. Michael was almost three-years-old. I'd had Michael in Washington State while we were living with Rick's mother, also named Judy, like me. I wished Judy or my mom could be here. Rick worked long hours and I was alone most of the time. We had friends who would watch Michael while I was in Landstuhl Regional Medical Center giving birth.

Rick was just getting home from his mid-shift (11 A.M. to 8 P.M.) when my contractions got regular and strong. I automatically started the Lamaze breathing that I learned from sneaking out of my bed and over to the stairs when my mother taught childbirth classes. "Take a deep cleansing breath, now exhale slowly." I was suddenly, painfully, homesick. Labor was a welcome distraction. We took Michael to stay with our friends.

Rick got us to the hospital in record time (at one point running off the road into a construction site!). Landstuhl was a lot like the first hospital in Washington State. I was hooked up to a monitor to follow the baby's heart rate, the contractions and to check my vital signs. Rick sat in a chair in a corner while they were prepping me then moved to my side. Suddenly, I was startled by the monitor's alarm. The nurses said that the baby's heart rate slowed to almost nothing and I had to roll on my side. The nurses helped me move. Next thing I knew, I was on my hands and knees. "Anything to get the baby *off* the umbilical cord!" one nurse said. "It may be caught between the baby's head and the bony pelvis." I immediately understood. "The baby's head is squeezing the umbilical cord with every contraction and cutting off oxygen and blood flow. Is my baby going to be all right?!" Rick squeezed the top of my hand. "Don't worry," the nurse was professionally calm and reassuring. "We can move you into the Emergency Room for a C-section if we need to."

They checked on me and the baby often. I had to have Pitocin, a drug to make my contractions more consistent, and was given something else to take the edge off the pain. When it was time for me to push, the nurses helped me get into position. The doctor and nurses made sure everything was sanitary. I had to have an episiotomy which was given with a numbing medicine.

I pushed the baby out into the doctor's hands and my heart sank. Unlike Michael, who cried out as soon as he was born, our second baby was very blue and very limp. Rick and I watched anxiously as the doctors worked on him. They asked, "What's his name?" Rick and I responded "Jeffery." At his name, Jeff started to turn pink. We signed with relief. He was healthy, after all. The nurse put him in my arms. We were parents of two boys.

We were still in Germany when the Gulf War started. We still lived in Hefersweiler. I was pregnant again but would not be giving birth at Landstuhl Regional Medical Center. The military hospital was mission-ready to receive the casualties of Desert Storm. I would be giving birth at a German hospital (Krankhaus) in Kaiserslautern, Germany, 80 miles southwest of Frankfurt.

My mom ignored all the warnings about the risk of flying into Frankfurt, Germany, during the impending war in the Persian Gulf. She flew out from California to take care of Michael and Jeff, which was a huge relief. Here we were, expecting baby three, and Rick was preparing to be sent to war.

The German hospital was an entirely different experience. Not necessarily worse, just different. For one thing, they don't monitor your contractions continuously. Nor do they monitor the baby's heart rate. I was in a small room with the doors open, people coming and going, other patients walking by. A nurse came in, seemingly an eternity apart from the last time. Few spoke English. They came in, did their work, and left. I needed Pitocin again to make my contractions stronger and more consistent. They inserted the IV and gave me the medicine, but nothing to take the edge off the pain.

I asked for help because the pain was so intense, but they said it would slow my contractions and that I would be fine. When it was time to deliver, a lady—I presume a doctor—came in and moved into position to deliver my baby. She didn't put on any protective clothing. The baby's head was large so I needed an episiotomy. A contraction hit me just as she pulled out her scissors, so I didn't see Rick's eyes widen and his face go pale. Afterward, he said he almost lost it, "She pulled out these HUGE scissors and preceded to snip, snip." No pain medications. She just told me to close my eyes.

I pushed and pushed. Soon we had another son, Christopher Jacob. The nurses bathed him in the sink in the room, wrapped him and put him into an incubator with another newborn from the lady in the next room. Luckily, hers was a girl. No wristbands to make sure the babies went to the right people, just the labels on their bassinets. You couldn't keep the baby in the room with you.

I was in a room with three other women who had all had C-sections. No curtains separating us, so if the doctors or nurses needed to look at stitches or check anything, everyone could see. I asked to go home the next day because I wanted to keep my baby with me. They made me sign a paper stating I understood I was taking the baby out of the hospital against their advice and he might die.

Thankfully, the expected wave of Desert Storm casualties never materialized. Only one person (that I am aware of) was treated there in all the months they were closed.

The two facilities, Landstuhl Medical Center and Kaiserslautern Hospital, are not far from each other. Landstuhl is run by the Americans, so Jeffery was born on American soil. Christopher Jacob was born in a German Hospital, on German soil.

When we came back to the U.S., I learned about a couple in Germany who could not have children. I carried their baby for them. Christopher Nicolai was born in a California hospital with both of his German parents in the delivery room. He is now a tall, good-looking German teenager who speaks fluent English. Of his four half-brothers, he is closest to Christopher Jacob.

We've had many adventures as a military family. Rick learned computer networking and turned it into a career. Michael grew up to be a computer whiz. Jeffery joined the Marine Corps. Christopher Jacob started college this year with plans of directing movies. Our fourth son, Joshua, was born in California and is starting high school.

Being a military wife gives you experiences you don't expect. My birth experiences in Germany were both harrowing and both very different. I can understand how my mother and mother-in-law must have felt when they gave birth.

It all went so fast! Rick and I will be empty-nesters in four years! The first two boys have serious girlfriends, so I think the circle of life is starting again. I suppose we can expect the unexpected.

~JUDITH LYNNE TURNER

With thanks to my mother, Lanie Adamson, for encouraging me to write.

Gratitude and complaining cannot co-exist simultaneously.
Choose the one that best serves you.

~KAREN WALKER

Sixteen

Like most teenagers, my fifteen-year-old applied her typical appraisal of "no big deal" when I told her of my upcoming deployment to the Middle East. She'd grown up in a military household, but more often, it was her father who left for months at a time. I had anticipated a stronger reaction.

I wasn't going to be gone long in terms of days or weeks, but I was going to miss days of importance—Thanksgiving, Christmas, New Year's, and worse—her birthday. Sweet sixteen. The birthday that is expected to magically transform a young girl into the portals of womanhood—complete with ceremonies and traditions like cotillions and parties and first kisses. Sixteen is a delicate age for most girls. A delicate balance exists between child and woman. Wanting the best of both worlds, my daughter was perched on a craggy spot between the two. A misstep in any direction could send her falling down into the valley below. I wanted to be there to catch her if she faltered; to save her from the painful journey.

Twenty-eight years of service in the Navy, however, had made an impression on me. I was expected to place duty to my country over my self-imposed duty to be home throughout my child's adolescence. Try as I might, there was no sure way to appease my country, my daughter, and me without leaving one element short. As a senior enlisted leader, I had an obligation to my troops to be there for them and to set an example of self-sacrifice and self-confidence. I ultimately decided that I could set the example for my troops and for my daughter. If I wanted my daughter to treat commitment seriously and respect the sacrifice that it takes to commit to anything, then I had to honor my own obligations. Perhaps she would resent it at sixteen, but I hoped that when she was older, she would understand that I had to go.

We planned out nearly everything before I left. I commandeered a hall closet and stocked it with enough feminine hygiene products to last a year. (God forbid, she might have to ask her Dad to make a midnight Tampax run.) We shopped until we dropped so that she would never stumble into the embarrassing mode of having to ask her father for anything but food and a ride to school.

I was hungry to hear my family's voice and assure them that I had arrived and settled in. I was fortunate enough to have access to a phone on a semi-regular basis. The first time I called home, my daughter refused to speak to me. I was wounded, but chalked it up to that period of time in the first several weeks when a parent deploys. I used to call it "crash" time. When my husband set out on a mission, the first two weeks after leaving and the two weeks following homecoming, the entire household was thrown into chaos. The children misbehaved. Electrical appliances in the house died. My car would stop running. And no matter where we lived at the time, whatever naturally occurring natural disaster for that area would threaten—hurricanes, tornadoes, earthquakes, etc.

The Middle East, in its own way, is a beautiful place. The hollow voice singing the evening call to prayer traveling with the wind over the flat desert is hauntingly beautiful. Upon hearing it every evening, I paused to say a prayer for my family, particularly my daughter. I assumed my duties and kept busy taking care of my Soldiers, Airmen, Sailors, Marines, and Guardsmen.

Over the weeks, though, my husband was trying to let me know that our daughter was not doing well. She was becoming depressed and withdrawn. Normally a gifted student, she was taking an academic dive. The school was concerned enough to call us and suggest counseling. She stayed in her room whenever she wasn't in school. I could hear the fatigue in his voice. My spouse was trying to run our business, manage the household, and care for our daughter simultaneously. I was so far away and helpless to do anything to assist.

At the same time, the holidays are difficult times for servicemen and women overseas. I did everything possible to keep spirits up as we kept a wary eye out for any service member displaying signs of depression or suicidal tendencies, the whole time hoping that someone might do the same for my own child.

I chided myself for being so selfish. Some of the men and women working for me were experiencing hardships far more paralyzing than my worry over a depressed teenager. Unfortunately, there are deployment situations which become miserably routine. The wife or girlfriend sends a "Dear John" letter and departs with the contents of the checking account to take up with her new love. Young couples—apart for the first time—succumb to the pressures that long separations infuse. Several servicewomen had children who were infants and toddlers; left home to be raised with Grandmother or Auntie while Mother cries herself to sleep every night in her tent. I had no right to be miserable, I told myself. But I was. I protected each service member as fiercely as any parent; I considered it an honor to be a surrogate parent to these young men and woman.

Over the holidays, we received cards and letters by the boxful from U.S. citizens. Every precious one was appreciated. But it was impossible for us to respond to each one, so we divvied them up and I answered quite a few. So many of them were chatty, happy, greetings from teenage girls wishing us well. I prayed for chatty, happy greetings from my own teenage girl, but she remained detached and cool.

It was difficult to carry on as a caretaker for the troops within my control while not revealing that I was as broken and homesick as they were. Leadership is a heavy burden—the younger kids look at you and think that you are strong and wise. The older ones know better, but admire you for keeping up the appearances. Once a leader loses respect, the foundation of the team begins to crumble, and only disaster can follow. I was not about to allow that to happen to my troops. As a woman, I was obligated to every other service woman not to crumble. I did not give in to my emotions and let them control me or interfere with what had to be done. Neither did my daughter. She fought for her mental freedom and won.

Four years after the deployment, I still carry the guilt. I still wish I could have been home for her sixteenth birthday. But she has proven that sacrifice, strength, and resilience—all symbols of the armed services, can make a

strong and silent impression on the youngest of minds. She is in her second year at college in cadet training with the Army Reserve Officer Training Corps. Soon she may hear the call to prayer across the sands beckon her to make some difficult choices in the name of duty.

~ELIZABETH OBERG, MASTER CHIEF PETTY OFFICER, USN (RC), RETIRED (E9)

Without courage you cannot practice any of the other virtues.
~MAYA ANGELOU

Worry a little bit every day and in a lifetime you will lose a couple of years. If something is wrong, fix it if you can. But train yourself not to worry. Worry never fixes anything.
~MARY HEMINGWAY

Every day I remember some little detail of our times together that makes me smile and carries me through the day. It is the small moments that have built our love and makes the time apart manageable. I focus on the moment when he comes home and how great that feels. The reason I can carry on with my life when my husband is away is because . . . the love we share when we are together can carry me through the lonely times when we are apart.

~MONICA SHEPPARD, PEDIATRIC PHYSICAL THERAPIST
Wife of Navy Lieutenant Geoff Sheppard, Operations Officer/Speechwriter for Naval Surface Forces

Passion, Purpose and Patriotism

Freedoms

They were quiet. They must be tired, they're so quiet, I thought. I'd just picked up my roommate and two friends at the airport in the early 1990's. They'd spent ten days in Russia, teaching people English. I was asking a million questions and getting short answers.

"Was it life changing?"

"Yes."

"How so?"

"The people are so hungry for God, freedom, things American."

"What did you like the best?"

"The people."

"Why?"

"They were so loving."

And, on it went. I kept asking them if they wanted to get something to eat or drink. They said no, but when we arrived at the apartment, they did want something . . . a tall glass of ice water. Seems they couldn't get clear, cold, clean water in Russia. They were so thankful for that simple drink.

After she'd had some rest, I asked my roommate what impressed her most about her trip. She said she'd never again take America for granted: the grocery stores, the highways, the gas stations, the clean water.

My dad heard that story and concurred, "I was so happy to be back in the States after two years in the Army, that when I landed at the Anchorage Air Force Base, I got down and kissed the ground. I would've walked to Texas from there if I had to."

Some of us have to lose our freedoms to appreciate them. As a journalist, people pick on me sometimes about the liberal, biased media . . . but

I like to remind them that they'd be unhappy without the freedoms that come with the First Amendment.

Say thank you to a service member. Say thank you that you can walk where you want to, write what you want to, say what you want to, worship where you want to. If it weren't so good, so many people wouldn't die trying to get here. May God bless America!

~LORRI ALLEN, SPEAKER, THE SOUNDBITE COACH, RADIO SHOW HOST
www.SoundbiteCoach.com

Because all of us believe and understand in the fabric of the common bond of why we call ourselves American is to care for the men and women who wear the uniform; and when they take off the uniform, we care for them when they are veterans.

~STEVE BUYER

As we look forward to freedom, the shining city on the hill and the best days of America lying ahead, it is the men and women in uniform who protect, defend and make us proud to whom we should look and give thanks every night.

~ROBIN HAYES

I studied the lives of great men and famous women, and I found that the men and women who got to the top were those who did the jobs they had in hand, with everything they had of energy and enthusiasm and hard work.

~HARRY TRUMAN

It's in the Stars

Every time I hear the National Anthem, the tears flow from my eyes like that stalwart flag does fly.

The symbol of the flag and its stars represent so much.

Moved to tears, infused with pride, humbled by the commitment and sacrifice of those who fought bravely for our liberty.

White stars on our banner of freedom represent 50 States united in purpose to form a great nation. Blue stars told all during the Great War, a family member proudly serves from this household. On seeing these white flags with blue stars every man, woman and child dug in at home as other fought abroad. Blue stars were covered in gold, a shroud of honor in the passing of one who perished in service, the ultimate sacrifice. A flood of feelings overcome me when listening to the Star-Spangled Banner.

I look to the heavens, I send a prayer of thanks to those who are still watchful to see we are still standing strong, proud and free and our flag is still here.

Our flag is still here, flying over the Capitol and still there on the battle field and on every memorial marker in remembrance.

Our Star-studded flag is still here flapping in the gentle breeze in front of every American's home on Independence Day reminding us to hope, dream, create, live and be grateful to be an American alive today in the Greatest Nation on Earth.

I look to the heavens and see the light in the night from above guiding the land of the free so there will be a home for the Brave.

~DR. LONI ANDERSON L.AC.

God bless those who served our country including my father Gerald Anderson, a Norwegian American, who showed others the way through the invaluable maps he made to guide missions to success, to my step-father Herman Ameen, a Lebanese American, who fought in Normandy. To all the Gold Star Mothers who lost a son or daughter in service to our Country.

Through Faith & Pride

Patriot. The word's meaning became fixed in my soul July 4, 1983, as I stood with the United States Marine who became my husband. In evening rain, we held hands beneath the Washington Monument illuminated against the night. Above the United States Capitol, thunderous fireworks in red, white, and blue pierced the dark sky. Among thousands, I stood beside this Marine whose face, lifted toward the flag, revealed a reverence I'd never seen.

My own patriotism intensified when later, my now retired, Sergeant Major, escorted me to an Evening Parade at Marine Corps Barracks 8th and after returning from Vietnam. With his six-foot frame at stoic attention during the National Anthem, I stood completely awed. Spellbound, I watched two companies of Marines impeccable in dress blues enter the grounds. The instant crack of 150 steel-plated rifle butts striking the concrete deck in exact unison sent chills across my skin.

An hour later, after precision mirror performances by the Marine Corps Silent Drill Team and hearing *The Stars and Stripes Forever* by "The President's Own" Marine Corps Band, I believed my heart could contain no more pride or humility. Then, a lone Marine bugler appeared atop the oldest Marine Corps barracks in the nation. With my hand against my heart, I reverently watched as the United States flag slowly descended in the glow of light to the hands of two waiting Marines. For the first time, in person and with tear-filled eyes, I heard the beautiful, mournful notes of *Taps*.

Two decades later I held my Marine's hand as we listened to those mournful notes resound in a Georgia chapel after the death of another true patriot. My husband's only child, my step-son, Sergeant Patrick Tainsh, had been killed in action in Baghdad, Iraq on February 11, 2004. A *Purple Heart*, *Bronze Star*, and *Silver Star* recipient, Patrick was a proud U.S. Army Cavalry scout with 2nd Armored Cavalry Regiment, Eagle Troop. When *Taps* played for Patrick, not only fell tears of sorrow, but tears of honor.

I had been Patrick's *bonus Mom* since he was 13. And his only Mom after his birth mother died when he was 17. As a military wife, I had watched my husband, David, roll socks, underwear, and t-shirts into tight cylinders to fit with other clothing into a single military bag for deployments to Japan, the Philippines, and *Operation Desert Storm.*

But, sending a son to war and, having him return beneath a flag, took a heart that I wonder at the miracle that kept it from bursting. Not only have I grieved for the 33-year-old son who never was to marry the love of his life and bring grandchildren into our world, but I grieved for my husband whose only child had been taken from physical sight. I couldn't replace Patrick, and I couldn't fix my husband's broken heart as I struggled with my own grief for both of them. My faith was all I could turn to along with writing.

Through the emotionally difficult days that followed, I asked God to lead me to do what I should to be the wife and Mom I needed to be. Since the dark day of our notification on February 12, 2004, the sun has continued to rise and the heavy veil of grief's darkness has lifted from our hearts, although missing and remembering Patrick will never cease.

Together, my husband and I discovered ways to honor Pat and his fallen comrades by sharing our family's story through the book, *Heart of a Hawk: One Family's Sacrifice and Journey Toward Healing,* and providing royalties in memory of Patrick to the *Tragedy Assistance Program for Survivors* of military personnel. We share our journey and faith with other grieving military families and speak to groups about the pride we will always retain and revere as a military family, even through our darkest days.

Looking back, through hardship and pain that has allowed me to grow as a woman of faith, I would not trade my life for anything else since July 4, 1983: that wonderful evening, when I stood in the rain beneath the Washington Monument with the Marine who became my husband, the husband who brought to my life a son who lived life large, and also served a purpose greater than himself.

I know that through faith, and pride, and the promise that in God's time all things will be beautiful, the heart of this military woman has, and will, continue to be given the strength and courage needed to remain the proud wife and Mom of great patriots.

~DEBORAH TAINSH, AUTHOR OF *HEART OF A HAWK: ONE FAMILY'S SACRIFICE & JOURNEY TOWARD HEALING*

Wife: USMC Sgt Major David L. Tainsh (Ret.)

Gold Star Mom: U.S. Army Sgt Patrick Tainsh, KIA 2/11/04 Baghdad

www.heartofahawk.com

www.deborahtainsh.com

The area where we are the greatest is the area in which we inspire, encourage, and connect with another human being.

~MAYA ANGELOU

Women are the real architects of society.

~HARRIET BEECHER STOWE

In politics, if you want anything said, ask a man;
if you want anything done, ask a woman.

~MARGARET THATCHER

We can do no great things, only small things with great love.

~MOTHER THERESA

The quiet voice inside says, "That's the way it should be . . . "

~OPRAH WINFREY

The Cost of Our Freedom

Immediately following the tragedy of 9/11, I grabbed my journal to confide how I felt. I'd like to share this in memory of all the dear souls we lost that day—yet most of all for those family and friends who remained . . .

Casualties of war on U.S. mainland soil
Dig deeper—rip our skins with a treacherous knife.
Blood burst—then splattered
Lives all around us—shattered.
Not only the human corpses within buildings and planes—trapped
The outer rings of families, friends, and special acquaintances—snapped
With a vicious kick
A bruised purple lick,
Then tear out our hearts and feed them to vultures
That hover now at the sites
At the end of the flights.
Where were all the people going?
What were they saying at this time?
In the air—imagine—knowing
People at coffee stations—into mugs the coffee flowing
Unaware in moments they'd be casualties to terrorist crime.
Hearts beating, hands feeling, feet walking
One moment—then
Hearts yanked out, hands and feet blown apart
Heaven sent.
Has this world ended?
Has a new one just begun?
A place we once defended—
Now blown to tiny fragments for some psycho-minded fun.
Sadness purges my inner-core

continued

Tugs at my intestines
While they wrap around my throat.
Shut off the surging roar
From the results of despicable sins.
God bless the souls, the hearts, and the lives that have vanished.
Stolen lives of precious beings—all of their memories lost.
Mend the holes of those who remain in their dear ones shadows
Where sadness penetrates like flames in gray coals.
Seethe through the madness with fury and fire—at such great cost.
I feel as if I've crawled into the depths of a lucrative spy novel,
The pages sweaty from swift turns—as my heart grovels
To be released from the misery trapped beneath
As death shatter all illusions—the victims of the tragedies bequeath.
I hear the faint cries languor all around me
Loved ones lost
Such an enormous cost
We live in the United States of America—are we really free?

~SUZAN TUSSON, CPCC, AUTHOR, SPEAKER, LIFE COACH FOR WOMEN
www.wisewithin.wordpress.com
© 2009

We as Americans must provide the vision of the American way, the way of freedom, integrity, innovation, leadership, friendship and dreams for every American. We must believe in our country, our creator and ourselves and have the faith that even in the face of adversity our efforts can and will make a difference. . . .

~CARL MORRIS, POET ON AMERICA AND VALUES
www.apassionforfreedom.com

Romance in the Ranks

Issued a Family

Matt and I have been married to each other for a total of three months, but we have been married to the Corps a total of two years. We have lived through Basic Training as best friends, PA School as engaged, and finally duty stationed as engaged and married. Even as a newlywed, one of the toughest jobs is to remember you're not only married to your spouse, but to the Corps as well. Your little family soon becomes a much bigger family comprised of everyone you work and interact with. You share holidays, changes of duty stations, but most of all you share a commitment not only to protect and serve, but to love and help.

When we first moved into our duty station, we needed help. I suggested hiring movers, but Matt reminded me we already have built-in movers, his fellow Marines. Over the next few days of moving, I soon found myself surrounded in a house full of boxes and people I didn't know. In the short time it took us to move, I discovered something else. By the end of the move, all the people who helped us not only were my husband's coworkers, but became my friends. The people I turned to for everything from "it's too heavy I need help lifting" to help assembling all our furniture that was in a box.

There is one particular military spouse that told me it's not the family you leave behind; you're gaining a new one. When she told me this on the first day of moving in, I could never have imagined how right she truly was. Our new family is quite large now, gaining new members with every rotation, but I will never forget my first taste of how truly amazing it is when a Marine walks in and walks out family.

~KRISTIN RONDEAU-GUARDIOLA, UNITED STATES MARINE CORPS

Military Romances

"**D**an, before you head off for Guam, I have to tell you something that's been on my mind," I said to my 30-year-old son. "I know you just broke up with Barbie after three years, and you're not looking to jump into a serious relationship. But you're going to be in Guam for three years, and I predict you'll meet *the one* while you're there."

"What?" Dan, a helicopter pilot in the Navy, exclaimed, "No way, mom, I don't want to get into an international marriage, where we have to decide if we live in her country or mine. I want my kids to grow up with their whole family, and that's harder to do in separate countries. Besides, three years isn't necessarily going to be enough time to meet, fall in love, and get to know someone well enough to marry them. Look what happened with Barbie," he said.

"Yeah, but you and Barbie had some good things going for you for awhile. You were both heading off in vastly different career directions, so it's not surprising you pulled apart. Be on the lookout, that's all I'm saying."

To my delight, three months into Dan's Guam tour, he was sent home for a short visit around Christmas. Casually, he mentioned that an Air Force girl would be stopping by on her way home to Maine. My ears perked up. Stopping in San Diego . . . on her way to Maine? Hmmmm.

Liz was not a pilot, but a hospital administrator. Turns out, her family lived in the same city as my in-laws. She grew up there, so we had lots to talk about. In high school, she won 13 scholarships playing tennis, and chose the Air Force Academy in Colorado. Dan's sister lives in Colorado. Hmmmm.

During the next two years, we heard more about Liz here and there, but Dan wanted to keep a lid on it, lest we start planning a wedding. By the time they were both sent stateside to Pensacola, we were not surprised, but pleased. Meanwhile, my youngest step-daughter, Linda, joined the Navy after high school graduation. My husband had spent six years on USS Constellation aircraft carrier, and they were the best years of his life. He regaled Linda with the opportunities he'd had for world travel, education, and partying. She bit!

She had a good head for math and computers, but there were few spots for women in Cryptology, so it took almost a year. After Boot Camp in the Great Lakes, she was sent to Pensacola, where she met up with her step-brother, Dan and his girlfriend, Liz. They celebrated her graduation together. Dan and Liz bought a house, and Linda reported to her first ship in Hawaii, while the happy couple planned their wedding. Sadly, Linda reported before the Cinderella wedding and drawn swords of fellow officers.

Meanwhile, far from the loneliness of Boot Camp, and the twilight zone of Pensacola, Hawaii was the happiest time of Linda's life. Who wouldn't be happy on a ship with sixty women and three hundred men? And Hawaii! She adored exploring its beauty. Her adventure continued when they set sail for Africa, Australia, and adventure. While out to sea, she formed a relationship with a handsome sailor. About six months into her new life, she called, "I'm pregnant." She was just 20. We were shocked, disappointed and certain that this would be the end of her career.

Sailor boy did not want to be a daddy at age 21, and wanted nothing to do with the baby, *hmmmm* babies—twins. We offered to adopt them; Linda wanted to keep them. So we offered to take care of them. Joey and Lizzy were born on April 14 and 15, and were as different as their birthdays. There are no real happily-ever-after stories, of course. But some situations can be made to work. Liz and Dan just celebrated their third anniversary and have a wonderful life together. No children—yet. Linda was gone very little the first year, but a month after the twins' first birthday, she was sent away for 11 months of training, ending up in Maine, where her new ship was being built. She came home twice during that time, and sailed into harbor just before the Lizzy's and Joey's second birthday. In the next six months, she'll be gone all week and home only on weekends. After the beginning of the year, she will go away for about six months. And, that will be the pattern of her career, but she and the babies will continue to live with us, to provide them with continuity and stability.

People, usually other new moms, often say, "Oh, I could never do that, I could never leave my babies." Of course, that's understandable. It is not

the best way to raise children, but it is better than some of the alternatives. These babies have a mother who loves them enough to re-enlist for six years, to provide them with day care, medical coverage, and overall better care than she could provide on her own. We adore these children, and they bring greater purpose into Grandpa's life.

The daddy? He's never seen Lizzy or Joey, nor did he tell his parents about their twin grandson and granddaughter. But Linda sent them photos of the grandbabies. Each birthday and Christmas a package arrives. We want the children to grow up bathed in the love of the family who wanted them.

~NANCY CANFIELD

Love is missing someone whenever you're apart,
but somehow feeling warm inside because you're close in heart.
~KAY KNUDSEN

When two people love each other, the don't look at each other, they look in the same direction.
~GINGER ROGERS

When you realize you want to spend the rest of your life with somebody, you want the rest of your life to start as soon as possible.
~FROM THE MOVIE WHEN *HARRY MET SALLY*

A woman may be able to change the world, but she will never be able to change a man.
~AMY SNOWDEN

"The Ensign Said She'd Marry Me!"

Let's face it: I joined the Navy to find a husband. I figured the Navy had a monopoly on guys that looked like they came out of an Old Spice commercial, so what a great place to look for 'Lieutenant Right.' How true! By the time I left Officer Candidate School, in March of 1973, I was already engaged!

Now that I have the guy, I thought, I could focus on my career. That involved getting stationed with "Dave" in Groton, Connecticut, while he attended Submarine School. I was stationed at a Command that supervised the Submarine Shipyard at Electric Boat Division in Groton.

My adventure began the day Dave moved me into a room at the Bachelor Officer Quarters (BOQ) on the Submarine Base. This green-coated-cinder-block-cubicle of a room was questionably decorated from floor to ceiling with Technicolor pictures of naked (and apparently cold) women, thoughtfully left for me by the last tenant. Dave's inability to see my problem with this room left me speechless. He left to cool off. I set off in search of another room.

Now, in a BOQ, you never know whom you will run into as I so happily discovered. Maybe it was my long brown hair or my tomato red wool poncho that attracted his attention, at this point, all I remember that day is that I met Superman. LTJG Troy Erwin—with his Navy issue glasses—looked exactly like Clark Kent. I had to look twice. As I breezed into the BOQ lounge, he got up immediately and we exchanged introductions. I asked for his help in changing rooms and, like any worthy superhero, he was able to save the day by getting me ensconced in a more appropriately decorated cubicle, conveniently located right across the hall from his room. He made it all look effortless.

As I felt my heart fill with gratitude toward Troy—among other remarkable sensations—I guiltily looked down at my emerald and diamond engagement ring. I think I pretty much knew from that moment, that my life with Dave was now iffy at best. Within about two months, Dave and I realized that this relationship just wouldn't work. We parted ways as friends, probably because I agreed to buy the ring from him. I loved that ring; I had picked out every stone.

Once Troy and I began dating, he proudly gave me a tour of his 'boat.' Troy was the assistant weapons officer aboard the post World War II diesel submarine USS Greenfish SS 351. As I awkwardly maneuvered myself down the narrow, vertical hatch of his boat, I was profoundly glad I wore pants. Next, I was almost knocked flat by that "aromatic" smell of a diesel submarine that you never forget. This scent is a unique combination of diesel, food, pipe and tobacco smoke and the unmistakable smell of lots of hot, sweaty men. Maybe, I pondered, this is precisely why there are no women on submarines!

One night when Troy was the Duty Officer on Greenfish, I was keeping him company. When he left to go do ship's rounds, he asked me to answer the phone if it rang. However, it did not occur to either of us how this would appear to whoever was on the other end of that phone line. Phone rings:

[My female voice] *USS Greenfish, Ensign Debs speaking, this is not a secure line, may I help you sir or ma'am?*

[Male voice] *"DAMM!"* Slam goes the phone!

Then it rings again. So again I answer:

USS Greenfish, Ensign Debs speaking, this is not a secure line, may I help you sir or ma'am?

[Male voice] *"!??! Damm! No Way!"*

Finally, the phone rings a third time and after I answered it the same way the caller said:

"DAMMM IT! There's women on submarines! Damm! Women on submarines! I can't believe it, The Navy's going to hell!" Slam goes the phone so hard this time, it hurt my ear!

I could have explained to the caller who I was, but then, what fun would that have been?

Men! You 'gotta love them. Often as not, they have no idea how what they say is going to affect you. It just sounds innocent to them. So when Troy tells me that he has orders in hand to the diesel submarine in the Philippines, USS Grayback SS 208, and asks me if I will wait for him after he leaves, he is utterly dumbfounded by my answer. I had heard all about that "bachelor boat' in the Philippines. Lots of partying, in and out of port, no responsibilities other than the ship, just a really fun tour—for him.

"No, I won't write to you in the Philippines, and no I won't wait for you to return." I tell him. "If you are interested in any kind of a long term relationship with me, you will just have to get your orders changed to a 'Boomer' out of New London. I just can't wait for you. I have a life to live. If you want to live it with me, you have to make some decisions."

Be still my heart! The very next day, Troy changed his orders to a "Boomer out of New London," the ballistic missile submarine USS Benjamin Franklin SSBN 640. That one phone call changed both our lives. The tour aboard Franklin was far more career enhancing, and this critical change told me that we were going to have a life together. Now all he needed to do is ask me to marry him. Hmm, time to think about rings again!

Finally, one hot night in August '73, Troy and I went out for ice cream. I was feeling hopeful! Along the way to the ice cream shop, he showed me every charming chapel he could find. Each time we entered a chapel, I thought, *"This is it! He's going to ask me now, for sure!"* but he didn't. *"What is he waiting for? We can't be stationed together until we are married! Time is passing!"*

Finally, as our evening is waning and we are headed back to the base, I decided to "nudge" things a bit by casually describing the guy I plan to marry. Hopefully, he will see that I am describing him! Finally, he says to me *"Well, will you marry me?"*

"I don't know, is this the real thing, or are you just exploring the question?"

"This is the real question, will you marry me?"

"Well, I don't want to rush into anything . . . but I have considered marrying you, so yes, I would love to marry you!"

Finally we reached the Submarine Base, and as the proud Marine guard rendered a snappy salute, Troy, happily called out the window to him: *"The Ensign said she'd marry me!"*

Epilogue

We eloped on October 19, 1973. 36 years, three kids and two dynamic careers later, Troy is still my superhero, still going to sea in the Merchant Marine after retiring from the Navy, and we are still very much in love with each other.

~TINA D. ERWIN, CDR, USN (RET.)

The flower of a woman's wisdom blooms within her heart.
~LAUREL BURCH, ARTIST, "CELEBRATING THE HEART OF WOMANKIND"

I love you not only for what you are, but for what I am when I am with you. I love you not only for what you have made of yourself, but for what you are making of me. I love you for the part of me that you bring out.
~ELIZABETH BARRETT BROWNING

Nobody has ever measured, even poets, how much a heart can hold.
~ZELDA FITZGERALD

We do not fall I love with the package of the person; We fall in love with the inside of the person.
~ANNE HECHE

More Than Missing

Baby tea roses with a hint of apricot,
 Edging the wedding white buds—
Are arranged in lead crystal, which
 Sits bedside, atop Battenberg lace.

She awakens to this every morning.
 Eyes open to a room surrounded;
Provided with her "comfort things."
 A framed picture holds memories.

He's been absent nine months—
 Was expected home last fall,
 No word as to his whereabouts
 The Marines have informed her.

Married barely two years, they are
 Still newlyweds in her mind.
 He did not leave her with child.
 No resemblance of him to love.

continued

Intermittent e-mail ceased long
Ago. All communication is lost—
Kate's soul mate is missing, but
She is more than missing him.

War is sacrifice; but does anyone
Care to know hers—the alone hours
The deep cut inside, the unknown?
It's personal. God, it's personal.

She's grown weary of the spin doctors,
The rhetoric, the "just for oil",
The unending political machine.
His fight she sees as noble.

She opens her eyes this morning,
Pushes thru various shades of gray—
Puts on the ritual pot of coffee,
And emerges into a jade bath.
Glances at the sterling which
Adorns her left hand, and reflects . . .

~LEE A. BARRON~
Copyright © 2006

Beneath a Goodbye

Heart like a lamb. Beating softly and warmly,
I curl into you. Knowing you will leave.
Fearing I will grieve and fall desperately
back. Into a pit. Beneath a bluff where
only wind, hail, and earth caress my face.

Heart like a lion. Proud and roaring,
I hear your call. Feel your pull as
it rips my chest. Tearing, stripping
and consuming. My fingers curl
around your head, and cling.

Heart of a father. Bleeding and shredding,
I see your pain. Knowing you will leave.
Fearing they will grieve and flail
into my open arms. Their tiny hands
pushing, their eyes welling. Again.

Heart of a soldier. Thriving and pounding,
I believe in you. Knowing that thump,
that beat that drives you, may come home
in a box. Fearing loss. Hoping for peace.
Standing beside you. 'Til death do us part.

~MELISSA SELIGMAN~
Author of The Day After He Left for Iraq
Host of Her War Her Voice, *a podcast for military wives*
www.dayafterheleftforiraq.com
www.herwarhervoice.com

Setting the Bar

Unknown Influence

Back in 1995, I was a Lieutenant Colonel in the Air Force Reserve. My assignment was a six-month tour in Budapest, Hungary as the native language-speaking Deputy Commander on the Military to Military Contact Program for the Military Liaison Team. I left my four children, five- to 12-years-old, behind with my capable, fully-employed husband as I set out on this assignment. Needless to say, his support was critical and instrumental in my successfully fulfilling this mission.

Near the end of this tour of duty, I was invited to be the guest presenter in Graz, Austria to speak on issues generally pertaining to women serving in the military. After overcoming much red tape, including a myopically uncooperative supervisor, I was finally permitted to go give my speech—in German, no less!

Much to my surprise, I wasn't forewarned that after reading my prepared remarks in German, that there would be a 30-minute question and answer session, also in German. I went on to tell them the *Rozi* story as best I could, which was then followed by pertinent questions regarding how I balance a military career, being married, the raising of our children, and the like. The evening was mentally draining, but went reasonably well, I thought.

When I got back home to Calabasas, California after the end of my tour and the speech, I received a call from a writer for the *Reserve Officer Association* (ROA) magazine, a monthly publication for Reservists. The caller informed me that he was about to write an article about me, and that he would publish it in the upcoming January issue. I asked him what he was going to write about, and he said he already had most of what he needed, and he just wanted a couple of additional details.

As I soon found out, the article was about that speech I gave in Austria. He went on to tell me that I wasn't informed before my appearance that there would be a female member of the Austrian parliament in the audience. I also did not know that one of the then hot issues during that particular session of Parliament was a debate regarding their country's allowing women into military conscription—and that the member of parliament in question happened to be against that! Yet, after hearing my speech, this lady had changed her mind; and, hers was actually the deciding vote that would allow women to enlist into the Austrian military from then forward!

Needless to say, I was stunned! I had no idea that I, as a military woman and mother of four could possibly exert such an influence over a significant national issue such as this. The subsequent headline in the ROA magazine read something like: *Reserve Officer Determining Factor in Austrian Defense Policy.*

So, what do I feel is the moral of my story? It's that you just never know the power and influence you possess as a woman serving in the U.S. Armed Forces. Welcome the opportunities that cross your path. Go forth and be heard. Embrace your unique skills. And, above all, be immensely proud of the service you unselfishly dedicate to your country.

~COLONEL ROSEMARY "ROZI" HEREDY, USAFR (RET.)

I am a woman above everything else.
~JACQUELINE BOUVIER KENNEDY ONASSIS

When you have decided what you believe, what you feel must be done, have the courage to stand alone and be counted.
~ELEANOR ROOSEVELT

Chaplain School USMC Training

When I reported to Chaplain School, I was fortunate to know that I was going to serve with the Marines at my first command. There was additional training that went a long with this. One part was a weekend with a Marine Reserve Infantry Unit . . . Mortar Battalion. Here, being a man or woman didn't matter (there were no other women but me) doing the job mattered. In fact, no one knew there was a woman in the unit until we made our first stop in the march. In full gear and packs, we marched eight miles through the sand and dirt roads to the mortar range where training would occur. There are no trucks to carry the weapons, just people, so as you march you take your turn carrying parts of the launchers. Some parts you can carry a long time, others, like the 50-pound plate, only a few minutes.

Our training Gunny who came with us gave me simple encouragement. "Once they find out you're a girl, don't you let them carry anything for you . . . even if you can only carry the plate for a few steps, you take it, and give it to the man behind you." It was an incredible experience. By the time we had made our first stop and the discovery was made that there was a female in the group, it didn't matter. I had carried my share and done my part, and was immediately accepted as part of the unit. Some of my male Chaplain counterparts, however, did not heed the Gunny's similar advice to not let anyone carry anything for them. They spent a good part of the experience just with each other.

Now I didn't have clue about what a Chaplain could do to be useful on a training mission. It was drilled into our heads to stay out of the way, never pick up a weapon (Chaplains are non-combatants), and never interfere with a mission. So, I learned how to load mortar rounds, had the Marines teach me about their jobs, and learned that the strawberry dessert in the Meal Ready to Eat (MRE) could be bartered for some really good stuff. I learned the importance of clean, dry socks and proper foot care. I dug heads and learned how to pitch a shelter. I had to obtain another shelter-half because you only carry a half and your shelter mate carries the other half. Since I was the only woman, they decided I probably should have a whole shelter to myself (just a little bigger than a pup tent). I had the luxury suite. It was disappointing that we Chaplains were not going to be allowed to stay the whole time with the Reserve unit . . . I would, however, have this experience again.

This one small experience would provide me with incredible knowledge in my future commands. Marines don't care what color, religion or gender you are. If you do your job, carry your weight, and help your comrade when he or she is down, you're accepted as a Marine. Chaplains and Corpsmen are treated with immediate respect in the Marine community. You can lose that respect quickly if you do not do your job.

When I reported to my Marine Base, I was assigned to the Base Command Chapel and the Family Service Center. I was a little disappointed with this because I would not have any field experiences this way. It didn't take long, however, before I found a small battalion whose Chaplain was stationed on another base and didn't come to see them. I met them when I needed volunteers to get Christmas trees for the Chapel and someone told me to go to the LAAM Battalion—they were always looking for something to do. My six to eight volunteers became almost the entire battalion as we traversed the forest on base to find just the right trees and greenery. For the two years I was there, I was their "additional duty" Chaplain.

Another aspect of serving with the Marines for Navy personnel has to do with the uniform. While Navy personnel serving in Marine units may wear Marine uniforms, they may do so only with the permission of the command. They must also maintain rigid physical standards in order to wear the uniform. There are no overweight or out-of-shape Marines.

The Marines also knew what they were doing when they designed women's uniforms. They didn't take men's uniforms and make them in women's sizes, they had a designer specifically design a uniform that a woman could

work in and still look professional: tailored, princess-seamed over-blouses and tailored slacks. The cami uniform is all the same, plain and functional.

Serving with the men who were on the "pointy end of the spear" is an incredible experience. Later, when I served with Navy commands, I would add other women into my experiences. I spent the first several years in the military hearing the phrases "I never saw a woman Chaplain before." Or, "Never worked with a woman before . . . "

"Neither have I," I responded.

~DARCY LOVGREN PAVICH
Chaplain/Stand Down Coordinator, Veterans Village of San Diego
www.vvsd.net

I don't measure a man's success by how high he climbs but how high he bounces when he hits bottom.
~GENERAL GEORGE S. PATTON

Women are the architects of society.
~HARRIET BEECHER STOWE

Once a woman is made man's equal, she becomes his superior.
~MARGARET THATCHER

If you're willing to do the work, you will eventually become what I call a woman who is in full possession of herself.
~OPRAH WINFREY

Proud to Be in the Military

Joining the military was my ticket to Germany. You see, ever since I took a German class from my dynamic teacher, Mrs. Irwin, I was hooked and vowed I would travel to Germany, and perhaps live there forever. Fast-forward five years. I was called out of my high school English class, "Jennifer, the counselor wants to see you." I've never been in big trouble before and I think my classmates and I were mirror reflections of each other, surprise-wise. Going down that very long hallway, I couldn't imagine why I was called out of class. I waited outside Mr. Richard's door, suppressing the urge to throw up or at least whimper loudly. "Jennifer, good to see you. Go ahead and sit down. Jennifer, do you know why I called you out of class?"

"Um, no, sir." Feeling immensely guilty (for what)?

"Congratulations, Jennifer, you've made it into the Air Force Academy!"

"I'm not in trouble?"

"Should you be?"

"No."

"Well, good job!" I walked back to class feeling confused, happy yet worried. Getting into the Academy and committing to become an officer for at least five years after graduation . . . that meant the next nine years in a uniform. Wow, heavy stuff for a teenager.

I am now almost 44 years old and my Air Force Academy 20th reunion is coming up. I think back on all of the experiences I accumulated during those nine fleeting years. Yes, I did get to Germany during an especially historical moment—a month after the Berlin Wall came down. While at the Academy, I tested my courage in so many ways. Soaring a glider on my own, jumping off a 30-foot diving board in full fatigues, going through a simulated POW camp and survival training, and taking a lot of engineering classes even though I was a fuzzy major (political science), thoroughly tested me.

Besides courage, I learned the true meaning of team spirit and sticking together, whether it meant doing push-ups in unison when someone got in trouble, picking up one of our classmates if they fell down, pulling all-nighters together for those tough classes, or running side by side and encouraging each other during physical fitness tests. I thought being at the Academy was my biggest challenge. As a new 2nd Lieutenant, butter bar, I learned differently. Imagine entering a squadron and being assigned the head of a department where the majority have years more experience and they know it. I heard a Master Sergeant was really not happy I was coming to Berlin, especially after finding out I was a brand new 2nd Lieutenant (strike one), a woman (strike two) and an Air Force Academy graduate (not a zoomie!—strike three). Besides an unhappy Sergeant, our message center was isolated from the rest of the Air Base.

I affectionately called it Berlin's Basement. Our message center had no windows and I remember the darkness leading down to the sealed double-doors. I eventually got another position on the sunnier fourth-floor.

I learned much as an officer over the next three-and-a-half years. I made some poor decisions and some really good ones. When they pinned on my Captain bars shortly before it was time to head back to the States, I reflected on all that had happened. I had tested myself in so many challenging situations and had met a lot of interesting people in Berlin's melting pot.

My next assignment was March Air Force Base, Riverside County, California. I had limited technical expertise and tried to treat people with respect, listening and being there when it counted, staying calm, and using available resources wisely. Again, I made some good decisions and some I wish I could erase. I never stopped trying to progress, and the military affords many opportunities, especially if you're willing to take initiative. I still can't believe I designed health and fitness programs for Berlin Air Base during my two assignments at March AFB as a side job! Being in charge of the weight management program at the Base Commander's request, creating a Passport to Health, writing health newsletters, and organizing health seminars are just a few of the many highlights. After getting my Master's Degree in Public Health, I decided to leave the military since my new husband had a local business and the military had only one position as a Health Promotion officer.

My husband laughs when I say everyone should be in the military for at least a year. It is a character-building, unique experience. Twenty-six years ago I had to choose between a scholarship to UC-Berkeley and the Air Force Academy. Robert Frost said it well, "I chose the path less traveled by and that has made all the difference." I have tremendous respect for all who have served our country. I get angry when Hollywood portrays the military as a bunch of buffoons or someone downplays the military as a last option.

I still remember my grandma's comment when she heard I was going to the Academy, "Hey, you got good grades, why are you going into the military?" It started out as my ticket to Germany and a free education. I wish I could tell you it was for nobler reasons, but I'd be lying. As the years went by, I developed a much deeper love and heartfelt respect for my country and for those who protect this great country's borders. I'm proud to have served in the military.

My special request is that you take time to thank Veterans or soon-to-be enlisted personnel. Thank you. Two simple words. Every time I thank the Veterans in my classes or relatives of Veterans they truly do appreciate the acknowledgement.

~JENNIFER PIGEON

You really have to take charge of your own career.
Nobody is going to do that for you.
~DARLENE KERR, EXECUTIVE VICE PRESIDENT, NIAGARA MOHAWK
Excerpt from Playing with the Big Boys *by Debra Pestrak*

Looking Back

L ooking back keeps me thinking forward. Reflecting on the day I said, "I will," started what I perceived to be a military journey. It proved to be much more than my desired wish to expand my education and travel endeavors. I captured a greater understanding of who I was and how I fit into the scheme of the military infrastructure.

The military afforded me the opportunity to learn and to apply that learning in both local and remote sites of God's good Earth. When I said, "I do" to a humanitarian mission to Honduras, I had no idea it would prove to be the single most moving experience of my career or of my short life time. I practiced as a Nurse Practitioner for the first time—which deviated from my usual Reserve assignment. I was honored to fulfill this awesome responsibility.

I watched a Third World experience from a first-class seat. I saw true poverty mixed with a sweet spirit of humility. We nursed wounds, extracted loose and decaying teeth, and witnessed four-year-olds nurse from their mother's breasts for lack of viable food sources. I listened to chest sounds, mistaking the movement of worms that had migrated into the lungs at night, for a respiratory condition. I saw nits in the curls and matted hair of little girls dressed in their Sunday best just to meet our team.

We arose at the crack of dawn to prepare for each day's journey to a new village. The recipients of our compassionate care, old and young, formed one orderly line longer than our eyes could see preparing for their long-awaited visit. We drove upon rugged roads and narrow, poorly standing bridges. It was not unusual to pass along a road and return on that same road to discover that a huge hole, large enough to consume our Hummer, had amazingly appeared. Because of this, we completed our mission and returned before dark as no street lighting was available. During these travels, we were reportedly witnesses to a vicious cycle and our modern medicine served merely as a Band-Aid effect. The medicine used to kill

the worms would soon surrender it effectiveness. The worms would return until the next humanitarian tour.

Life is a process. Many lessons did I learn. We take very basic needs for granted. I conserve more, I listen with my heart much more thanks to the language barrier, and I am much more grateful for every resource available to me. As I look back, I realize my experiences made me not just military savvy but a warrior for all mankind. I look ahead to take advantage of any and all avenues by which my brother and sister can be made stronger.

~LT COL MARY L. WOOLDRIDGE, USAFR (RET.)
Chief Nurse Executive (1997–2008)

I find a woman's point of view much grander and finer than a man's.
~KATHARINE HEPBURN

Never doubt that a small group of thoughtful, committed citizens can change the world. Indeed, it's the only thing that ever has.
~MARGARET MEAD

We must believe in ourselves or no one else will believe in us; we must match our aspirations with the competence, courage and determination to succeed.
~ROSALYN SUSSMAN YALOW, U.S. MEDICAL PHYSICIST

You may have to fight a battle more than once to win it.
~MARGARET THATCHER

Souls Are Called: Living with Loss and Grief

The Power of Prayer in Healing Grief

Everyone talks about praying for the family of the person who has died, but what does that mean exactly and how does it really help them? What are you praying for when you pray for the person who has died?

Prayer helps to heal grief by lifting the burdensome weight of the darkness from your aching heart. When you are profoundly sad, you find yourself engulfed in the darkness of your most exquisite pain. When people pray for you, they send you the blessings of their compassionate hearts. It is the brilliant energy of that blessing that begins to dilute the darkness or the hopelessness that you may be feeling.

Prayer sent with love to grieving family members clears the darkness they wake up to each painful day after someone they love has died. Prayer helps them think about what they have to do next. Prayer helps them to be considerate with their children and other family members who may also be grieving. Prayer sent with sincerity enables the grieving family to remember that the often seemingly endless days will not, in fact, last forever.

Prayer sent to a person who has died helps that person through the darkness of the initial shadows of death. Prayer sent in love to this person transitioning from life to death to the heavenly world helps to light the soul's way. Prayer sent during any type of grief situation gives people something profoundly important to do when they feel as though they do not know how to help. Prayer is the fabric of your healing foundation, and it should begin as soon as you learn of the death.

What Type of Prayer Should You Initially Send?

When you first hear of a death, you are filled with shock. You can't believe that it has happened. Once you are able to take a moment to pray, you may find that the following types of prayer are extremely meaningful.

- You can immediately begin to pray silently to God that light and love be sent to every member of this grieving family.
- You can pray that they have the strength and courage to face the days ahead.
- You can pray that each person remembers how much the deceased loved one adored him or her and the family.
- You can pray that the healing salve of love fills the family's aching, broken hearts.
- You can pray that each person in the family will be clear headed enough to make the wise decisions that the days ahead will demand, no matter how badly that person feels.
- If you are grieving, you can ask God to help you to make these decisions regarding your deceased loved one.
- If it is you who must bury your son or daughter, husband or wife, parent or friend, pray that you have the wisdom to do the right thing in every moment.
- Pray for the light of knowledge to know what to say to heal your own heart as well as the aching hearts of all those around you.
- You can ask that angels of transition be sent to the soul of the person who has died to light that soul's way to the heaven world so that he or she will not be lost.
- You can even pray to understand the purpose of this death, no matter how senseless or untimely it may seem at the moment.

Prayers that you create from within your heart are the most powerful ones you can send, because they come from your very core, your most compassionate and loving soul. These are the prayers that are sent with the power of love.

What if you are too distraught to create your own prayer? What can you do? There are many wonderful prayer books out there that you can easily use. Whatever effort you make, prayers heal—no matter when, where, or how often you send them.

Everyone Is Grieving Something

All people who have ever felt true grief know that, as they begin to talk about their particular pain, they encounter other people who are also grieving. People will tell you about what happened to them. Some people will find themselves going back to their initial sense of grief as they try to comfort you.

The more you work through your grief and talk to others, the more you get a larger sense of the tremendous amount of silent, private grief that literally millions of people are experiencing in every moment. For some, this is a comforting thought. For others, it is no comfort at all.

We are all going to experience some type of grief in our lives. Some experiences just come to a tragic and sudden end. Even though death brings an end to a physical relationship, it does not destroy the love we have for that person. As you experience this, you begin to understand this tremendous dynamic—everyone is grieving something. Perhaps realizing this will enable you to open your compassionate heart to people everywhere who are suffering any type of grief.

Being sensitive to those who are grieving does not mean that you feel sad all the time. It means that you learn to develop a loving heart that readily sends out love and knows to send a prayer whenever you hear of anyone grieving. Eventually this love lives within you, and you begin to send out love to every grieving person as part of your daily prayers. The energy of a compassionate heart helps you to heal as well as to progress spiritually.

~TINA D. ERWIN, CDR, USN, (RET.)

Excerpt from The Lightworker's Guide to Healing Grief
© 2009

Times I've Cried

I had a splitting headache as I was walking down the noisy hallway of the elementary school where my sister taught. Crowds of screaming kids were as far as the eye could see. "We just don't pay teachers enough," I thought. Why on earth anyone would want to face 20-plus kids confined to a classroom every day, and try to teach them something is beyond me.

I had just spent the afternoon with my sister's first-graders talking to them about my recent deployment to Iraq and thanking them for their support for our troops. I'm not accustomed to addressing classrooms of kids, but while I was deployed during Thanksgiving and Christmas, they sent me those turkeys that you make by tracing your hand on a piece of paper and those snowflakes cut from white construction paper. They even coordinated a message of support through a local radio station and emailed it to me. So, to express my appreciation for their support, I presented to the school an American Flag that I had raised in front of the building where I worked in Iraq, complete with a certificate signed by my Commanding Officer.

As I continued down the hallway, I felt someone grab at my sleeve. I turned around and saw one of the little boys in my sister's first-grade class. "Excuse me, Dr. Arnold, I have a question I forgot to ask while you were in our class." Oh great, I thought, more questions about scorpions. "Sure, what is it?" I asked, trying my best to be patient. He looked up at me and asked, "Are people in the military allowed to cry? I never see them crying on the news."

I stood there in my service dress blue uniform, completely dumbfounded. "From the mouths of babes," I thought, forgetting about my headache. Why was he asking me this, anyway? Did this kid and his friends really think just because we're in the military; we're not allowed to cry? Do kids these days really think it's not okay to cry? I'd better choose my words carefully.

All kinds of memories flooded into my mind of times I cried during my years of service as a Navy Physician at that time. There were all those circumstances that seemed silly later, but were a big deal to cry about at the time . . . like, when I didn't get the internship I wanted, or when I finally really left home to my first duty station, or when I first moved overseas and really missed my family, and those relationships with men that just didn't work out. Then there were the times that I still get sad thinking about, like the time my mom called me to tell me about my dad's stroke, the friends I had lost to aircraft mishaps and suicide, and the friends who ended marriages or relationships because of deployments. I thought of all the patients and their families with whom I had to share the bad news of loss. This ranges from the death of a child to the death of a fellow service member.

Until then, I was trying to avoid all those raw memories of my recent deployment as the Officer in Charge of a casualty evacuation program in western Iraq. These were the ones that kept ruining my sleep and kept my stomach tied in knots. These were the memories of young men and women wounded or dead, their bodies lifeless, burned, or dismembered, the young children in Iraq who know nothing else but war, and their families who have suffered so much for so long . . . Then, there were the injured detainees who scared me the most—like the guy with the broken arm we transported to Abu Ghraib prison. Thank God he wasn't wearing any explosives.

There's nothing like flying in a helicopter with someone who looks at you like he wants to kill you and everyone else. This was a recurring nightmare of mine for a while. Not only that, but this was the first time I had to really be in charge of something with several flight surgeons and corpsmen looking to me for leadership and support. I felt responsible for them being in harm's way, as well. These folks were evacuating casualties every day. I was only flying with them a couple weeks a month, so I could do my job better to support them and earn my flight pay. Most of these corpsmen and doctors were brand new. If I was struggling with resolving all this, they really must have been . . . and for that, I felt guilty.

I looked around and the hallway was empty except for the first-grader and me. There's no way I'm getting out of answering his question. I needed to answer him as much as he needed the answer. I knelt down next to him and told him that his question was very important. I explained to him that people in the military have feelings, too, and when they hurt, they cry, usually somewhere that feels safe to them, which is usually not in front of a camera. Most of the time, there is nothing to cry about, but sometimes something happens that saddens us, and we go somewhere to be alone and just cry . . . like that day one of our helicopters full of Marines crashed into the ground, and turned into a ball of fire. Nobody survived. A friend of mine lost a close friend in that crash, but had to stay at work because he had a job to do, and there were no days off in Iraq. Hopefully, he found the time to grieve.

Wait a minute. Maybe that's what the kid was asking. Did we actually take the time to mourn, or did we just go on back to work like nothing happened? I told the child that whenever a service member dies in combat, that member's unit has a memorial service shortly after so the people in the unit can take the time to grieve. The body of the service member is brought home to the family to do the same. We never leave anyone behind. I remembered one flight in which we stopped at one of the field hospitals to pick up several Marines killed in action. We called them Angels, as all patients have to be triaged and categorized by urgency for medical attention. Several Marines helped us with the stretchers; the Angels were in body bags. Other Marines lined up and saluted the Angels as we carried them by and loaded the helicopter. These were fellow Marines from their unit, and all of them cried.

There is nothing that says people in the military aren't allowed to cry, I told him. I also explained that the people who report the news want to respect the privacy of the military member and the family. I wanted him to understand that the news can't capture everything, and many things happen that he won't see on the news.

As I was walking him back to his classroom, he asked, "What's the matter? You look sad, like you're going to cry."

"Nothing," I said, "I'm just glad to be home."

~SARAH J. ARNOLD, MD/MPH

Commander, Medical Corps, United States Navy

Thy Will Be Done: Notes on Grieving

Grief respects no person and reveals itself in numerous ways: disappointments, broken and unfulfilled relationships, destruction of possessions, but especially the death of something or someone dearly loved. The grieving process, its length of time, and lasting affects depends on each individual's view of life and loss on planet earth, their abundance or lack of faith and other belief systems.

The greatest balm for grief is communication with others who have walked the same path so to validate the roller-coaster ride of emotions and that with time the raging fire of grief lessens to glowing embers that never let us lose memory of the one we so loved.

I have observed that those who carry grief with the greatest of dignity are those strong of faith in a Creator of the universe and see planet earth as just a pass through. One's true faith shines in the darkness as well as in the light. And it is only through darkness that one's faith can flourish or die.

It's okay to be angry at God, even to say a number of curse words. Lightening didn't strike me. But God's love did because ultimately I knew that although I was angry about the death of a son and cursed God's will, God was the only one that could bring me back from the depths of an abyss. And "When I let go and let God," He did.

A number of months after my husband and I learned of our son's death in Iraq, I was walking on the treadmill feeling the weight of grief in my heart and saying quiet prayers, seeking understanding and peace. Later while channel surfing I came upon the spiritual motivational speaker, Wayne Dwyer, on PBS. His words brought a peace to my soul: "We are not human beings having a spiritual experience; we are spiritual beings having a human experience." Everything about life on earth seemed to become so very clear.

I've professed my faith in God and saying the Lord's Prayer from the time I was a child. I never truly accepted the words into my life until experiencing the death of a son at war.

"Our Father who art in heaven, hallowed be thy name. Thy kingdom come, *Thy Will Be Done*, on earth as it is in heaven . . . " I now say this prayer and conclude with "Father, fill me with the strength and courage to walk the path of your will so I can be a light for you through the darkest times" as I also remember that even Jesus asked his Father to remove the cup of pain from him, but then concluded with, "Not my will, but thine be done."

"Life is not waiting for the storm to pass. It's about learning to dance in the rain," wrote Vivian Greene.

For those who desire to help the grieving, you must own a strong heart and gentle spirit. Please just be willing to listen, to share tears, or send a thoughtful note to say "Hello, I'm thinking of you." If you offer help, please follow through if you're asked. Don't be one with empty words. It only adds additional pain and disappointment to the grieving. If you knew the loved one of a grieving person, don't be afraid to share stories. You have a gift the grieving desperately need.

~DEBORAH TAINSH, AUTHOR OF *HEART OF A HAWK* AND *BEYOND THE FOLDED FLAG: COPING, COURAGE & FAITH*

© *October 17, 2009*

We understand death for the first time when he puts his hand upon one whom we love.

~MADAME DE STAEL

When you are sorrowful look again in your heart, and you shall see that in truth you are weeping for that which has been your delight.

~KAHLIL GILBRAN

The Last Breath

WHERE AM I?
I am afraid
You're in the hospital
It's okay
I will stay right here for you

I don't hurt anymore but it is hard to breathe
I have given you something to take care of the pain

Promise me you will stay until I go
Don't worry . . . !
I am here just for you
You are my date tonight

Your hair looks like my mom's when she pulls hers back
I bet she is proud of you

You smell just like the Lemon trees back home
I am Kathleen but my friends call me Kath

My name is Tom
but the guys call me Sunshine 'cause I am from Florida
Kath, you are so beautiful
Thanks
You ain't so bad yourself
You got a girl back home?

No one special, Just friends, I am only 19
Kath, does it hurt to die?

continued

I am seeing a bright light
Kath, I don't want to go
Tommy, it's wonderful where you are going
Tommy, go in peace my friend
I am sure glad I got to know you
That's it
Let it all the way out
I am here for you, helping you cross over
Close your eyes and follow the light
I love you Tommy
You are my Sunshine

~SGS KERRY "DOC" PARDUE~
©2004
National Chaplain, Medics & Corpsmen (2008–2010)
Poems In The Keys Of Life: Reflections of a Combat Medic
www.medics-corpsmen.org, www.kerrypardue247.com

I've seen and met angels wearing the disguise of ordinary people living ordinary lives.
~TRACY CHAPMAN

Angels do find us in our hour of need.
~AMY HUFFMAN

The Most Beloved Soul

The good Lord was walking through heaven one day and spoke to the souls waiting to return to earth.

"I need a volunteer to go back to earth." He said.

Instantaneously all hands went up in an effort to be recognized.

"You don't understand what I'm asking of you." He said. "I need someone who would need to travel at a moment's notice."

A few hands came down.

"Someone who doesn't mind being alone for days, weeks, months as their parent travels the globe to protect others rights and freedoms."

More hands dropped, leaving only a few remaining.

"This person must have the patience to wait long hours as the daily workload keeps their parent away, often with guidance from a neighbor who was once a stranger, but was placed in the same area with a loved one who had the same mission."

All hands dropped at this time.

The Lord looked around and said "Yes, this is a tough task to ask of a soul. The one who rises to this mission may spend time alone, need to be strong and mature for their parent's sake, and sometimes have to leave many friends as they move to a location which is often far from their last home. However, the benefits are that you will have a parent who loves you and will do their utmost to make your sacrifices and patience rewarding. They will provide you with the tools you will need in adulthood to respect your home and country for the sacrifices made by prior military service men and women, to be able to make decisions based upon the best outcomes, and a respect for the diversity in your own country that is not tolerated in others."

At this time, a single hand rose . . .

And Kevin Michaels (Kenny MacDonald) became the Lord's Most Beloved Soul.

~JOLITA WAGONER, AZCS(AW), USN (RET.)

Look for the beauty in things.
~MAYA ANGELOU

Be willing to believe in a greater way about yourself.
Let your heart be receptive to God's Spirit and guidance.
Have the courage to make the decision to allow the possibility of greatness
in you. Take risks beyond your boundaries, and God is right there with you.
~MARY MANIN MORRISSEY, AUTHOR OF *LIFE KEYS*

A strong, positive attitude will create more miracles then any wonder drug.
~PATRICIA NEAL

I've learned from experience that the greater part of our happiness or
misery depends on our dispositions and not on our circumstances.
~MARTHA WASHINGTON, WIFE OF PRESIDENT GEORGE WASHINGTON

Let your light shine.
Shine within you so that it can shine on someone else.
Let your light shine.
~OPRAH WINFREY
O, The Oprah Magazine, *March 2004*

Every once in a while life hands you a moment so precious, so overwhelming,
that you almost glow.
~UNKNOWN

Times Sure Have Changed

That Woman

Some stories we do not know about until after they have happened. This one is more about my Senior Chaplain than about me and is a statement of the times in which I served. When I reported to my first duty station as a new Navy Chaplain, I was the only woman Chaplain anyone had ever seen on this marine base. There were no female Marine officers, only a few Navy nurses and doctors, and one barracks of Marines and Navy Corpsmen and dental techs (which also housed the battered women's shelter—another wonderful story about women Marines).

Not long after I reported for duty, the Senior Chaplain was ordered by the Commanding General "to prevent that woman from preaching in the Base Chapel." "That Woman" was me. It was okay if I taught Sunday school, sang in the choir, counseled the troops, went on deployments, served on the Family Advocacy Committee and, generally, stayed away from anything religious that men are supposed to do. This was my first—and only—experience of a member of the line community showing any form of discrimination. And I did not experience it personally because my Senior Chaplain decided that he would disobey that order. I didn't find out about it until Commanding General was transferred and my Senior Chaplain retired.

My Senior Chaplain paid for that decision. He was planning on retiring anyway, he said, but I know he was given a less than charitable fitness report from the general. It wasn't a lawful order so official charges could never be brought against him. I know he heard about it regularly.

~DARCY LOVGREN PAVICH

Chaplain/Stand Down Coordinator, Veterans Village of San Diego

www.vvsd.net

From Grandma Grunts to Tony Lamas

Fresh out of high school, with Liz Taylor eyes, dark hair, and an hourglass figure, Nola accompanied her best friend Shirley to a meeting with an Air Force recruiter. The recruiter said, "The military is no place for a woman. You'll lose your freedom. People will shout orders at you from dawn until dusk. You will march until your feet feel dead and then you'll march some more," he warned. Then he told them the advantages, "You'll learn a trade and get a chance to travel. If you finish three years, after discharge you can go to college under the G.I. bill. Or you could make a career in the military."

In 1953, career choices for women were limited to teacher, nurse, secretary or wife. Women who sought adventure found few socially acceptable options. Prior to 1948, when President Truman signed the *Women's Armed Services Integration Act*, women like my mother Nola, could only serve during war time, unless they were nurses.

Nola and Shirley enlisted on St. Patrick's Day, 1953. Giddy with excitement, the girls counted down the days. Nola's father, a retired Navy Lieutenant Commander, drove her to the bus depot in the sleepy town of Oxnard, California. That morning she would catch a plane to Lackland Air Force Base in San Antonio, Texas. In the dark, early morning hours the sky lit up from an atomic bomb test blast in Nevada. "This is my lucky day," Nola beamed.

Flying into Texas, Nola suffered her first doubts. In contrast to the fertile citrus and avocado groves of her California home, the dry, dusty Texas landscape appeared ominous. Exhausted from hours of travel and no sleep, the women were led to barracks for a short rest. Before dozing off, Nola and her bunkmates shared childhood memories. Nola spoke of summers riding horses with her relatives in the warm colorful glow of Star Valley, Wyoming. Her grandfather, a two-term Senator for the State of Wyoming, raised 12 children on a large ranch. Her beloved uncle served as a physician in the Navy. She shared stories of moonlit nights on the ranch singing cowboy songs with her cousins.

The next morning they were issued wrap-around dresses that resembled hospital gowns without the gap in the back. Uniforms would come later after measurements. They awaited their new uniforms with the stomach tickling charge of a Jitterbug competition. Fatigues consisted of navy-blue cotton slacks, crisp powder-blue blouses and a smart bill-less flight cap. She loved the look of her size 4½ Li'l Abner fatigue shoes that resembled miniature, black, lace-up aviator boots. A medium blue skirt and jacket, cap with a bill, and Grandma Grunt shoes comprised the snazzy dress uniform.

For three months of Basic Training the women learned to fold their nylon stockings into the shape of little boats, spit shine their Grandma Grunts and Li'l Abners to a patent-leather glow, and make their beds so you could bounce a quarter off of them.

Nola loved marching because she could sing. "We're the girls of Flight 16. Fight, fight, fight for victory!" They received all the same training as the men, except their standard issue rifles contained no live ammunition. All of the women dreaded KP duty. Petite women, like Nola, cleaned pots and pans the size of small bathtubs. From 3:30 A.M. to 4:30 P.M. they stood working. Nola tried to lead everyone in song but the Tactical Instructor shouted her down. "No singing! You just earned more KP."

But more daunting than KP was a test that separated the women from the girls: could they endure forced exposure to tear gas? After a brief lecture, the women were assigned three tasks. First, they had to enter a vapor-filled room while wearing a gas mask and lift the flap of the mask for a second. Next they had to enter the room with masks off and quickly put them on as the gas clouded the room. The final test required them to take off the gas mask and slowly walk, not run, out of the gas-filled room. One woman refused to participate after completing the easier task of lifting the flap of the mask. "They can cut off my toes. I won't do it!" she cried.

In 1950, deep into the cold war, America had joined with UN troops to protect South Korea from communist rule from the North. World War II was still a fresh wound in the American heart, and the threat of fascist leaders and communist conspiracies covered the front pages of the daily newspapers. A survey of thousands of servicemen in the 1950's found that most of the men believed the number one reason women joined the service was to meet men. But for the women surveyed, meeting a man was the last reason. Brave women like Nola wanted to help, to serve, to make their own mark on the world.

After Basic Training Nola received orders for radio operator training at Keesler Air Force Base in Biloxi, Mississippi. There she learned Morse code and military intelligence codes, and studied weather patterns. She made it to the equivalent of a corporal before her skinny, but charismatic boyfriend, Mark, did. When Mark received orders to Mather Field in Sacramento he ripped a two-dollar bill in half. He gave one half to Nola saying, "When you decide to marry me we'll use this bill to buy our marriage license." Later, Nola got orders for Mather Field to the very same squadron. Like the atomic blast on the day she left for Basic Training, this seemed like a lucky omen.

Nola and Mark eventually bought a marriage license with that two-dollar bill taped together. They married, and when Nola was three months pregnant (with me) the Air Force discharged her. It would take two more decades before women with children could continue to serve in the Armed Forces of the United States.

Mark and Nola had their second daughter and later divorced. As a single mom, Nola worked for a labor attorney, a big city mayor and a mental health clinic. She would pop out of bed after dawn, as if responding to some internal reveille. The mission to serve, to belong to something greater than self, beat in time with her heart.

Today, Nola still serves her community. At 75, she lives alone and holds a full-time job at a non-profit corporation serving abused and abandoned

children. When a new donation comes in, or one of the kids gets a scholarship for college, she beams with joy and can't wait to tell us all about it.

In a corner of her lovely condo sits her old leather saddle on a stand. Next to the saddle you'll see her well-polished red Tony Lama boots. It's easy to imagine her slipping on those boots, throwing the saddle on her Arabian mare, and riding off to another big adventure.

~GINA SIMMONS

Psychotherapist, Co-director of Schneider Family Services

www.manageangerdaily.com

In every girl is a goddess.

~FRANCESCA LIA BLOCK

Accepting what others see as your strengths is crucial to your continued growth. Compliments are a gift. Did you accept it?

~RHONDA BRITTEN

Only I can change my life. No one can do it for me.

~CAROL BURNETT

Somewhere out in this audience may even be someone who will one day follow in my footsteps, and preside over the White House as the president's spouse. I wish him well.

~FIRST LADY BARBARA BUSH AT WELLESLEY COLLEGE
1990 COMMENCEMENT

The Last All-Female Company

It was my senior year in high school and I was planning to go to a four-year college just like the rest of my peers. Near the end of that year, I decided that I wanted to travel the world with hopes of being stationed aboard a ship. I met with a few recruiters and decided on the U.S. Navy. I graduated high school in June of 1991, and shipped off to Boot Camp December 2, of the same year.

When I went through Boot Camp, I was part of the last all female company to complete Basic Training before women were fully integrated into the Navy. After being in Boot Camp for ten long weeks, I graduated on February 14, 1992. It was one of the best Valentine's Day gifts one could receive.

I went from Orlando, Florida to Meridian, Mississippi for four weeks of Yeoman apprentice school. While in school, I received orders to Glenview, Illinois. Once I figured out I would not be traveling, I started going to college. My admin officer helped me focus on the fast track to an officer promotion through NROTC.

In the meantime I was having lots of fun dating and meeting great people. I grew up fast as a child and the military seemed like a good fit. I had a lot of great guy friends and one set me up on a blind date with a guy within my squadron. We started secretly dating because he was a few ranks senior to me. We also worked at the same command. My husband and I were married after six months, and at the time we had to request permission from our command. With this huge decision I was disqualified for NROTC, so I continued going to college and received my Bachelor's Degree in Business Management.

Soon after receiving my college degree, I decided to separate from the Navy after almost seven years. The decision was made because it was very challenging for both of us being on Active Duty with no children when it came time for new orders.

For the next few years, I supported my husband the best I could through many deployments and duty stations. When we were stationed in Lemoore, California, I interviewed and was chosen to be the Command Ombudsman which was a unit that consisted of 650+ sailors and Marines. I fulfilled this role for two years to help empower spouses to deal with anything, from family emergencies to broken down cars. I am proud to say that in July of 2007 my husband retired after serving our great country for 20 years.

~KARRIANN GRAF, YN2—U.S. NAVY—VETERAN

www.karrianngraf.com

Adventure is worthwhile.

~AMELIA EARHART

If you don't like something change it;
if you can't change it, change the way you think about it.

~MARY ENGELBREIT

Don't compromise yourself. You are all you've got.

~JANIS JOPLIN

Obtacles are those frightful things you see when you take your eyes off your goal.

~HANNAH MORE

Life's challenges are not supposed to paralyze you, they're supposed to help you discover who you are.

~BERNICE JOHNSON REAGON

40,000 Men and Me

What did you do in the war, Mommy?

What did you do in the war, Mommy?
Why, not much, son, I would answer
I typed on an old Selectric typewriter
and faked taking dictation as best I could.
I tried desperately not to fall asleep
while the Major was mulling over his next sentence.

I took every opportunity to sneak out,
to leave the building, get outside.
No I didn't smoke, I needed to get warm.
Viet Nam had two seasons: wet or dry, and always hot
But the stark gray government buildings
were stuck at 58 degrees.

We worked ten-hour days, seven days a week
They said it was to keep the soldiers from getting into trouble
And besides, the war doesn't take weekends off.
But I'm not a soldier, I'm not fighting, I wailed,
and I promise I won't get into trouble.
It didn't matter. We're all in this together—40,000 men and me.

If I took the Army bus to the office,
Someone would always strike up a conversation
"What's a nice girl like you doing here?"
As if I were a novelty, a celebrity, a circus act.
If I walked to work, there would be whistles,
cat calls, offers of a ride.

continued

When I accepted a ride—which I seldom did,
there were offers, questions, propositions.
If I turned down a ride, even with my friendliest smile,
I would sometimes hear
"Stuck up" or even "Bitch" hurled at me
as the jeep screeched away.

I know they were only lonely
for their girls, wives, mothers, sisters at home.
To talk to an American girl would be a treat.
I understood, and yet, it was hard
always being in the spotlight
The unwanted center of attention.

What did I do in the war?
Very little. Secretarial duties were negligible.
My main responsibility seemed to be to provide "eye candy" for GIs
I was one of the few round-eyes—and probably the youngest—
of the female type to grace this huge army base
of 40,000 men—and me.

I loved it!

~DEE DEES~
©2000

Trailblazers

Army Guinea Pig!

I certainly did not start out looking for a career as a guinea pig. The day before I boarded the plane for my freshman year in college at Utah State University, I received a brochure about the wonders of Army ROTC. It looked interesting, and I read that participation could help pay for college. Since there wasn't any extra money for my college years, I filled it out and mailed it.

Saturday morning, 8:00 A.M., I was called down to the dorm office for a phone call. That turned out to be from the university Army ROTC recruiter asking me to come in for a visit. That was the first year that Army ROTC was open to women at colleges across the country. To shorten the story, eight college freshmen women joined the program that first year. Three years later, when I graduated and received my Army commission, I was the only woman left in the program.

Along the way I learned how to ski cross-country—there was a lot of opportunity for that going to school in Utah. I climbed mountains and rappelled down real cliffs (most ROTC students had to rappel down the side of the walls at their universities!) and I parachuted out of a perfectly good airplane—twice! I also learned a great deal about my own capabilities, and limitations, and developed a level of confidence that I hadn't experienced before.

College Army ROTC students have their own version of Boot Camp, a six-week course of basic training between junior and senior years. I attended mine at Fort Lewis, Washington and was one of 60 women in training with about 1,000 men. Again, this was the first time women had been included. As there were no female Army drill sergeants at the time, we "borrowed" one

from the Marine Corp! During the six-week course, we received about 60 hours of separate training from the men, as the Army was still determining how best to integrate military training for men and women. And, our Marine Drill Sergeant spent a fair amount of time working to convince the training developers that there should be no separation, we should receive the same training as the men, which eventually did happen, just not that first year! My fondest memory is of the barracks and the extreme lack of sleep. We had sufficient time for sleep, but after the first week it was more passing out half-way down to the pillow and snapping awake when the alarm went off!

With that behind me, I applied for the Army's Military Intelligence Counterintelligence Branch and was, again, among the first group of women accepted. This time, there was no separate training—it was six months of togetherness learning how to be a spy! Not that we would ever have that experience in peace time. But, some of the training was actually fun, like spending a day in Tucson, Arizona practicing surveillance and following a "mark" throughout the city. There were stories of a student being arrested for soliciting when she followed her teammate into a bar at 9:30 in the morning, and had a conversation with him that appeared to be, well, soliciting!

Once training was complete, I received my first assignment with the 25th Infantry Division stationed in Hawaii—nice work when you can get it. Up to that point, I had never in my life lived near a large body of water, and I suddenly found myself surrounded by an ocean. I wondered if there were people who ever complained about being stationed in Hawaii, but I loved living on an island with a beach—any beach,—within a 30-minute drive!

Once again, I found myself among female guinea pigs. An infantry division generally has thousands of men assigned. When I arrived I was one of about 165 women, 16 of whom were officers. That was an interesting time, it was a period of history when military women were labeled in a very unfavorable way; equality and sexual harassment were new topics, and women officers were not always respected for their rank. I expected that challenge and I worked hard, along with the other women in the division, to show

that we belonged there, could do the job, and should be as responsible for defending our country as the men we worked along side with. It was a time of learning and growth for the Army and for me.

I left Hawaii, and the Army, with so many wonderful stories and memories, some funny and fun, some not so much. But my growth as a woman, as a person, during my service is something I will always cherish and remember with pride and gratitude.

~VALERIE HODGSON
Captain, U.S. Army, Military Intelligence
www.healthyhappens.com

Courage is the price that life exacts for granting peace.
~AMELIA EARHART

Assertiveness is not what you do, it's who you are!
~CAL LE MON

You were born an original. Don't die a copy.
~JOHN MASON

Success is the result of perfection, hard work, learning from failure, loyalty, and persistence.
~COLIN POWELL

I believe that you are here to become more of yourself and live your best life.
~OPRAH WINFREY

Of God and Gender: The First Women on Ships

When I first reported aboard my ship there were many in the command who had never worked with women officers of any kind, and especially not Chaplains. A good number of the officer community on the ship were LDO's and Warrants who had worked themselves up from the enlisted ranks into the officer community. In essence, they were the experience and soul of the ship. When you're new to a command, and I was, ask a Chief or an LDO.

Most of the women officers on my ship were just out of college, 22 or 23 years old. I had a little advantage being 30. And, despite some of the prejudices, the job title of Chaplain often superseded gender. I remember very clearly a crusty old Master Chief who would frequent my office and bluster about girls working for him and how could the Navy allow women on ships, and how the Navy was going to hell. For weeks, and even months, I let him rant and rave and carry on about how women were ruining his Navy. I finally asked him, "Master Chief, am I ruining your Navy?" He replied, "No, you can stay . . . but the rest have to go."

There was never a complaint from the women who worked for him about mistreatment, rudeness or prejudice. He truly hated that women were serving on ships but never let it get in the way of his treatment of those who worked for him. He treated everyone the same.

The rumors about these first ships which had women crew were incredibly untrue as most rumors are. A sister ship of ours was dubbed the love boat because of the pregnancies reported on board. We faced the same issues, but the news never caught wind of us. Some of those pregnancies were planned between a husband who was at home and a wife who was serving. A very few of those pregnancies were ones that always happened, except now not to a woman in another port but a woman who served on the same ship. Even fewer of those pregnancies were no different from the many men who came to my office with the list of reasons why they simply

could not go on a deployment, a frequent one being, "My wife is pregnant and I can't leave her."

The actual facts were that the women were more demanding of the other women than the men were. A young female sailor would hear quickly from a more senior female if she was allowing a man to pull her weight, or relying on "helplessness" to gain assistance. If you weren't doing a job, it was more often a woman who would pull you up than a man.

On the down side, however, there were cases of sexual harassment in the early days (and I'm afraid from what I hear, still today) which never saw the light of day. The consequences were too severe for the woman who reported inappropriate behavior. I'm not talking about political correctness but, putting hands where they didn't belong and threatening careers if sexual favors were not granted. These were not commonplace, but they did occur and they were only addressed when the woman could not put up with it anymore.

Thankfully when they came to our Commanding Officer they were dealt with properly without regard to rank or gender. I believe the fact that the CO, XO and senior staff on the ship were exceptional leaders of high character created an overall atmosphere of fair treatment. It also helped that there were some women in high places in the command. At that time, however, there were very few senior women enlisted on board. I only recall two specifically: one an LNC and another SKC. It was often difficult for our young enlisted women to break the barrier between officer and enlisted. A Chaplain is the exception to that rule, so here being a woman was a great advantage for our young enlisted women. They could come and talk with me and not appear to be breaking any rules.

~DARCY LOVGREN PAVICH

Chaplain/Stand Down Coordinator, Veterans Village of San Diego

www.vvsd.net

Rebellious Brat Earns Congressional Gold Medal

Betty Guild's childhood talent was rebellion. When other kids were discovering their skills and mapping a life path around them, Betty was perfecting rebelling and squashing her guilt feelings over having to lie to go her own way.

She rebelled against her mother's plans for her only daughter. Loving her mother and wanting to please her did not create a desire to cook like a gourmet, sew for the poor, join the Junior League, attend charity luncheons, nor play a respectable game of bridge.

Born in Hawaii, surrounded by two brothers and seven male cousins, it wasn't surprising that Betty wanted to be one of the boys. They were doing the fun things. Her immediate goals were being a catcher on the neighborhood baseball team and a strong paddler in an outrigger canoe.

While playing baseball, Betty honed skills that were uniquely useful in her future barraging of the boundaries. She could burp on cue, spit through her teeth and crack her knuckles. As a catcher without a mitt, she broke fingers and learned to play on through pain and do what needed to be done.

Betty was naturally drawn to tales of the freedom of flight and exploring new worlds. Amelia Earhart was her idol. Amelia came to Hawaii to attempt a new record, to become the first woman to fly from Hawaii to the West Coast of the United States and the first aviator to do it solo. She spoke at the University of Hawaii on the night before her flight. Betty's enthusiastic, 14-year-old face in the front row captured Amelia's attention and she favored Betty with a long chat after the lecture. Betty confided that she wanted to learn to fly more than anything in the world, and Amelia invited her to come to Wheeler Field the next day to watch her takeoff. Betty was thrilled.

Betty was at the airfield early and Amelia greeted her and gave her a tour of her plane. They waited hours for the weather to clear. Finally they watched Amelia taxi to the runway; Betty held her breath when the throttle opened and Amelia started down the runway, the gleaming Lockheed Vega's engines roaring, and the plane accelerating.

Amelia achieved another first and Betty's dreams of piloting were set.

Later that year, when a friend asked her to be his first passenger after he earned his pilot's license at age 16, Betty felt a twinge of guilt over the lies she would tell to take that ride but guilt didn't stop her. Betty thought the J-3 Cub looked like it was held together with a few pieces of cloth and wire and had second thoughts about saying yes to the flight but she couldn't let him know that she was afraid. She held in her cries of alarm when the little plane hopped down the uneven gravel runway in a gusting wind. Betty was at last airborne.

The ride was rough as the plane slowly climbed toward the mountains. The plane seemed smaller and flimsier in the turbulence and Betty kept up a litany of prayers. She promised God that if He'd just let her get back on the ground safely, she'd never fly again. That promise lasted until they were back on the ground. In minutes, as the scared part of her fled and the elated part took precedence, Betty was ready to go again.

Betty fell in love with flying the way other pilots did, becoming enthralled with the view from the sky. That particular capacity for rapture is in the genes; most people are either petrified by being helplessly suspended in the air or immune to the sight as if it were nothing but a dusty, faded out-of-date schoolroom globe. But when Betty looked out onto the verdant escarpments of the Pali Cliffs on Oahu, she knew bone-deep that this was the correct view for her, from the air, not from horse or car or foot. At first sight addicted to the wonder, Betty had yet to know how much sacrifice and effort that wonder would cost but she did what she had to do for that bird's-eye view. She was on her way to becoming an aviation trailblazer and heroine in service to her country, a description that still has her laughing, but at 14, she was just another teenager who found ways to sneak out without parental permission to do what she felt like doing.

Perhaps history is always made like this, by people who think, to hell with asking for permission.

On December 7, 1941, the Guilds awakened to the rat-a-tat of gunfire and the roar of airplanes and the explosions of bombs at Pearl Harbor. From their many-windowed home built high on a hillside south of Honolulu they could see the tracer bullets from some P-40s chasing planes in and out of cumulus over their heads. They rushed back into the house and turned on the radio.

"The enemy is attacking us!" the announcer shouted. "All military personnel will return to their bases immediately!"

For a few days, the radio was the Guild's only contact with the outside world and reports came that barges filled with hundreds, even thousands of Japanese were landing on the north side of the island. They watched dozens of military trucks full of soldiers racing off in that direction. Enemy parachutists were reported landing on the hills above their house. They were warned to expect another attack. They listened to President Roosevelt's declaration of war and wondered how soon the invasion would continue.

Military wives and children were evacuated to the mainland. Betty's submarine-captain cousin urged her to help when the military developed a desperate need for office workers to fill essential slots vacated by the departing wives. Few locals were interested in working on the base that would be the main target when the enemy returned. Four days after the Japanese attack, Betty answered that call to service and started working in the office of the Captain of the Yard, across the harbor from battleship row.

As the war expanded with an urgent need for more pilots to ferry aircraft, Betty utilized her special talents in her second call to service. She had earned her Private, Commercial and Flight Instructor licenses and had amassed enough flight hours to qualify for training. She was in the first class of the WAF (later named WASP) in 1943 (43-W-1) and the Air Transport Command 6th Ferrying Group at Long Beach, California.

Of the 25,000 women who applied to join the WASP: 1,830 qualified; and 1,102 completed training. They flew 78 types of aircraft and ferried 12,650 planes to where they were needed. They towed targets, tested aircraft and trained male pilots. Thirty-eight women died during their service. Betty freed pilots to go to the front by flying 2,500 hours in all types of aircraft around the United States.

Though the use of women pilots in the military was "experimental" in World War II, the WASP produced permanent gains in the status and freedom of American women. Twenty-nine years elapsed before women were allowed to fly military aircraft again.

The talented and courageous women who survived flying for their country were not rewarded with veteran status and military benefits until March 8, 1977 and earned the Congressional Gold Medal in 2009.

~NORAH O'NEILL, AIRLINE PILOT, AUTHOR
Friend of WWII WASP Betty Guild Tackaberry Blake
Daughter of Pearl Harbor survivor Captain John W. O'Neill USN, Retired
www.norahoneill.com

The basic difference between being assertive and being aggressive is how our words and behavior affect the rights and well being of others.
~SHARON ANTHONY BOWER

You cannot please everyone.
The sooner you get this, the better off you'll be.
~CATH KACHUR-DESTEFANO

"Women Can't Teach Class"

The early 1970's was a time, when military women working for the Submarine Force, was not just unheard of it was unthinkable. However, around 1973, that changed when my Officer Candidate School [OCS] classmate and I were assigned to work for the Submarine force in New London, Connecticut as brand new Ensigns. I was sent to work for the Supervisor of Shipbuilding, Conversion and Repair, Electric Boat Division in New London, CT, the ultimate submarine shipyard. My friend was sent to work at Submarine School, as an administrative assistant.

You have to understand that the United States Submarine Force is probably one of the most elite private men's clubs in the world. They have the coolest toys, even cooler than jets, because submarine missions are an ever clandestine, hush-hush, never discussed type of work. Submarines truly are America's first line of defense, carrying nuclear weapons, and torpedoes. If you are going to work for this select group, you really have to be the best of the best because these guys deliberately "sink" (submerge) their ships. This is a remarkable group of men with an utterly unique shared experience, which makes Submariners a very close group. So, how do a couple of green female Ensigns fit into this mix?

My job at the Supervisor of Shipbuilding office was to be a CMS custodian. This meant that I had the impressive task of receipting for all cryptographic/communication material for all 688 class New Construction Submarines under something called the CMS or Communication Material System. Quite a bit of responsibility for a brand new Ensign, but then what I loved about the Navy was that sometimes they do give you a tremendous amount of responsibility immediately.

After about two years, my friend at Submarine School was offered the job of being the Aide to the Admiral at Submarine Group Two. This was an outstanding opportunity for her, and she took it. However, the Commanding Officer at Submarine School requested another female officer to replace her, so I was "traded" or sent to Sub School to fill her spot. We are now both Lieutenants' Junior Grade.

Upon my arrival at Sub School, I had an interview with the Executive Officer (XO) of the Command, a Navy Captain. He politely asked me what I would like to do now that I was there. Being still somewhat new to the Navy and not terribly politically savvy, I told him the truth: I wanted to teach class. To this he stiffly replied, *"This is Submarine School. Women can't teach class. We don't allow women to teach our Submariners."* To which I replied, *"Of course women can teach class—how hard can it possibly be? Men do it."*

I suppose I thought the XO would see the humor in my response to his question, but needless to say he didn't and I was buried away in the bowels of Sub School. I had a depressing windowless office and was assigned the challenging task of opening mail for a Lieutenant Commander. I didn't get to *answer the mail*. I was only allowed to *open the envelopes*, which took all of ten minutes a day. How many ways can you spell boring?

Finally, I was so bored, I urged my boss to let me go to Instructor School, if nothing else, so that he could literally get me out of the way for a while. He readily agreed because I was driving him nuts asking for more things to do.

Once fresh out of three weeks of Instructor Training, I now had the necessary credential to teach class because I had become a qualified instructor! I don't think it occurred to anyone that I would actually want *to apply* my newfound instructor qualification to meaningful work.

I lobbied every one I knew, up and down the chain of command, to allow me to teach class. I also had to convince them that I had a specialty to use, which was teaching submariners how to manage crypto material. After all, I had already been successfully managing mountains of it for an entire class of submarines. Teaching one CMS custodian how to handle material for one ship could not be that hard and they already had a curriculum for this set up.

Once again, I am called to the XO's office to discuss my desire to teach class. I figured I had to keep trying: no guts, no glory! I also knew that returning to envelope opening would never be career enhancing.

Even though the XO still tells me no, I suspect that at least he respected my courage and determination and perhaps that is why he encouraged me to speak to the Commanding Officer (CO) of Submarine School about my request.

The CO of Sub School was willing to hear me out. By now, I had become somewhat more politically enlightened and I used this once-in-a-lifetime opportunity to point out that allowing me to teach class would not just benefit him, but the whole Navy. I reminded him of the Chief of Naval Operation's program to place more women in non-traditional jobs, and I described how wonderful it would be to bring such positive publicity to Submarine School. Not only that, it would show that the CO of Submarine School, was a progressive visionary—which actually he was. More importantly, I told him, I was qualified to do the job.

All Hands, the Navy magazine did a wonderful article highlighting Ensign Tina Debs, the first Female Officer instructor in the history of Submarine School. The article prominently discussed the CO of Sub School and how open-minded he was. Everyone walked away from the experience feeling like they won something. However, for me, each day just got better and better. Not only was I able to teach submariners how to manage cryptographic material, I found myself literally locked in a sealed vault with about 28 of these great guys every day! Talk about an amazing atmosphere! As I earned a measure of respect among the other instructors, I was invited to update the curriculum for the class.

Other opportunities presented themselves and I took each one, including becoming the Chief Inspector for the CMS system for all the submarines on the waterfront. My proudest achievement was the invitation to teach the Sealed Authenticator System. This was the process by which authorization to launch nuclear weapons was conveyed to the Submarines and then authenticated. I taught this critical system to Commanding Officers, Executive Officers, Navigators, and Weapons officers. Not only did I love my now exceptionally career enhancing job, I also made contacts with hundreds of Submariners which turned out to pay political dividends for the next 20 years.

When you work for the perhaps the finest organization in the world, the bar is set high. Meeting that bar stretches you in every conceivable way. I spent most of my career working for the Submarine Force and I will always be grateful to those courageous and open-minded men at Submarine School who took a chance on me and allowed all of us to make a difference.

~ TINA D. ERWIN, CDR, USN, (RET.)

Mama Was a WASP

While most other babies were being crooned to sleep with Brahms's Lullaby, my twin brother, sister, and I slept peacefully to strains of "Zoot Suits and Parachutes." Other children only knew that socks went on feet. We proudly told our friends that socks showed wind direction. When some mothers took their youngsters to the movies, we stood beside Mama and watched planes take off. When she sighed longingly and talked about a "beautiful ship," we knew she meant the big silver aircraft perched on the end of the runway. Before their time in the wild blue yonder came unceremoniously to an end, WASP pilots were used to introduce newly designed, experimental aircraft and overcome male reluctance to fly the B-29 bomber. Over 60 years have passed since the first of these wings proudly flew on jackets of women who would make history both for the military service and for their country. Within two years, they logged 60 million flight miles in domestic wartime service and flew every plane in America's World War II arsenal. They were called WASPs: Women's Air Force Service Pilots.

~ EILEEN MCDARGH, SPEAKER, SELF-TITLED KIDS OF WASPS (KOWS)

Author of Gifts from the Mountain: Simple Truths for Life's Complexities

www.eileenmcdargh.com

© 2009

Flying High

In 1979, I entered Vanderbilt University as a freshman. I attended college on a United States Air Force Reserve Officer Training Corps (USAF ROTC) four-year scholarship. When I graduated, I earned the commission of Second Lieutenant and went to Columbus Air Force Base, Mississippi for my first assignment on Active Duty.

There, I spent a year learning how to fly the T-37 and the T-38 after which I was awarded my silver wings as an Air Force Pilot. My first assignment was to Langley AFB, Virginia to fly Operational Support Airlift (OSA) for the 375th Wing, 1402d Squadron, Detachment 1. I flew there for three years where I attained the rank of Captain, became a flight examiner instructor, aircraft commander in the C-12F and had the opportunity to fly some of the highest dignitaries in the military and civilian world. OSA is a unique mission and is entirely devoted to flying distinguished visitors to and from important meetings and conferences to any destination.

During my tenure at Langley, I flew Senator Kennedy, Representative Dan Daniels, the U.S. Ambassador to West Germany and innumerable general officers. One of my most enjoyable tours was a short mission to Ramstein AB, Germany where I spent two months in support of United States Air Forces in Europe (USAFE). I was one of the last pilots to fly the Berlin Corridors, which were soon removed with the end of the Cold War and the opening up of the skies over Eastern Europe. Aside from flying, I served my Detachment as the Unit Executive Officer, directly handling the day-to-day operations of the office of the Commander.

After Langley, I moved to Dover AFB, Delaware, where I spent the remainder of my career on Active Duty flying C-5s for the 457th Air Wing, 9th Airlift Squadron. I served in support of the liberation of Panama from General Manuel Noriega. I was a member of the first—and only C-5 Aircrew—permitted to remain overnight at the remote station in the USSR,

Semipalatinsk, Kazakhstan, where we were supporting our troops analyzing Soviet nuclear testing for the START Treaty.

I was the first aircraft commander qualified in Combat Aircrew Training (CAT) which was a program designed to readily supply combat-ready aircrews at a moment's notice anywhere in the world to perform any mission required by national security interests. I also served as an air refueling Aircraft Commander throughout our two-year tenure in *Operation Desert Shield* and *Operation Desert Storm*, now known as The First Gulf War.

While at Dover, I slid right back into the job of Executive Officer for the Commander and, while there, completed Squadron Officer School in residence at Maxwell AFB, Mississippi.

In 1992, I left Active Duty and briefly served in the Reserves at Dover. Before long, however, I was hired by Detachment One of the National Guard Bureau, stationed at Andrews AFB, Maryland. There I worked for the next 13 years as a Boeing 727 pilot, flying the highest dignitaries in the world to locations that spanned the globe. I've been to Argentina, Greenland, Mongolia, Okinawa, Canada and everywhere in between. The majority of our flying took place in the former Soviet Satellites as we supported the United States Congressional Committees on their delegations to evaluate American expenditures and interests abroad. These missions are commonly referred to as CODELs. I also flew the Defense Advisory Committee on Women in the Services (DACOWITS) to conferences and other important activities.

While flying the B-727, I was able to see such marvelous sights as the Waterfalls at Iguaçu, Brazil; the remains of the Berlin Wall in Berlin, Germany; Thule AB, Greenland in minus 70°F degree weather; Buenos Aires, Argentina; the highest peak in South America, Aconcagua; do a low-level fly-by of Mt. Rushmore, South Dakota; Bratislava, Romania; Sophia, Bulgaria; Vilnius, Lithuania and many other exotic places.

While at Andrews AFB, I completed Air Command and Staff College and earned my Master's Degree in History from Washington College,

Chestertown, Maryland. In 1996, I graduated from Catholic University's Columbus School of Law and became a practicing attorney in the civilian world while continuing to fly for the District of Columbia National Guard. Around that time, my Detachment was reorganized under the 113th Flying Wing, and it was our Wing that first flew over the smoldering remains of the western wall of the Pentagon on September 11, 2001.

We were immediately activated and posted within the District to defend our nation's Capital as it was under direct attack from an unknown enemy. I remained on Active Duty until I retired as a senior Major and Flight Examiner in the B-727, and an Aircraft Commander in the C-21A in 2005. It's been a great experience and a wonderful career.

~ANNE ARMSTRONG

It's the moment you think you can't that you realize you can.
~CELINE DION

No life is so hard that you can't make it easier by the way you take it.
~ELLEN GLASGOW

Intention without action is useless.
~CAROLINE MYSS

Surround yourself with people who take their work seriously, but not themselves, those who work hard and play hard.
~COLIN POWELL

USAF Female Warriors Lead the Way

Airman First Class (A1C) Elizabeth (Liz) Jacobson was 21-years-old when she became the first USAF Security Forces member to be killed in action in Iraq. She also was the first Air Force female to be killed in action in Operation Iraqi Freedom. She was posthumously awarded the *Bronze Star* and *Purple Heart* for her bravery and service. Airman Jacobson was killed on a convoy near Camp Bucca, Iraq, on September 28, 2005 when her vehicle was hit by an improvised explosive device (IED).

Liz had been in Iraq for just over three months. Her fellow Airmen noted that "Liz was a great trooper. She always sought the hardest challenges and she never gave up. She worked very hard to get on the convoy section and had only been working it for a couple of weeks when the incident occurred. She was a bright and intelligent young lady who cared deeply for her country and the military."

"She was an outstanding Airman who embraced life and took on all the challenges and responsibilities with extraordinary commitment to her country, her comrades and her family," said Col. Scott Bethel, 17th Training Wing commander at Goodfellow AFB, Texas, the Base from where Liz was deployed. "Her dedication to the U.S. Air Force and serving her country was evident in all aspects of who this young lady was," he added.

Liz Jacobson epitomizes the increasing and important role played by females in the USAF Security Forces, one of the largest career fields in the USAF. Over the years, female security force members have become an integral part of the force. They go most everywhere that their male counterparts serve and they serve with pride, passion, and dedication to their team members, the security forces career field and the USAF. It is not surprising that a female was the first security forces member killed in action in Iraq.

Given the ever increasing role of female security force members, it is equally not surprising that the Air Force "Top Cop" and Chief of all security

forces is Brigadier General Mary Kay Hertog. She is a career security police officer and the daughter of a retired security police officer. Over the years General Hertog worked her way up through all the commissioned ranks and became the first female to lead the Air Force Security Forces. General Hertog is now Director of Security Forces, Headquarters U.S. Air Force, Washington, D.C. She is the focal point for force protection within the Air Force and is responsible for planning and programming the security for more than 30,000 Active Duty and Reserve components' security forces at locations worldwide. She provides policy and oversight for protecting Air Force installations from terrorism, criminal acts, sabotage and acts of war, and she ensures security forces are trained, equipped and ready to support contingency and exercise plans.

She has been a tireless advocate for watching over all the thousands of troops in her command and she is particularly proud of her female *warriors.* She is an outstanding role model for all her troops and particularly females who were able to see, first hand, that one of their own had climbed to the top and that the path was there for them to follow.

Brigadier General Hertog recently celebrated another "first," as she was promoted to Major General. She thus became the first security forces chief to make a 2nd Star while serving in that position and the first female security force member to achieve that accomplishment.

The heart of a military woman is vividly illustrated by these two outstanding women, A1C Jacobson and Major General Mary Kay Hertog. Two women, one at the bottom end of the rank structure and one at the top end. Both are outstanding examples of "female warriors" in today's USAF Security Forces. One made the ultimate sacrifice, the other continues to do everything she can to blaze new trails and continue as a great leader and role model for her Airmen.

~DAVE COULIE

Information on Elizabeth Jacobson: http://vspa.com/ElizabethJacobson.htm

Bio on Major General Hertog: http://www.af.mil/information/bios/bio.asp?bioID=7996

No Women Allowed

Noumea, New Caledonia 1981: Out of a 200-person crew on the ice-breaker, only ten-percent were women; and, of those, only three of us were officers. This was a time when women serving aboard ships were a bit of a novelty, even in the United States. No matter where we went, we seemed to stir things up just by being there. When we pulled into Noumea, our captain accepted an invitation to attend a reception hosted by the French Navy. All 25 of our officers were "encouraged" to attend (both male and female).

We certainly turned a lot of heads when the three of us walked into the room. This traditionally male club didn't even have a female head (restroom). Yes, the women were quite a topic. I overheard it several times in different conversations. Finally, one brave Frenchman explained it to me, "Women are not, under any circumstances (including open houses) permitted aboard French Navy vessels—period." Therefore, the invitation to tour their ship was not extended to the three of us.

~JEANNE CASSIDY, CAPTAIN, USCGR (RET.)

Having faith in a Source greater than and one with myself has empowered me to breakthrough every setback in my life — and I would not trade any of those events for the character it's developed in me. God is always working Her plan! Walk every day with faith!

~SHERYL ROUSH, SPEAKER, AUTHOR OF *SPARKLE-TUDES!*™

Never be afraid to trust an unknown future to a known God.

~CORRIE TEN BOOM

Tributes and Accolades

Setting a Great Example for Others to Follow

Twenty years ago, as an Army Major at Fort Lewis, Washington, I had the honor of serving as Secretary to the General Staff of the 9th Infantry Division (Motorized). Our commander was Major General John M. Shalikashvili, who later became a four-star general and Chairman of the Joint Chiefs of Staff. But this story is not about him; it is about his wife, Joan.

Many outstanding military leaders accomplish great things and achieve fame. However, their wives achieve equally great things, but without the fame. From here, I will depart from normal storytelling style and simply present an award recommendation I wrote for Joan Shalikashvili. It tells the story of a great military spouse.

Mrs. Joan Shalikashvili is nominated for the Forces Command Certificate of Appreciation for Volunteer Service for her exceptionally distinguished contributions to the welfare of soldiers and family members of the 9th Infantry Division (Motorized) and the entire Fort Lewis Community.

From the day of her arrival at Fort Lewis in June 1987, Joan and her husband Major General John M. Shalikashvili, established a tremendously successful command climate in 9th Infantry Division (Motorized) that is second to none. She helped promote a caring climate throughout the command by showing that she cared. Her enthusiasm and encouragement motivated others to serve the community and their units, and helped make Fort Lewis the fantastic place to live and work that it is today. Her vast contributions include both significant personal volunteer service; and, training and developing officers and enlisted wives throughout the command.

In her role as first lady of the Division, she demonstrated exceptional organizational ability in her development and support of other wives in their roles as part of a command team from Division down to company level. She encouraged strong family support groups in every unit, ensuring chains of concern were established at every level. This organization proved invaluable during a battalion deployment to the Sinai for duty as Multi-national Force and Observers, a unit deployment to Honduras with Joint Task Force Bravo, numerous deployments to Yakima Firing Center, two brigade rotations through the National Training Center, and other unit deployments to Europe and Korea. Because of the network Joan had established, family members stayed informed and their needs were met during these challenging periods of separation. Each month, Joan spent countless hours gathering information from all post activities to share with leaders' wives in both the officer and noncommissioned officer channels, working extremely well with the wife of the Division Command Sergeant Major to ensure that all soldiers and their families were cared for, regardless of rank.

Mrs. Shalikashvili recognized that one person cannot do it all, so she developed an ambitious program to train other wives throughout the command. She organized a group of wives to design and conduct seminars for company-level leaders' wives from all units in the Division. These seminars covered communication skills, meeting management, family support groups, providing information through newsletters, leadership styles, protocol and etiquette, group norms, brainstorming, and what it means to be a leader's wife. The seminars proved successful and were repeated for battalion-level leaders' wives, enhancing the command climate and support level in 9th Infantry Division units. Joan also worked with wives of brigade commanders to share her invaluable insight and experiences with them. With her charming personality she quickly made every woman feel at ease and comfortable.

Joan also played a key role in the development of semi-annual off-site conferences for battalion and brigade commanders, and command sergeants major, and the Division staff, as well as, their spouses. She orchestrated exciting agendas for the spouses and utilized local talent to deliver content covering self-esteem, delegation, seminars or conferences production, health risk assessment, and enhancing unit and community life through information exchange.

Each event Mrs. Shalikashvili organized or attended increased future community service by attendees. The inspiration that made this possible was Joan's personal volunteer service. During her two years at Fort Lewis she spent over 2,100 volunteer hours working with Army Community Services (ACS). Each Friday, she spent three hours at the ACS Volunteer Desk warmly greeting new arrivals, providing them with welcome packets and guiding new soldiers and their families to the many sources of help, service, and recreation on the installation and in the surrounding community. She has faithfully and energetically served on the Commissary Council, Army and Air Force Exchange Service Council, Officers' Club Council, and Family Advocacy Council. She actively supported the Youth Services Booster Club, the Fort Lewis Red Cross, and the Washington State Special Olympics.

Joan was also instrumental in establishing the Octofoil Clinic, the medical clinic on main post providing direct care to family members of Division soldiers. She gave her personal time, money, and energy to the development of the clinic, including purchasing curtains, organizing a painting party, and providing waiting room toys. Through her dedicated efforts many other wives were inspired to also volunteer their services.

Mrs. Shalikashvili also provided outstanding support to the Officers' Wives' Club (OWC). She attended all general membership, special, and executive board meetings and provided appropriate policy guidance on all OWC matters. She served as an advisor to the Welfare, Budget, Nominating, Round-Up, and Holiday Bazaar Committees. Joan hosted numerous functions such as Newcomers' Coffees, Tour of Homes, and appreciation luncheons in her home. She was always available to anyone at anytime for anything—day or night. Her warm personality and tireless efforts over the past two years enabled OWC to successfully raise over $70,000 for community welfare.

When wives think of Joan Shalikashvili, the words that come to mind are: caring, loyal, loving, warm, kind, down-to-earth, heart of gold, conscientious, organized, dedicated, selfless, devoted, true volunteer, giving, sharing, standard setter, and more! Joan made the 9th Infantry Division (Motorized) a true family—one that cares and has spirit. Her distinguished service to soldiers and families at Fort Lewis truly merits recognition beyond the installation level. Joan Shalikashvili richly deserves the Forces Command Certificate of Appreciation for Volunteer Service.

The commander of I Corps and Fort Lewis, Washington, Lieutenant General William H. Harrison, endorsed the award recommendation with a handwritten note to the four-star commander of U.S. Forces Command: "Joan Shali truly has made Fort Lewis a better place to live, to work, to train and to play. She and John are the epitome of the Command Team— I strongly recommend your approval of this award." The award was well deserved—and approved.

In this day, with significant numbers of American troops stationed all over the world, and especially in two major zones of conflict, it is reassuring to know that there are many outstanding military spouses doing extraordinary work in support of those troops and their families. Joan Shalikashvili is a great model for others to follow.

~ROY CRAWFORD, LIEUTENANT COLONEL, U.S. ARMY (RET.), ADJUTANT
GENERAL'S CORPS

If you're not having fun you're not doing it right.
~JOHN F. KENNEDY

A dream doesn't become reality through magic; it takes sweat, determination and hard work.
~COLIN POWELL

Guardians of the Pacific Graveyard

Gentle wind becomes driving rain
Severe weather advisory comes again
Jagged rocks beckon thirty foot seas
On our sixty foot fisher, misery

An ink black night with no horizon found
But that deafening wind, the banshee's sound
Like a blind-side hit, no way to know
Rogue wave's impact, our ship, she rolls

Lights flicker, Oh God, the engines fail
Terror strikes, the captain goes pale
We're taking water . . . have no control
In Davy Jones' grasp, his icy, deadly hold

Emergency power, then Marconi's gift
No time to waste, quickly key the switch
MAYDAY! MAYDAY! Give our long and lat
God does anyone hear us? No sound . . . just static

Then God's voice crackles back, or so it seems
"I have your position fixed" responds Coast Guard Station Cape D
HOLD ON NOW LADS! The skipper barks and commands
"The Coastie's are comin' so against Davy we stand!"

The helo arrives on station, like an angel in the night
But our fisher's badly listing, and pitching too high
DON'T DROP THE BASKET! It'll tangle in our gear
The crew's hope for salvation, again fades, disappears

continued

Then through the cold black, pierces yet another light
Fear . . . confusion . . . reality, it's a 47 Motor Life!
Her twin diesels a fury, driving headlong into the storm
Her crew steeled against the cold . . . focused, calm

Over before it begins, the fisher's crew now safely on board
Their vessel succumbs, The Graveyard of the Pacific claims one more
But no souls for you tonight Davy, you haunting Son of a B
Because we are The Guardians of the Pacific Graveyard,
Coast Guard Station Cape D

~KENNETH ZAPP~

Epilogue

To all the brave men and women of the United States Coast Guard, and especially those of CG Station Cape Disappointment: Thank you for your selfless
acts of service and ongoing, unrecorded bravery—"There is no greater love
than a man should lay down his life for his friends." (John 15:13) In loving
memory of our son, FN Scott Bradley Long, who lovingly gave those MLB
diesels their fury. Until we, too, come home to meet you in Heaven, *Semper
Paratus.*

~KEN AND KIM ZAPP

*From Mom's heart and Dad's pen, in honor, admiration and pride of their son, Scott
Bradley Long. Apr. 2, 1982—Feb. 12, 2005. Fallen on earth, but now raised in Heaven with
rejoice at another son's homecoming.*

Scott B. Long, FN, Coast Guard, Cape Disappointment

I Would Give My Life

In 1990, our Unit, 45th Station Hospital, was deployed in the 1st Desert Storm. I was Chief Nurse and had to involuntarily transfer Nurses from the 313th MASH to the 45th.

I remember a phone call to two nurses, both of whom I knew personally, professionally, and militarily. They had a seven-month-old baby girl at home. I called and informed them I needed to take one of them—not both—and I would let them make the decision. I did not want to take both of them away from the baby, and at that time, we had the ability to let them decide. Twenty minutes later they called back saying, "The baby is going to the grandparents and we are both ready to go." I tried to discourage them from both leaving, but they insisted they were ready. They went and served admirably.

Later that night, I went home and talked to my husband and 93-year-old grandmother about the amazing choice this couple had made. My grandmother asked me if I had volunteered to go, and I quickly informed her I had signed an agreement years before saying if I was called, I would go. She had a hard time understanding that, but my husband said, "We both knew you had something else in your life to do, so we will be here when you get home."

My Assistant Chief Nurse was an AGR Nurse at that time. Her name was Captain Joyce Clarkson. She arranged special, extra time for my husband and me (nine hours) and then I was off, out of country, to go forward and make assignments at the 7th Medical Command. She remained behind with the Unit at the MOB site to complete the deployment paperwork, close the Unit, take care of the troops, and was to meet up with me later.

When I learned the Unit was to be sent to 17 different locations after the main body arrived overseas, I tried repeatedly to call Captain Clarkson to inform her. For years, the soldiers in the 45th had been told they were training together because if they were ever deployed they would go as a Unit, to a fixed facility (we even knew the location), and would all remain together.

Captain Clarkson was never available, and I could not understand why. December 25, I found out why, as I entered an aircraft looking for her. I was informed she had taken my name out of the lottery, and volunteered to go to Saudi, so I could stay as Chief Nurse with "our" troops. She didn't want me to know because she knew I would fight for her to come with all of "her" soldiers.

She had remained with "her" soldiers up until they deployed. At the last minute, while trying to help a soldier (and having already changed into civilian clothes to catch a plane so she could go spend the last 25 hours with her Mom and Dad), she was not allowed on the tarmac to see her soldiers off. I had to face all of our great Soldiers and inform them they were being split up, and help them to understand the reasons why. In those days, the terrorism was rampant and, Saudi was not the place any nurse wanted to be—yet Captain Clarkson went in my place, and took care of soldiers that needed her nursing expertise.

All of the 45th soldiers performed their duties to full expectation. Those who went to Saudi had extremely frightening experiences, and suffer more trauma than any of us who were filling in needs in other locations, but not in the forward area of the battle.

What people need to hear is that *any deployment*—no matter how short or how long—takes human beings, family members—away from home and into very dangerous and unknown situations. There were a great many grandparents who went with us. It is extremely frightening for families to not know where their soldier is and when they might hear from them again. In those times, there were no cell phones. There was one AT&T phone for 183 people, but no time to stand in a two-to-three-hour long line to try to call home. We were busy turning a relatively small hospital into a larger capacity facility, and worked many long hours to be prepared for the unknown number of casualties.

It was not until my husband's death, that my daughter shared with me his December 24 experience and her "meltdown" after I left. She had a very loving husband who was extremely supportive of her. She also had two beau-

tiful little girls to whom she had to try to explain why Grandma was not here for the family's holiday activities and, not for Christmas either. She felt very alone and frightened, not knowing where I was for a long time. Everyone needs to know deployments are terrifying for everyone; and, no matter how much you may dislike the conflict it is so important to support the troops.

LTC Clarkson, my then Assistant Chief Nurse, and I are probably the closest friends each one of us has ever had to this day. I would give my life for her as I know she put her life in jeopardy, going to Saudi in my place.

Please support the troops you know. Send them prayers and positive thoughts each and every day, because you never know what they might be facing in their own minds and hearts today.

~COLONEL LARRIE NOBLE, (RET.)

If we have to use force, it is because we are America.
We are the indispensable nation. We stand tall.
We see further into the future.
~MADELEINE ALBRIGHT

More than 48 million men and women have served America well and
faithfully in military uniform.
~STEVE BUYER

Our men and women in uniform deserve the best intelligence possible to
help them protect America.
~CHRIS CANNON

Putting Heart Into It

My parents, and their friends, were part of Tom Brokow's Greatest Generation. I came along as part of their baby boom. Growing up, I remember vividly visits from Vi, one of my mother's friends. She had both joined the Air Force during the War and had been married to an Army Officer. Her friends and I are blessed that she is still with us, but that's another story. This story is about her service and how she shared her gifts.

When the Army found out Vi could sing, and sing she did—with the USO. After her discharge she stayed with the USO for a time, continuing to go around the world entertaining the troops wherever the troops were located.

She never visited us without bringing presents and I looked forward to each visit, keen on hearing her stories and anxious for some small, exotic gift I know was part of the trip. I still have some of her travel gifts—cuff links from Norway, a print from Japan; the ski sweaters have long-since worn out—to remind me of her journeys and her visits between shows and travels.

Vi's stories were seldom about her travels, but they were rich in detail about the shows she and her fellow entertainers put on, in remote locations, under trying conditions and with sparse props but always, always, with an eager and supportive audience. One of her favorite gambits, when serving as Master of Ceremonies for a show was to dedicate a song, usually one of her favorites, like "Summertime" to the person on base who had been there the longest.

The men and women who made up her audiences were her joy and she would tell us interesting anecdotes about audience members seen from afar, and warmer comments about those she had shared time with.

One story she recounted lingers, no doubt a product of the times. During one trip with her troupe to Iceland (and the Arctic Circle Command), to perform "Pajama Game," they broke the larger group down into mini-troupes of four or five who fanned out to visit even the smallest, most remote, bases. While there, and during a performance, the loudspeaker announced, "Would the men from unit "X" please report for duty." The men left quietly and nothing further was said. The next day, in speaking with one of the pilots, Vi found out the base had been buzzed by a Soviet bomber. Fighter planes were scrambled and the bomber was followed back toward Soviet airspace.

The details have faded in my memory, but her joy in her work and her passion for her audiences was apparent. From that time as a little boy, I remember both the high profile Bob Hope trips to visit the troops that were televised, and Vi's stories, perhaps to much smaller venues where the performances may have been even more important, that were heard about only by a few.

They say all performers have their heart in their work. On those special stages, in dark times, where the show might easily have been the last for some audience members, that heartbeat becomes even more special, or so it seems.

~JOHN REDDISH, BABY BOOMER AND FAN OF SERVICE MEMBERS

Basic beauty lies in the way a woman walks;
it is health and an attitude to life.
~NANCY ASTOR

If the eyes are looked upon as the windows to the soul.
then a smile must be the doorway the heart.
~UNKNOWN

WWII Flight Nurse

The movie *Saving Private Ryan* looked authentic to Army Air Force Flight Nurse Lieutenant Merilys Brown. She would know since she was one of the first females on Omaha Beach just days after the June 6, 1944 D-Day invasion of France. As soon as the Allies got a toe-hold, the combat engineers with their bulldozer tanks started to blade out a crude airstrip just above the beach. They laid down the metal interlocking Marston matting and the first U.S. combat runway was put into action on French soil. Because the C-47s hauled in combat troops and equipment they could not paint red crosses on the sides of the planes. So when the aircraft lifted off of Omaha Beach they were not protected under the *Geneva Convention* as non-combat medical planes.

A makeshift tent hospital was set up next to the runway and the injured allies, as well as German troops, were triaged to determine who was seriously wounded enough to be flown back to England, but not so serious that they would die in transit. Medical evacuation from the battlefield by air was new to the Army. Prior to WWII, the wounded were transported in trucks, field ambulances, and two-wheeled handcarts. The landings on Omaha Beach were the first time C-47s with one Flight Nurse and one Medical Technician were flown into a hot combat zone to get the wounded out of France and back across the English Channel.

A thousand-bed field hospital was established in Prestwick, Scotland and the C-47s were flown directly to it after clearing French airspace. In the first days after D-Day a single C-47 Air Evac crew could fly three missions off Omaha Beach in a day. Lieutenant Brown was temporarily posted at Prestwick to fly C-54 Air Evac missions out of Scotland using that vital air bridge, transporting the wounded on a 13-hour flight back to New York. Many of these wounded patients had never been away from home before joining the Army, never been wounded in combat, and never been on an

airplane. All three created increased stress factors for the Flight Nurses on the long trip to the United States.

The first class of Army Flight Nurses completed training in February of 1943. Over one million patients were evacuated by air during WWII, with 4,707 wounded transported in one day. In WWI, all the wounded returned to the U.S. on troop ships and actual military hospital ships. In WWII, one fifth of all patients returned to the States by Air Evacuation. Speed saves lives in combat. The Army Air Force had 500 Flight Nurses and formed 31 Medical Air Evacuation Transport Squadrons to meet the needs of the seriously wounded in WWII.

I met now retired Captain (Army equivalent Colonel) Merilys Brown of the U.S. Public Health Commissioned Corps at the Labor Day weekend 2007 convention in Colorado Springs of the WWII Flight Nurses Association and the Society of Air Force Nurses. There where seven combat tested, WWII nursing aircrew members at the convention. These nurses aimed high before the phrase was fashionable. They set the standard for today's Air Force medical evacuation flying missions.

~MAJOR VAN HARL, USAF (RET.)

Editor's Note: Contact the WWII Flight Nurses Association and the Society of Air Force Nurses to be in contact with this Veteran's organization.

Did You Know . . . ? When allied armies reached the Rhine, the first thing men did was pee in it. This was pretty universal from the lowest private to Winston Churchill (who made a big show of it) and Gen. Patton, who had himself photographed in the act.

~WWII HISTORY BUFF COL D. G. SWINFORD, USMC (RET.)

Yes Sir, Ma'am, or Honey?

Wow, Our Little Girl is an Air Force Officer? Even as a young child, Christine, our second daughter, had a unique ability to problem-solve and influence others to peaceful solutions. She could see the playground group who was excluding someone and calmly alter the guidelines to bring the outsider into the circle. She would see opportunities for leadership when others simply saw problems. She also adored her father, Dwain, a former Air Force officer who retired from the National Guard.

So why were we surprised one night at the end of a month when she called us from Seattle where she was living while going to community college? She said she had good news and bad news, which did we want to hear first? Her dad said, "Give us the good news." "Well, I am dating the cutest Air Force National Guard Recruiter," she replied. "You don't even have to tell us the bad news, it is that he needed to make quota and so you joined up?" her Dad said. "Gosh Dad, that would not be right, but I did sign up from one of his friends," Christine sighed.

As always, she threw herself 100 percent into everything she did. She took advantage of all the training, exercises and mentoring available to her. Moving up the enlisted ranks, while finishing college and working fulltime in retail management, she honed her ability to get things done and be organized. As a single mother, she made sure her personal family was well taken care of and then served her extended family, the United States of America.

In 2002, she was called on to go to United Arab Emirates (UAE) working as communication support for the Air Force. While there, an opening for an officer opened up in her home squadron. She realized that she had a small window of opportunity to pursue the paperwork, testing and training in order to become an officer. The age limit to apply was 35 years old, and she was within four months of that date.

She says, "This was a natural extension of my career goals and an opportunity to display what I believed in and who I wanted to be. I am extremely proud to be a part of the Air Force National Guard. Their mission, which is one I can totally represent with pride, is to support and defend the Constitution of the United States against all enemies foreign and domestic. This includes building up communities where we serve."

As for her role as a woman in the service, she says it has never been a disadvantage, nor has being 5'6" and 128 pounds. She says, "Being one of six children in a military family taught me how to get along, negotiate and be a team player. Those skills have served me well in thinking of ways to make adjustments in how I accomplish my goals. I respect myself and I treat others with the same respect and that is how you lead."

In 2008, the Northwest was hit with record snowfall and unprecedented blizzards. The Washington National Guard units were called on to shovel snow from the roofs of neighborhood schools so the children would be safe. Local families brought them hot chocolate, sandwiches and thank you messages for the work they did. Working in local areas to build and strengthen communities by providing service of time, talent and treasure (monetary donations) is one of the special hallmarks of the National Guard. As a member of the command staff of the unit, Christine encourages all members to take an active part in their own communities and neighborhoods.

She says, "For my kids and other young adults I hope to set an example by upholding the core values of the National Guard: Excellence in all we do; Service before self; and, Integrity first. If they can emulate these standards and character traits, they will see and experience what makes America great and be proud to contribute to the freedom we enjoy."

As parents of Christine L. Wright, whether we call her sir, ma'am or honey, we know that America is in good hands with women like her in leadership positions.

~JUDY H. WRIGHT, SPEAKER, AUTHOR

www.ArtichokePress.com

© 2009

Wisdom

Lessons from Petty Officer Mama Bear

This is a story of power. This is a military story, but it doesn't involve shooting people or facing mortal danger. It is a story of how an 18-year-old young woman found personal power she didn't know she had.

When I graduated high school in 1981, I didn't have a dime saved for college. Funny thing is, I was absolutely certain I would go to college. I applied and was accepted at several schools and was even offered small scholarships to a few. I decided to go to the University of Puget Sound in Tacoma, Washington. My father lived in Williston, North Dakota, where there was an oil boom going on in the early 1980s. He suggested I come up there and find work. Sounded good to me, so the morning after graduation, we headed north.

After a very short stint at McDonalds, I met Dee, the head waitress next door at the Red Fox Inn. Dee said she could hire me full-time for $4.50 an hour plus tips. I made good money at the Red Fox and squirreled it diligently away, yet at the end of the summer, I only had about $2,000 in the bank. This didn't touch the $8,000 I needed each year for school. I faced a difficult decision. Either I would go to school and get student loans for the first year, hoping for scholarship money the following year (which the recruiter assured me would be available), go to one of the state schools that had accepted me, or . . . what?

My dad sat down with me and suggested the possibility of the military. He and his brothers had all served and were able to go to college when they were done "on Uncle Sam's dime." The Navy clicked with me and I called the recruiter. Before I knew it, I was signed up to go with a guaranteed job but I had to wait six months before starting. It was a very long six months in

cold North Dakota. On March 1, 1982, I found myself at the AAFES station in Grand Forks, North Dakota, pledging to "uphold and defend the Constitution of the United States of America." Off to the airport and Orlando, Florida, here we come!

Boot Camp is Boot Camp. Seventy-two of us were in our company and I followed my dad's advice to "keep my nose clean and mind your manners." I studied hard, followed orders, and sang in the chapel choir. When Work Week came, we were anxious to hear our assignments. The grand masses all went to the chow hall to work the food lines. Some were sent to the induction center to receive the new recruits. The company leaders got to stay in the compartment where we lived and pretty much do whatever they wanted. I was in the outskirts of that group so I was assigned the Recruit Division Master at Arms. The Division was the building where we lived and this position meant I reported to the woman in charge of the building, the actual Master at Arms. I was to report to the girl who was the current *holder of the mop* to get trained. While I don't remember her name, I was incredibly grateful for her training and will always remember her hearty "aye-AYE!" in affirmative response to requests. The most important thing, she told me, was to never piss off the Master at Arms. This woman was a she-bear and would rather rip out your guts rather than as look at you. Do exactly what she tells you and do it right. Definitely never ask for a favor.

I learned that my job that week consisted of changing light bulbs, unplugging toilets, and buffing the floors with one of those buffing machines school custodians use. I ran and fetched and answered with my own "aye-AYE!" and seemed to make my boss satisfied. Then the big assignment came.

Petty Officer Mama Bear took me outside and showed me a herd of dead washers and dryers and said my job was to put them into the flatbed truck parked nearby. There would be a group of *rejects* coming to help and my job was to make it happen. Rejects were men and women who, for whatever reason, were judged to be incompatible with the Navy and were on their way

home. Oh, boy. Tough guys. I was the good kid in school, did as I was told, got good grades. What was I going to do with these guys?

Here they came, a group of about ten men of between 18–30 years old. I could tell they were not there to work. As soon as they sauntered up and the "adults" left, they pulled out cigarettes, told jokes, leaned against the truck . . . generally anything but what I was asking them to do. "Ok, guys, we are here to load these washers and dryers into the truck. Let's go."

Chuckles, and rolling of the eyes, are definitely not going to get the job done and, definitely going to get me in trouble with Petty Officer Mama Bear. Something snapped inside me as I remembered the advice I got from my mentor: never piss off the Master at Arms, do exactly what she tells you and do it right. I was NOT going to get in trouble for these rejects. I called cadence for my company, for crying out loud, so I knew I had a loud voice. I was a Girl Scout, the drum major for my high school band, and our school's representative for Girls' State. I knew I had leadership in me.

"Alright, get those cigarettes out. We've got work to do and I'm not putting up with any of you. Now get to work!" I commanded their attention! Everyone froze. I heard a lot of "Sheesh, lady, relax," but they got right on it. Before you knew it all of the washers and dryers were loaded. I thanked them for their hard work and sent them back to their barracks.

When I reported back to Petty Officer Mama Bear that we were finished she seemed a bit surprised but I could also see a crack of a smile. She would never say so, but I think she was proud of me. That day, I found power within me that I really never knew was there. When push comes to shove and I need to get something done, I know I can do it. It's been over 25 years since my time at Boot Camp in Orlando, Florida. This story is one of the few I tell about my time in the Navy because it is about the day I found my power.

~PAMELA WILSON

What Makes Your Heart Sing?

It was a difficult time in my life, having just turned 21. I had been a difficult and lost teenager making poor choices whenever there were choices to be made. I had my excuses. After all, my father had been an alcoholic and left us when I was 14. My mother had to work two jobs to make ends meet. She worked from eight in the morning to midnight six days a week, so as a teenager, I was left to roam the streets. I did that . . . and I did it well.

Somehow I managed to graduate from high school and I went to work for the printing company where my mom worked. Still a lost soul, I continued to make my poor choices but I had a dream that I would break away from the mid-sized Kentucky town I had been raised in. Even then, I knew in my heart that if I was ever going to make anything of my life I would need to break away from the family and friends that encouraged me in ways that did not serve me.

Soon, I went to work for an attorney's office. I was so proud of myself for getting the job. Almost as soon as I started in the position, it became apparent that because of my lack of discipline and my lack of self-confidence, I was going to sabotage it. After six months, they fired me. I was absolutely devastated. I decided, then and there, that I was going to the recruiter's office to enlist in the Air Force.

I passed the tests with *flying colors*. I could have my choice of any career field. I thought and evaluated and chose the position of Early Warning Radar Repair Technician. I chose it because I wanted to learn something that no one else I knew would know. I decided I wanted to learn about electronics because I did not understand electricity, and I wanted to know the magic of it. This career field had the second longest training time of all the career fields in Electronics—40 weeks.

After six weeks of Basic Training at Lackland, I was assigned to Keesler Air Force Base in Biloxi, Mississippi. I was assigned to a short-term squadron even though I was there for the long-term. Most of the women would

come and go within nine weeks—except for about ten of us. Because we were there for so long, we had a lot of freedom and we got to know many of the instructors.

One day, just a month before I was scheduled to go to Makaw Air Force Station at Neah Bay in Washington State, my friend, Eleanor, and I decided we would go to the Airmen's Club. Butch, who had been our instructor in Basic Electronics, was working there. He invited us to a party that night at the apartment he shared with two other instructors. One we knew—Mike. The second roommate, Randy, we did not know. I had seen him at the Airmen's Club working but we had never been introduced.

Eleanor and I went to the party; and Randy and I met. We stayed up all that night talking. About four o'clock that morning, he lent me his car to go back to the barracks and I was hooked. To make a long story short, 2½ weeks later we were married at his apartment. Because I was due to go to Washington State the next week it was critical that we act quickly. Interestingly enough, I know that, because I was such a lost child at that time, if I had not gotten married quickly I would have sabotaged our relationship. Randy and I have been married 33 years. Sometimes, despite what appears to be illogical, when we just trust in what seems right for us, it works out for the best!

My Air Force experience is still part of who I am today. I am a strategist and business coach. I help CEOs and entrepreneurs make good leadership, life and business choices. My military experience is the foundation for the discipline, courage and trust I have in my life. It is that foundation that has helped me to know that I am valuable, and that I have the ability to do anything I set my mind to do. It taught me that I have a lot to offer those around me.

I have accomplished much of which I am very proud, but our children are the shining stars of all of my accomplishments. We raised our two children to believe in themselves. We stopped the cycle of alcohol and drug abuse within my own family that had been started in my father's family.

Both of our children have graduated from college, and my son graduated with his MBA. I attribute the strength of character within them to the lessons that I taught them, based on what I learned in the Air Force.

If I was going to offer one piece of advice to a young person considering enlistment, I'd say be in your integrity. If it makes your heart sing, go for it. Do you feel great pride at being an American? When you see the American flag flying, do you feel the tingling in your body from your head to your toes? If so, you might be made of the right stuff. Trust your heart. If you are looking for that inner strength to make good choices, the military will teach you. We only go around once. *Trust your heart to lead you!*

~KATHIE BOBBITT, EARLY WARNING RADAR REPAIR TECHNICIAN, AIRMAN FIRST CLASS, USAF

www.kinesisdevelopment.com

Face a challenge and find joy in the capacity to meet it.
~AYN RAND

Every time you meet a situation, though you think at the moment it is an impossibility and you go through the tortures of the damned, once you have met it and lived through it you find that forever after you are freer than you were before.
~ELEANOR ROOSEVELT

If you want to accomplish the goals of your life,
you have to begin with the Spirit.
~OPRAH WINFREY

The Secret to Life

Shhhhhhhh . . . I've got a secret. The secret to life isn't about what happens to you, it's what you do with what happens to you. I was a high school dropout; but my story doesn't start there. Statistically speaking, 85 percent of us grew up in some form of dysfunction. Statistics also say that high school dropouts lack the tools necessary to succeed in life!

I was born to two alcoholic parents. When I was a little girl, only five-years-old, my mother, a raging alcoholic left me in a store. When I was 12, she died of alcoholism; and my father died emotionally. By age 16, all my dreams were shattered and stomped on so I rebelled, dropped out of high school, and ran with the bad crowd. At age 18, I came home to find a note . . . of EVICTION on the door of the house where I lived with my father! My father had packed up and moved to Florida and left me in Texas to fend for myself! So I moved into a small apartment with a mattress, a night stand and a Doberman Pinscher named Shema; the only family I had left. I grew up in dysfunction and I dropped out of high school. Statistically I didn't have a chance and that's the bottom line! The secret to life is what you do with what happens to you.

One day, when I was riding on the back of a friend's Harley motorcycle, I suddenly realized I was taking a back seat in my own life and letting circumstances steer my path! That realization led me to decide to experience what I call *risk.*

RISK stands for Realization Initiates Spontaneous Knowledge, which is a four-step approach to a new way of life:

R—Realize all change starts with you.

I—Initiate the change by taking action.

S—Spontaneity occurs as a result of initiating the change.

K—Knowledge of a new way of life is the overall result.

Risk is taking a small chance for a big reward. I took a risk and learned how to ride a Harley, and went from the back seat to the front seat of the

bike—and my life. I took control of the handlebars of my life, and have steered myself to a bright, successful future. No matter what happens to you, you can too!

At 19, I *realized* it was up to me to make my life work. I *initiated* the change by getting my GED and joining the Air Force. *Spontaneity* occurred throughout my military career. I earned two Associate's and a Bachelor's degree, the highest level of professional certification in my career field, and enough awards and decorations to fill a small museum. *Knowledge* of a new way of life was the overall result. I retired as a Master Sergeant in April 2003.

Thirty-two years ago, I was a high school dropout with a horrible past and no chance for a bright future. I worked hard to fight against the loser expectation that statistics, society and my parents put upon me. I have often thought about my decision to drop out, and wish I could have graduated high school and attend my class reunions. Today, I am known as the Pink Biker Chic; a Harley riding bad biker chick, military veteran girlie girl who loves pink! Go Pink!

RISK starts the cycle of spontaneity in your life. Statistically speaking, I didn't have a chance, but when I took a *risk*, knowledge of a new way of life was the resulting gift.

This year, I gave my daughter the gift my parents just couldn't give me; a life filled with love, support and discipline that led her to her high school graduation, which in turn was *my* very special gift 18 June 2009, when my daughter received her diploma and graduated from high school on my birthday. *And*, I received another very special gift when nine days later, this high school dropout was invited to attend her 30-year class reunion!

You see, the secret to life isn't about what happens to you, it's what you do with what happens to you!

~ELDONNA LEWIS FERNANDEZ, MASTER SERGEANT, USAF (RET.)

http://pinkbikerchic.com

COACH

My son announced that he was joining the Army National Guard. He was 17 and a junior in high school. I didn't know what the National Guard was, except that since 2001 they were fighting in Iraq and Afghanistan and helped during hurricanes. The thought of my son coming home in a coffin kept swirling in my head. Kenneth wanted us to talk to the recruiter. He couldn't sign up if we didn't sign the parental consent form. "Yeah," I thought, "I've got the power."

I don't know how we ended up in the recruiter's office. I know I didn't want to be there, nor did my husband. We didn't come from a military family and growing up we didn't know anyone who joined the military. We moved from New York to north Florida, and this is where we had our first experience with people in the military. We lived near two, very large Navy bases. Several people in our community were in the Navy and a few were in the Army. I would see them wearing their uniforms.

In New York, we had a monthly ritual with our children. We would go into the city early on Saturday to the World Trade Towers. There was a great shopping atrium on the bottom of the Towers. We would have coffee, hot chocolate and croissants on the stairs and watch the Chinese brides get their pictures taken. The atrium was beautiful and made a beautiful backdrop for wedding photos. I still remember seeing the brides in these beautiful white gowns, white shoes and black stockings. They changed into traditional Chinese wedding gowns several times during their wedding day. The stockings were for their Chinese gowns. The American gowns were only for photos. After breakfast, we went across the street to Century 21, a great store, walked to Canal Street so Kenneth could buy his gadgets and gawk at the electronics, and then to Chinatown for lunch.

That is what we thought about on 9/11, our Saturday morning ritual. We thought about all the firefighters we knew who were fighting the fires, and who eventually died that day. Andrea, my daughter was sent home because

she was so devastated. Kenneth seemed alright. *Easy going* is a good term for Kenneth. Never up or down, just steady.

Back in the recruiter's office I was wondering how 9/11 affected him. "Is this why he is joining?" I ask myself. I'm sitting on a squishy couch, arms crossed; and, Kenneth is squeezed between me and his dad, whose arms are also crossed. We are not happy. The recruiter is happy, chirpy and in her uniform. She is very talkative. I'm cool and not talkative. She talks and talks and finally I say, "I don't believe you." She is surprised and quiet. Then she shares about her husband, and says he is a Captain in the Army and is now in Iraq. I ask for his email address. She declines my request. However, she is willing to ask him the questions that I want to ask. I tell her I want him to answer the following: "What is it like to be in the National Guard? Why is he in? Why does he stay?" She says she'll let me know when he responds. I don't believe her.

I am an overprotective Mom. I didn't trust the recruiter and didn't trust the Army. I decided to do some investigative reporting. I was going to learn the truth so I could say to my son "No, you can't join because . . . " As a motivational speaker, I travel a lot so I decided to use the travel opportunity to ask questions. I stopped every person I saw in uniform. If you were wearing a Veterans baseball cap I was going to talk to you. I brought many beers for soldiers, though I don't drink, except for a glass of wine every six months or so. I was on a mission. I wanted to know. *Why did you join? What do you get out of it and why do you stay in?* Many were shy. Some were really animated. All shared five core themes. Over and over I heard them. They spell the word *COACH.*

C—CAMARADERIE Everyone, female and male, mentioned the camaraderie. There is a sense of being part of something really important together. There is LOTS of laughter among military personal but there is also this deeper connection that crosses generations, wars and services. They belong together, to their unit, their battalion, their branch and their country.

O—OPPORTUNITIES   Almost every person I spoke to shared about the opportunities they received. Young people 22-years-old in charge of budgets of over $5,000,000 and more. Many shared about the concept of *promote to potential*. You are given opportunities to manage projects, meet VIPs and do amazing acts of bravery because a superior is confident in your ability to get the job done—or there is no one else to do it. So, even if you don't think you can do it, you have to accomplish the task.

A—ADVENTURE WITH DISCIPLINE   Going to different countries, meeting diverse people, and overcoming challenges with courage. Adventure was mentioned but always tied to discipline. Everyone described the power of discipline. They say the discipline taught to them to be adventurous.

C—CELEBRATE   Every promotion is a celebration, every award is acknowl-edged. Transfer of command, retirement and death are all honored and celebrated. There is an understanding that each phase of service is an *honor* and is celebrated. The medals and ribbons all have a purpose. There are clear times for celebration, as well as, times for focus and courage. Both are important.

H—HELP A COMRADE   No solider will be left behind. Every person I spoke to became solemn about leaving a hurt soldier or fallen comrade. They would sacrifice themselves before they left someone behind. For those that lost their comrades and had to leave them behind there was deep, deep pain even after 30 years.

Of all the conversations I had—over 182—it was the dedication to their fellow soldiers that changed me and my decision to sign Kenneth's papers. My son is my light and my joy; and, I would do anything in the world to protect him. I would go to the ends of the Earth to protect him from harm. The pain I felt when I thought about signing his papers tore my heart. However,

after my interviews, I knew one thing for sure. That no matter what, if he was hurt or if something happened to him, his buddies would do everything they could to bring him home to me. They were are as dedicated to him and his buddies, as I would be. I wanted to him to experience COACH. And he wanted the experience.

My husband, David, and I proudly signed his papers and at seventeen my son, Kenneth R. Herbin became a United States Army National Guard Soldier. He has served for over six years and is becoming an officer. COACH has served him well.

~PEGINE ECHEVARRIA, SPEAKER, AUTHOR OF *SOMETIMES YOU NEED TO KICK YOUR OWN BUTT*

www.pegine.com

Remember, if you're headed in the wrong direction, God allows U-turns!
~ALLISON GAPPA BOTTKE

Laugh and the world laughs with you. Cry and you cry with your girlfriends.
~LAURIE KUSLANSKY

Do not follow where the path may lead.
Go instead where there is no path and leave a trail.
~UNKNOWN

When you're down to nothing, God is up to something.
~UNKNOWN

"Do-Over"

Late at night, when all alone,
With the thoughts deep in your head;
Do you think on happiness, laughter and joy,
Or do you dwell on thoughts of dread?

Does the sound of your voice as you spoke through the day
Bring a smile upon your face?
Or were the words that you spoke meant to harm others
Instead of words of kindness, acceptance, and grace?

As you look back upon your actions and choices,
Were they honorable and true?
Or in those late night thoughts in your head,
Do you wish for a "Do-Over" or two?

Good news my friends stuck in that land of dread
Longing for just one more shot;
As long as you're having those thoughts in your head
Finished . . . it is NOT!

Tomorrow will come with its good and its bad
And many choices you must face.
You can choose once again to speak harshly,
Or to speak words of kindness and grace.

Every new day is a chance for that "Do-Over"
To do it all again.
To rejoice in all our differences; to listen;
To learn . . . To be a friend.

Semper Fi,

~KELLEY MOORE~

www.WalkTheTalk.com

With Love, Your Family

It's the Military Way, It's the American Way

I was an Air Force brat, and I say that with the deepest affection and grati-tude because that experience has largely shaped who I am today. In fact, if it weren't for my father's military service, I wouldn't be here, let alone writing this story! Thomas Nicholas Kovacevic was what we called a *lifer* in the United States Air Force.

My parents met when my dad was stationed in Japan during the U.S. Occupation after the Second World War. It was not love at first sight for my Japanese mother. But, my father? He was a goner. After pulling out all the stops and courting my mother for a full year, he finally won. Mom consented to go out with him. Her initial reluctance was not only because he was an American G.I. There were also cultural traditions for her to consider. In Japan, if no sons are born, the designated daughter carries the family name. As an only child, the obligation fell to my mother to marry a Japanese man who would assume her last name, and give their children that name.

The romance was not ideal as far as my mother's family was concerned. But once they got to know the character of my father and his country, they fell in love with him, too, and set aside a cultural tradition that had been practiced for centuries. In February of 1955, my parents were married in a civil ceremony by a Justice of the Peace. Three and a half weeks later, they had a traditional Japanese wedding. My mother wore a bridal kimono and lacquered wig, and painted her face and hands white, like a Japanese por-celain doll. My father also wore a kimono for the ancient day-long ritual.

My parents' marriage is not unlike the military. They both are melt-ing pots representing diversity and integration. While there was still much racial intolerance in our country when my parents were first married, the opposite was true in the U.S. Military. By virtue of their world travels, U.S. servicemen came home with foreign brides and started families of mixed heritage. By virtue of their service, they learned how to cooperate and collaborate. By virtue of their commitment, they contributed wherever they served. My father served in small ways wherever he was, even when not in uniform. It's the Military Way. It's the American Way.

Compassion + Contribution = Community

Master Sergeant Kovacevic taught me compassion, contribution and community, not with words, but actions. I remember so well when we were stationed in the Middle East in Ankara, Turkey. I was in the third-grade. It was a hard time for us. There was no military housing for families, so we lived among the Turkish. The country was underdeveloped and the apartment buildings seemed to be built of sand. We couldn't drink the water or eat the food. We didn't speak the language. Frequent earthquakes rattled the ground and our nerves, and crumbled the buildings.

One particular summer weekend, as my sister and I were playing on the balcony to stay clear of the large population of dogs and cats plagued with rabies, we heard the anguished shrieking of a baby. Scared, we looked to our parents for cues and comfort. They recognized these cries were not coming from a child simply wanting attention. They were the cries of a baby in acute pain. Dad raced down the apartment stairs, following the sickening sounds of devastating pain. We followed, too, and discovered that our apartment manager's baby had been scalded. She had somehow managed to grab the handle of a boiling pot of rice and it toppled on her. I don't know what happened in the panic that followed, since Mom ushered my sister and me back home. She told us that Daddy was going to make sure the baby was taken care of. And he did. Yosef, the apartment manager, could not pay for his daughter's medical care, so my dad did. He bought them food and milk, too. Mom made and delivered meals to the family so they could devote as much time as possible to the care of their injured child.

Not long after that, a fire broke out on one of the bottom floors of our apartment building in the middle of the night. Dad helped Yosef with the orderly evacuation of the building and hauled and manned the garden hoses to spray down the flames while we waited for the arrival of firefighters. From that time on, Dad become the go-to guy when Yosef wasn't around—and sometimes even when he was! Out of these experiences, it ceased to be the Turks and the Yanks. It was no longer *us* and *them*. It was *we*—a priceless lesson that I carry with me today; a lesson in compassion, contribution, and perhaps most importantly, community. It's the Military Way. It's the American Way.

These are just a few stories of how my father's military service has served me. My life is rich with them. I am proud of my father and the 21 years he invested in the military. Even though he retired in 1970 and passed away in 1995, he will be in me and with me forever . . . in the way I live, in the way I love.

~DENISE YAMADA

Professional Coach, 7-time "Emmy Award" broadcast journalist

www.deniseyamada.com

©2009

I am the son of a man who dedicated his life to his country, family and the military, and I am a better person for it.

~TIGER WOODS, GOLFER

Did You Know . . . ? The youngest U.S. serviceman was 12-year-old Calvin Graham, USN. He was wounded and given a Dishonorable Discharge for lying about his age. His benefits were later restored by act of Congress.

~WWII HISTORY BUFF COL D. G. SWINFORD, USMC (RET.)

My Hero, My Mom

Lovelle knew she wanted to fly. She was eight-years-old, and her parents would not allow her to speak of flying in the house. At 17-years-old, in lieu of a New Year's Eve party in Los Angeles, California, Lovelle and her date had their first flying lesson January 1, 1937. After graduating from high school, another dream was fulfilled when Lovelle flew for Erle (Salty) Bacon, Stinson Flying Corporation in Los Angeles. Due to WWII, flying became difficult on the West Coast. Early in 1942, she moved to Phoenix, Arizona to work for Consolidated in accounting, and continued building flying hours. At noon on a Friday afternoon, Lovelle walked away from her job after reading an article in the newspaper about aviatrix Jacqueline Cochran's flight training program for women for the Army Air Force in non-combat.

The program was developed so male pilots could be released for combat duty. She wanted to be part of that program. The newspaper had no sign up information, so Lovelle wrote to the President of the United States. Her letter was answered with a form to fill out and submit. After an interview with Jacqueline Cochran in Phoenix, Lovelle was told that the first group of women had already been approved. But that did not deter Lovelle. She met again with Ms. Cochran in Indio, California; and, upon Lovelle's return to Phoenix, a telegram was waiting. Her orders informed her to report to Luke Field for a physical exam, then report to Houston, Texas. In November 1942, Lovelle was one of the 319th AAFWFTD that came to be called *The Guinea Pigs* because they were the first in the program organized by Cochran.

In April of 1943, Lovelle was assigned to the Long Beach Army Air Base, in California. She met her life-long companion a month later. Kenneth was also a pilot in the Army Air Force. They married in October of that same year. Every day was a dream; flying was serious and fun at the same time. For Lovelle, Long Beach had a party atmosphere, but she kept that "under her hat."

After the WASPs were deactivated in December of 1943, Lovelle left active service to become a full-time homemaker and mother of three.

Kenneth continued flying; it kept him away from home often. Lovelle kept up some flying when she was able to fly with Kenneth across the United States, and in the Middle East, Europe, Africa, Indonesia, Malaysia and Singapore. By her faith and Ken's skill, they weathered many storms together: weather, instrument failure, engine failure, forced landings and hostile fire. In every situation, Lovelle found something to smile about.

She never wrote about her flying or her travels, but she did write many prayers and affirmations. One of the personal affirmations of Lovelle Benesh, in 1984, reflects the depth of her devotion: "I am not alone. I am never without help. God is with me where I am. Right at this moment I am in the very presence of God. I can meet and overcome every challenge. I ask God to show me the steps that are needed to bring me these results that I so earnestly desire and give me the strength to carry through physically, mentally and spiritually. As these challenges are accomplished, my health will return and God's light will reveal my highest good. I am not afraid. The fears of the moment are temporary. They vanish as I call on my faith. I rise up and out of any kind of limitation. I can be free, well and happy. I can be all that I long to be. God blesses me. So be it. Thank you, God. I love You."

Lovelle's last few months were spent in a nursing home as she recovered from a stroke; and, every day, my hero, my mom, had a smile and a laugh, and told me to remember my prayers.

~MARJORIE BENESH

In tribute to J. Lovelle Richards Benesh ©2009

Woman's Air Force Service Pilot (43-W-1) WWII (1919–2008)

I was born in Harlem, raised in the South Bronx, went to public school, got out of public college, went into the Army, and then I just stuck with it.

~COLIN POWELL

Our Dad, Our Hero

It was the Sunday morning of Veterans Day weekend, and my family and I were attending a church in the town where we were vacationing. The pastor acknowledged the holiday with powerful words of appreciation for those who had ever served in the military, and then offered words of prayer for those who were currently overseas in harm's way. He then specifically thanked those in the congregation, asking the veterans to stand, beginning with those who had served in World War II. The silver-haired gentleman behind us stood first, with tears running down his cheeks. My son looked up at me and asked why he was crying, so I gently whispered in his ear that the man had most likely lost some friends in that war. He looked at him with the kind of compassion that only a child can muster. As a military wife, I smiled and nodded at the wounded Veteran with deep respect.

The pastor went on to invite the Veterans of the Korean War to stand, and then Vietnam. My children were very young and although they were aware that their daddy used to be a Captain in the Air Force, they had not yet come to understand the depth of pain that the Vietnam War had caused on so many levels. All three of them watched intently as their father stood proudly. The silent appreciation and respect that swept through the chapel was almost tangible, and I could tell that my children felt it too. When a tear trickled down the sunburned cheeks of their normally happy-go-lucky daddy, a sense of wonder seemed to fill each of them. In an instant, they all seemed to realize that they were not the only ones who thought their dad was a hero!

After each of the Veterans, retired and active, were honored, the pastor then asked the wives and children of the Veterans to stand by their side. My precious trio jumped to their feet and stood as tall as they could by their hero—their dad—the greatest man in the world. And as I rose to honor the man I married, I never felt so proud.

~ADRIA MANARY, MILITARY WIFE, SPEAKER, AUTHOR OF *MOMMY MAGIC*, AND *MORE MOMMY MAGIC*

A Soldier's Story

If you're reading this, and my mamma's sitting there, looks like I only got a one-way ticket over here. I sure wish I could give you one more kiss—and war was just a game we played when we were kids.

Well I'm laying down my gun. I'm hanging up my boots. I'm up here with God and we're both watching over you. Just remember this: I'm in a better place where soldiers live in peace and angels sing "Amazing Grace."

So lay me down in that open field out on the edge of town; and know my soul is where my momma always prayed that it would go.

And if you're reading this, if you're reading this: I'm already home.

The above excerpt from the song, *If You're Reading This*, by Tim McGraw, spotlights the sentiment echoed by the many loved ones who received letters like these from soldiers who didn't make it home. Or received the knock on the door telling them their son or daughter, husband or wife, mother or father made the ultimate sacrifice and died in combat.

In the Korean War, there were 33,686 casualties. In Vietnam, 58,209. Think about four of your friends. Each one represents over 1,000 families. Since in Iraq, over 4,000 brave men and women have died so that we may sit here and enjoy our freedom. Even though these most recent numbers are considerably less than those of previous wars, it by no means diminishes the pain and suffering of every family it touches. Families, friends, loved ones.

While there are literally thousands of stories to share, today I'm going to tell you a soldier's story—the story of Staff Sergeant Timothy Vichko. This soldier, like so many of them, saw the Army as a way to clean up his act. He dropped out of high school, and later got his diploma. He really didn't like having people tell him what to do, and certainly didn't like taking orders, so what better place to go? The Army, of course! He enlisted in the Army, where, over the course of ten years, he quickly rose through the ranks to Staff Sergeant.

In late August of 2001, he flew out of Boston's Logan Airport heading toward the West Coast on his way to a one-year tour in Korea. Two weeks later, another plane left that very same airport, and we all know their final destination: New York City. I mention 9/11 to set the scene and give context, because when Staff Sergeant Vichko left the States, he left behind his wife, who was six months pregnant with their first child.

Have you ever accepted a job where you would have to travel? Would you take that job knowing you'd be away from home for 15 months or more at a time? Away from your family! Our soldiers do . . . Staff Sergeant Vichko did. And continues to do it.

He missed the birth of his daughter, because he was serving a year-long tour in Korea. Two years later, he missed the birth of his son because of his eight-month tour in Afghanistan. He knew when he signed up there was a possibility of separation from family—all military folks do.

His daughter is seven-years-old and his son is now five. They've only known him a total of three years due to his tours. They've sacrificed spending precious time with their father, and he's sacrificed seeing them grow up. The Army doesn't let you come home for little things like the birth of your children, or anniversaries, or Christmas.

As we sit here comfortably, reading our *Harry Potter* novels and watching *American Idol*, my brother, Staff Sergeant Timothy Vichko, is sitting in Iraq defending our freedom, as one of fourteen American soldiers on a base training 600 Iraqi soldiers. I'm one of the lucky ones because he's still with us, alive and well. We haven't received one of those letters.

Every day, I think of him. I feel him in my heart, and more so when I hear this Lonestar song on the radio.

He called her from Iraq, from a lonely tent in Baghdad:

Just to hear her say I love you one more time.
But when he heard the sound of the kids laughing in the background, he had to wipe away a tear from his eye.

A little voice came on the phone, said, "Daddy, when you coming home?"
He said the first thing that came to his mind: I'm already there. Take a
look around. I'm the sunshine in your hair. I'm the shadow on the ground.
I'm the whisper in the wind, and I'll be there until the end. And I know I'm
in your prayers . . . I'm already there. (Excerpt from *I'm Already There* by Lonestar)
~KARA DEFRIAS, M.ED.

*Kara's younger brother is a career soldier. Both of her grandfathers served in the Army, and
her father and his brothers served in the Navy.*

Other things may change us, but we start and end with the family.
~ANTHONY BRANDT

When you look at your life, the greatest happiness's are family happiness's.
~DR. JOYCE·BROTHERS

Gray hair is God's graffiti.
~BILL COSBY

*I've definitely never had to look very far outside my family for inspiration.
I'm surrounded by unbelievable strength and courage. Even in very difficult
times, there's always been a lot of humor and laughter.*
~MARIA SHRIVER, INTERVIEWED IN *MORE* MAGAZINE, MAY 2004

*You don't choose your family.
They are God's gift to you, as you are to them.*
~ARCHBISHOP DESMOND TUTU

Eldonna Lewis Fernandez

A retired Air Force Master Sergeant with 23 years of honorable military service, Eldonna is an award-winning speaker with over 29 years of extensive leadership, management and supervisory experience. Affectionately known as the Pink Biker Chic™, she is a biker and empowerment coach for women—utilizing the PINK principles of—Power, Integrity, Nurturing, and Knowledge. The Pink Biker Chic™ programs are the GPS for feminine transformation. Women go from heels to wheels with beginner and experienced rider transformational workshops, luxury weekend bike trips, and week long touring rides. Women move from the back seat to the front seat of the bike and in their own life as they steer themselves to a bright and successful future. Her programs include individual and group coaching, and a one-week no-ride, no-lecture retreat in Maui with The Peaceful Woman.

http://pinkbikerchic.com

Sheryl Roush

Known as the Sparkle-Tude!® Expert, Sheryl is an internationally top-rated speaker, and was only the third woman to earn the elite Accredited Speaker designation from Toastmasters International, from 4 million members in 106 countries. She is the President/CEO of Sparkle Presentations, Inc., and an 8-time business owner, with 35 years experience in communication. Her keynotes, workshops and retreats rekindle the spirit, raise the bar, and create excitement. Sheryl has presented on programs alongside Olivia Newton-John, Geena Davis, Joan Lunden and others. A former Navy wife, she has great compassion and admiration for those who serve our country. Sheryl was twice crowned "Ms. Heart of San Diego" for her stellar contributions to women in her community.

www.SparklePresentations.com

Other Books Available from

Sheryl Roush

Corazón de Mujer
(Heart of a Woman in Spanish)

Heart of the Holidays

Heart of the Holidays with Music CD

Heart of a Mother

Heart of a Mother with Music CD

Heart of a Woman

Heart of a Woman in Business

Sparkle-Tudes!®
Inspirations for Creating Sparkling Attitudes
Quotations By, For & About Women